Liberating the Gospels

OTHER BOOKS BY JOHN SHELBY SPONG

Honest Prayer

Dialogue: In Search of Jewish-Christian Understanding
with Rabbi Jack Daniel Spiro

Christpower

Life Approaches Death: A Dialogue on Medical Ethics
with Dr. Daniel Gregory

The Living Commandments

The Easter Moment

Into the Whirlwind: The Future of the Church

Beyond Moralism with the Venerable Denise G. Haines

*Survival and Consciousness—An Interdisciplinary Inquiry into
the Possibility of Life Beyond Biological Death* (Editor)

Living in Sin?: A Bishop Rethinks Human Sexuality

*Rescuing the Bible from Fundamentalism: A Bishop Rethinks
the Meaning of Scripture*

*Born of a Woman: A Bishop Rethinks the Virgin Birth and the
Treatment of Women by a Male-Dominated Church*

This Hebrew Lord: A Bishop's Search for the Authentic Jesus

*Resurrection: Myth or Reality?: A Bishop's Search for the
Origins of Christianity*

Liberating the Gospels

Reading the Bible with Jewish Eyes

Freeing Jesus from 2,000 years of misunderstanding

❖❖❖❖❖❖❖❖❖❖❖❖❖❖❖❖❖❖❖❖❖❖❖❖❖❖❖❖❖❖❖❖❖❖❖❖

JOHN SHELBY SPONG

HarperSanFrancisco
A Division of HarperCollinsPublishers

For further educational resources exploring the ideas and issues addressed in this and other books by John Shelby Spong, contact:

Christianity for the Third Millennium
P.O. Box 69
Morristown, NJ 07963–0069
Fax: 201–540–9584

HarperCollins Web Site: http://www.harpercollins.com

HarperCollins®, 📖®, and HarperSanFrancisco™ are trademarks of HarperCollins Publishers Inc.

FIRST HarperCollins paperback edition published in 1997

Library of Congress Cataloging-in-Publication Data
Spong, John Shelby.
    Liberating the Gospels : reading the Bible with Jewish eyes / John Shelby Spong. — 1st ed.
    Includes bibliographical references and index.
    ISBN 0–06–067556–X (cloth)
    ISBN 0–06–067557–8 (pbk.)
    ISBN 0–06–067534–9 (intl. pbk.)
    1. Bible. N.T. Gospels—Criticism, interpretation, etc. 2. Bible. O.T. Pentateuch—Liturgical use. 3. Haftarot. 4. Synoptic problem. 5. Bible. O.T. Pentateuch—Relation to the New Testament. 6. Bible. O.T. Prophets (Nevi'im)—Relation to the New Testament. 7. Goulder, M.D. I. Title.
    BS2555.2.S65   1996
    226'.06—dc20   96–12598

04 05 ❖ RRD(H) 20 19 18 17 16 15 14

FOR

John Lanier Hylton

AND

Lydia Ann Hylton

◈

The newest grandchildren to enrich our wonderful life

Contents

Preface

This book was born as early as January 1991, when I was on sabbatical at Magdalen College, Oxford. At that moment I was working on the birth narratives of the New Testament and their implications for contemporary women. In discussing these matters with the Dean of Magdalen College, a New Testament scholar named Jeffrey John, he suggested that I might want to explore the concept of *midrash*, Haggadic *midrash* to be specific, that was present in the birth narratives. He also directed me toward the writings of Michael D. Goulder of the faculty of the University of Birmingham in the United Kingdom, about whom I had never heard. It was this suggestion that was to determine the immediate future of both my academic and my writing careers. To my regret I discovered first that most of Goulder's books were out of print. I was able to purchase his most recent work, a two-volume commentary on Luke, entitled *Luke: A New Paradigm*. My first impression was that it was the most expensive book I had ever purchased! It was also heavy reading. It would be two years before I would do a thorough study of this work. Jeffrey John's suggestion and some of Michael Goulder's insights had their effect on me, however, and this was clearly visible when I published my book *Born of a*

Woman in September 1992. The concept of *midrash* had become the lens through which I viewed the birth narratives.

Next I moved on to begin some new work on the resurrection narratives, and more and more I was enabled by Goulder and others to see these central passages of the Gospels through Jewish eyes. In the spring term of 1992, while a fellow at Emmanuel College, Cambridge, I wrote *Resurrection: Myth or Reality?* In this book I proposed that the Jerusalem Easter tradition was shaped in almost every detail by the Jewish festival of Sukkot or Tabernacles. I had made, almost unconsciously, my first major interpretive connection between Jewish liturgical practice and the shape of the Christian faith. I was, however, not yet aware of how important that connection would turn out to be.

During that same time, I also found in the Cambridge library a copy of one of Goulder's out-of-print books, *Midrash and Lection in Matthew.* I read it in its entirety. It was, quite frankly, the most exciting New Testament scholarship reading I had done in my professional life. Goulder documented for me the *midrashic* connections between the Gospels and the Jewish scriptures in mind-boggling ways, and he opened my eyes for the first time to the possibility that the Jewish liturgical calendar, far more than history or the memory of eyewitnesses, had determined both the shape and much of the content of the Gospels.

So dramatic was this learning experience that I did three things. First, I contacted Michael Goulder, told him of my interest in his work, and asked if I might come to Birmingham to spend some time with him. He was wonderfully receptive, and a genuine friendship began to develop. We have now made four journeys to Birmingham to spend time in dialogue with this brilliant and unusual man.

Second, I employed an English rare-books firm to search for copies of Goulder's out-of-print volumes. They were successful, and now each of his published works is a cherished possession in my personal library. Each of these volumes also bears the marks of a book that I did not just read, but devoured. They are penciled extensively, with underlines and comments, and I have copious notes on each of them in my files.

Third, I became convinced that I wanted to write my next book on the Jewishness of the Gospels, despite the fact that I had a contract for a quite different book with my publisher, HarperCollins. My first working title of this new book was *The Gospels as Midrash*. My editor at HarperCollins, however, discouraged that title for two reasons: First, *midrash* is not a familiar word to the general reader, he said, and second, Jewish people use the term *midrash* in a very strict and limited sense, which was quite different from the way I was using the term. I had seen that reaction in my closest rabbi friend, Jack Daniel Spiro, the first time I used the term in a public lecture that he attended. I do not ever want to be offensive to my fellow pilgrims within the Jewish tradition, so in this book I have used the word *midrash* only as the modifying adjective, *midrashic,* both to indicate the broadness of the way I am employing this concept and also to leave the word *midrash* to its special Jewish understanding.

My contract with HarperCollins was for a book on how one can continue to say the creeds of the Church with integrity while taking seriously the intellectual revolution that stretches from Copernicus through Einstein, and into the fields of astrophysics and subatomic physics, which has created what some call "the postmodern world." This book, which was to be called *A Believer in Exile,* now needed to be postponed. Writing is such an all-consuming vocation that one can hardly afford to focus in more than one direction at a time. My friends at HarperCollins agreed to this plan and allowed me to postpone *A Believer in Exile,* which is now scheduled for a 1998 publication date.

So it was that my consuming task from 1992 to 1995 was to explore the Jewish background of the Christian scriptures. My primary teacher, through his books as well as in correspondence, and through personal visits, has been Michael Goulder.

This man fascinated me not only with his writing but also with the personal journey of his life. His story was unique. It is fair to say that Michael Goulder is not a power in religious or ecclesiastical circles. Indeed, his work is generally ignored by that world. One reason for this is that his books are not written for popular consumption. They will never be part of the table talk of ordinary folk. They are closely argued, heavily footnoted, and lean quite frequently on the nuance found in a Greek or Hebrew word. They are also challenging to the orthodoxy of the contemporary religious consensus. Since they are not likely, therefore, to come to public attention, the traditional theological "defenders of the faith" do not have to deal with Goulder's arguments or insights. So a scholar like Goulder does not haunt the religious establishment. He tends rather to remain in the shadows.

There is one other reason, however, that I think is even more telling. Michael Goulder was at one time an ordained priest in the Church of England. Before plunging into graduate studies and an academic career, he had actually served as the vicar of a congregation. However, as broad as Anglican Christianity has tended to be theologically, the way that faith community understood its belief system became less and less adequate for this probing scholar. In 1981, after producing three of his most penetrating books, Michael Goulder resigned from his ordination and ceased to identify himself as a priest. He also ceased even to identify himself as a Christian, proclaiming himself to be "a nonaggressive atheist." Christian traditionalists who are more acquainted with the techniques of propaganda than they are with the demands of education find it hard to deal with a brilliant New Testament scholar who is an atheist. The easiest way to handle that situation is simply to ignore it. So Michael Goulder has generally been ignored in the academic circles that purport to be made up of "Christian scholars." It is a shame because the insights of truth, even the truth that lies buried beneath the words of the gospel, are valid no matter who the illuminating source of those insights happens to be. Truth, even Christian truth, can and does stem from the mind and pen of one who thinks himself to be an atheist.

I have come to know, admire, and respect Michael Goulder. He is gentle, loving, kind, and extremely personable. He and my wife seem especially happy in each other's company. He has never once been critical of or negative about my ultimate commitment to Jesus the Christ as my Lord. We have discussed those parts of the gospel story that stretch credibility to the breaking point when literalized. We have together sought to define the God in whose reality I believe and he rejects. Both of us love to probe the scriptures for clues to truth for Michael and clues to God for me, and both of us delight when we discover something that has generally been undiscovered before. I remember my joy when I came to the conclusion that Zechariah, the father of John the Baptist, was a *midrashic* creation, with his name stemming from the fact that John had been identified with the prophet Malachi, whose immediate predecessor in the Bible was the prophet, Zechariah. So John's immediate predecessor was called Zechariah. I remember even better Michael's amusement and his twinkling smile when he showed me that he had not only come to, but written about, this possibility years before it even dawned on me to explore the issue.

I have footnoted Michael Goulder significantly in this book, but there is a sense in which this whole book is my attempt to make accessible to the general public the insights of Michael Goulder. I am not a slavish disciple. He is not my only source of insight. I have drawn on the reading of a lifetime. Nor do I agree with Goulder in all his conclusions. Indeed, I have broken with my mentor at significant points in my story. The most striking disagreement will be on the "order" that organized the Gospel of Luke. For me it was the Torah. For Michael it was the attempt on Luke's part to harmonize Mark and Matthew, which are, Goulder will argue, Luke's only major sources.

But I do assume the validity of many of Goulder's premises. I no longer accept the popular theory of the existence of something called the "Q" document (Burton Mack, et al., to the contrary notwithstanding). That is a new conclusion for me. Yet all of the reasons for asserting the existence of Q disappear for me when Luke and Matthew are understood as liturgical and lectionary books. In this volume I will not debate or seek to justify my dismissal of the Q hypothesis. I will simply assume it. Those who wish to debate this are referred to the devastating argument against it developed by Goulder in the preface to *Luke: A New*

Paradigm. It was for me totally persuasive. I prefer to think that Q was nothing more or less than Matthew's own creative genius that emerged as he wrote his gospel as a *midrashic* expansion of Mark designed better to fit the entire liturgical year of the Jews.

I also dismiss the presumed "M" and "L" documents as separate sources of written or oral tradition. The M source for me was Matthew's personal creation based on Paul, or on the Hebrew scriptures, but not picked up by Luke so that it remained uniquely Matthean. L was that material peculiar to Luke's gospel that I think Luke himself wrote.

Luke, I am assuming, had Mark and Matthew before him as he created his gospel. He preferred Mark and followed him closely. However, Luke also adapted Matthew to his purposes, thereby requiring what came to be called the Q hypothesis, which simply suggested that Matthew and Luke had enough common material to postulate a common source. That common source was, in my opinion, that Luke both had read and would employ Matthew in the writing of his gospel. Luke, however, like Matthew, also created some new material based primarily on his understanding of the Hebrew scriptures, most especially Genesis and Deuteronomy. This was the material that in time came to be called the L source.

So this book assumes that Matthew had Mark before him when he wrote. Luke had Mark and Matthew both before him when he wrote; and John had Mark, Matthew, and Luke before him when he wrote. It is amazingly simple; and the lectionary theory presented in these pages answers almost all of the questions that the various source theories were designed to answer.

I am pleased to express publicly my deep admiration for Michael Goulder and for his work. I am delighted if I can popularize some of his insights and thus inject them into the theological debates of the academy that will ultimately project their content into the pulpits and pews of the churches of the Christian world. I would find it both ironic and exhilarating if the insights of my nonbelieving mentor, Michael Goulder, could help people to make meaningful and significant commitments to the Christian faith. Goulder's insights have significantly deepened my commitment to this Christ, and I want to acknowledge that publicly. Michael Goulder expands the parameters of our Christian faith story, and his work changes the nature of the questions we ask of our sacred sources. When we approach the Christ story from Goulder's perspective, we will stop expending our energy in an attempt to shore up the crumbling structures of traditional Christianity and instead we will return to the roots of that Christian edifice and there discover a Jewishness that will refocus us and allow a whole new understanding of Christianity to grow from those roots. This will, in turn, I believe, allow our world to be confronted with a new vision of a nonliteral but powerfully real Christian view of life. I write to seek to give shape to that vision.

I also have come to treasure my friendship with Michael Goulder. His many kindnesses to me and to my wife, Christine, are remembered with gratitude. By using his insights, I hope to expand the boundaries of Christianity to the place where people like Michael Goulder will once again feel comfortable calling themselves Christians. It would be the crowning achievement of my life if I, as an Anglican bishop, could preside over the liturgy that would restore Michael Goulder to the Anglican priesthood as one of our most creative scholars. If that privilege is not to be mine, then I would, if I survive Michael Goulder, desire to be present at his funeral, so that as an Anglican bishop I could proclaim to the world how deeply the writings of this self-professed atheist had enriched my Christian life and deepened my Christian devotion. That is a message that I yearn for my Christian world to hear. For now, however, I must be content simply to acknowledge that if I am the father of this book, then Michael Goulder is surely the grandfather. I am pleased to pay him the recognition that certainly is his due.

During the course of preparing this book, I lectured on its content both within the Diocese of Newark and beyond. Material from this book formed the basis of my New Dimensions lectures in 1994, which were hosted by the congregation of Christ Church, Short Hills, New Jersey, whose rector is the Rev. Leonard Freeman and whose assistant is the Rev. Victoria

McGrath. It was also a major part of the content of my fall diocesan lectures in 1994 held at St. Paul's Church in Chatham, New Jersey, where the Rev. Dr. Franklin Vilas is rector and the Rev. Margaret (Bambi) Koeniger is the assistant.

The Lenten Lectures of 1995 featured the content found in the section of this book on the passion story and Judas, and in 1996 they featured the resurrection tradition through the ascension and Pentecost. In both years these lectures were held at St. Luke's Church in Montclair, New Jersey, where the Rev. Robert Griffiths is interim rector and Mr. Bruce Smith is the assistant.

In the New Dimensions lectures in the fall of 1995, the material on Luke's gospel was delivered at Christ Church in Ridgewood, New Jersey, where the Rev. Margaret Gunness is rector and the Rev. David Ware is the assistant. In the diocesan fall lectures of 1995, the material on Matthew was delivered at Calvary Church in Summit, New Jersey, where the Rev. Christopher Brdlik is rector and the Rev. Gregory Cole is assistant. I express my gratitude to all of these people for their invitation and their welcome.

Beyond the Diocese of Newark, this material was tested primarily at the Chautauqua Institution in western New York in the summer of 1995 at the invitation of the Rev. Dr. Ross MacKenzie and his wife, Flora. There, in a building called the Hall of Philosophy, an audience of some 1,000 people, about a quarter of whom were Jewish, gathered each day for a week to listen, to question, and to interact with what was to become the content of this book. Their response convinced me that I was dealing with something that was real, exciting, and appealing to people far beyond that which those who abide within the traditional religious boundaries would even contemplate.

Just before mailing the manuscript to my publisher, I completed a sixteen-lecture tour of Canada under the auspices of the United Church of Canada. Three conferences were part of that tour. The first was held in the Five Oaks Conference Center about an hour outside Toronto and was directed by Yvonne Stewart. The second was held in the Prairie Christian Teaching

Center in Fort Qu'Apelle, Saskatchewan, and was directed by James von Riesen. The third was at the Knox Center of the Knox United Church of Calgary and was directed by Lorraine Hartry. To those three leaders, the people who attended, and the courageous United Church of Canada, I offer thanks for their welcome and enthusiasm.

Two people worked with me on this manuscript in a very close and intimate way. One was my wife, Christine Mary Spong. I have long appreciated both her love and her incredible talents, but before this book, I had never recognized her literary and linguistic skills. Her help on this volume was substantial, and it involved both style and content. She spent untold hours reading this manuscript and shaping its message. My admiration for her literary skills is now almost as high as my love for her has always been. So to her I express my gratitude and my devotion.

The second person was Lyn Conrad, my executive secretary. This was the first book I had ever done with Lyn, but she never flinched from this massive task. The material in this book has grown from lectures to chapters, from the spoken word to the written word, with version after version being placed into Lyn Conrad's user-friendly computer. She is a joy to know and a pleasure with whom to work. I do hope that the pressure of this task did not cause her husband, David, to face a diminished wife on those days when deadlines had to be met.

The other members of the staff of this diocese are inevitably affected by the fact that the bishop of this diocese is also an author. It certainly adds to their workload. They are a wonderful community of human beings whom I must salute with appreciation in this preface. First, I pay tribute to the members of what we call the core staff. That includes my partner in the episcopate, the Rt. Rev. Jack M. McKelvey; our chief financial officer, John George Zinn; our chief administrative officer, Michael Francaviglia; our personnel and public relations officer, Dale Gruner; our program officer, the Rev. Margaret (Maggie) Gat; and the Dean of our Cathedral, the Very Rev. Petero Sabune.

Next is what we call the support staff, which includes Cecil Broner, Rupert Cole, Gail Deckenbach, Charles Hayes, Karen James, Jeffrey Kittross, Robert Lanterman, Carla Lerman, Barbara Lescota, Patricia McGuire, the Rev. Harker McHugh, Peggy Mellors, Michelle Mitchell, Bradley Moor, William Quinlan, Joyce Riley, Lucy Sprague, Elizabeth Stone, Teresa Wilder, Anita Wortman, and Margaret Shirdel.

Finally, I express my gratitude to my family. Beyond Christine, my treasured wife, there are first our daughters: Ellen, and her husband, Gus Epps; Katharine, and her husband, Jack Catlett; Jaquelin, and her husband, Todd Hylton; and Rachel Barney; and then our son, Brian Barney. In the next generation there are our grandchildren: Shelby and Jay Catlett, to whom a previous book was dedicated, and John Lanier and Lydia Ann Hylton, to whom this book is dedicated. And last, but not least, I recognize with appreciation our mothers: Doolie Boyce Griffith Spong, who is approaching ninety, and Ina Chase Bridger, who is not approaching ninety. These are the people closest to our hearts, and they are the ones who, in the final analysis, make life as rich and sweet as it is.

Shalom.

John S. Spong
Newark, New Jersey
1996

Part One

✦✦✦

Understanding the Biblical Issues

The Crisis in Faith Today

Finding a New Question
and a New Starting Place

Did it really happen?

That is the question that people through the ages have always asked about the beginnings of their religious traditions. Certainly that has been the question asked of the gospel tradition of Christianity. Did it really happen? Did a virgin actually conceive? Did the heavens really open at the time of Jesus' baptism? Did Jesus walk on water or feed the multitude with five loaves? Did he literally restore sight to the blind, hearing to the deaf, and even more dramatically, life to the deceased? Did his resuscitated body walk physically out of the tomb at the dawn of Easter some thirty-six to seventy-two hours after his public execution? Did he rise from this earth and ascend into a heaven located just beyond the sky?

Traditionally, the only answers that these questions could possibly elicit were either yes or no. "Yes" was the answer of the believer. "No" was the answer of the unbeliever. In the years of Christian dominance in the Western world, the answer "no" was seldom heard in public places, for the pressure against doubting or questioning the conventional religious wisdom was enormous. The Bible had been proclaimed to be the literal Word of God. It was God's truth. It admitted to no error. Great theological systems of doctrine had been erected on the basis of this revealed Word of God. Belief in that creedal orthodoxy was equated with salvation. Unbelief was subject to condemnation.

Liturgical practices had been inaugurated by the Church so that these great objective moments of the gospel drama could be lived out annually and thus be riveted upon our memories. So at Christmas we heard the story of Jesus' birth, with all of its miraculous wonder that featured stars and angels, virgins, and close escapes into Egypt. During Holy Week we relived the literal drama of Jesus' suffering, from the betrayal, arrest, and torture, to his crucifixion on a hill named Calvary. At Easter we reveled in the stories of his restoration to life, which were replete with tangible proofs of his resurrected reality. He was seen by his disciples. He ate food before them. He invited them to handle him to make sure he was not a ghost. He opened the wounds in his hands and side to their tactile examination. On the Sunday of Pentecost, we celebrated the gift of the Holy Spirit and the birth of the Church complete with accounts of a mighty rushing wind, tongues of fire, and the ability to speak in the language of the hearer. Over and over, year in and year out, the liturgy of the Church flowed over the conscious minds of the people until these events became part of the cultural self-identity, thus enabling these concepts to be kept ever fresh in our memories.

The liturgy also served to make these defining moments in our faith story so dramatic and powerful that for centuries it occurred to no one to suggest anything other than that these were the objective memories of eyewitnesses who faithfully recorded them in the sacred text that came to be known as the Word of God. So to the question, "Did it really happen?" the believer would assert with great confidence, "Yes, of course. It happened just as the Bible says!"

But the Christian dominance of the Western world began to decline visibly by the sixteenth century, and with that decline the answer "yes" to the question, "Did it really happen?" became less and less secure. Believers had to face the fact that other answers were becoming conceivable. This shift did not happen quickly. At first, those few who would question or doubt publicly did so at the risk of some very real danger to their lives. Some were ostracized, others were excommunicated, and a few were even burned at the stake. To doubt or to question the literal truth of the Bible or the authority of the Holy Church was a dangerous occupation.

In this believing age, it never occurred to the Christian majority to ask whether "Did it really happen?" was the proper question with which to approach the Bible. That had been the unquestioned approach to scripture since at least the dawn of the second century. That was the way the Bible was read and interpreted by the leaders of the Christian Church. That was the way the "fathers" of the Church—Polycarp, Iranaeus, Chrysostom, Origen, Augustine, and Jerome—had taught them. Western consciousness in this era was such that it escaped the notice of the common mind that all of the fathers of the Church were gentiles of a Greek, Latin, or North African origin. It also did not occur to them to notice that the Gospels were books written by people who were Jewish, and that Jewish people did not relate to sacred history as if it were an objective description of literal events. Indeed, in the early years of the Christian Church in the Western world, a wretched spirit of anti-Jewish hatred was so pervasive that the very idea that the Gospels were the products of Jewish authors and that they represented a Jewish gift to the world would have seemed both incomprehensible and even revolting. So it was that the Christian Church locked itself into certain basic assumptions by which it lived and to which it admitted no challenge. Among these assumptions was that the Bible, especially the Gospels as the Word of God, were objectively true, that they described events of literal history, and that one could confidently assert that all that was contained therein did in fact happen just as it was written. This mentality produced a comfortable feeling of security that endured for centuries. It was, however, destined not to endure forever.

Inevitably, the day arrived when knowledge expanded to a place where biblical assumptions had to be challenged despite the personal cost to the challenger. The opening shot, at least in the public battle of ideas, was fired in the early years of the seventeenth century by a resident of the city of Padua named Galileo. Building on the work of Polish astronomer Nicolaus Copernicus, Galileo, challenged the common wisdom that the earth was a stationary body around which the heavenly bodies moved. This implied that the earth was not the center of the universe and therefore it might not be the object of the constant attention of its divine creator—the unwritten premise against which the whole biblical drama unfurled. The Bible portrayed God not only as the creator, but also as one regularly involved in the affairs of human history. This God had walked with Adam and Eve in the cool of the evening (Gen. 3:8). This Divine One had chosen one special tribe to be the elect people of God (Gen. 12:2–3). This deity had freed these people from bondage in Egypt (Exod. 13:3 ff.), split the waters of the Red Sea to facilitate their escape (Exod. 14:21 ff.), fed them with quails and heavenly bread in the wilderness (Exod. 16:13 ff.), and finally led them victoriously into the promised land of Canaan (Josh. 3:14 ff.).

Later, this God raised up prophets to speak the Divine Word. And "when the time had fully come, God sent forth his Son" (Gal. 4:4), said the scriptures. That was Paul's understanding of Jesus—who, he believed, had come forth from God at his birth and who, following his crucifixion, had returned to God by his exaltation into heaven. The God who dominated the biblical narrative was a God who was conceived of inside a worldview that Copernicus and Galileo had rendered all but meaningless. It was no wonder that the leaders of the Church reacted with such vehemence to the publication of Galileo's ideas, for they struck at the very heart of the Church's authority. The entire biblical frame of reference was challenged by Galileo's concepts. So the Church condemned Galileo and forced him to choose between recanting and death. The text used to challenge the work of Galileo was found in the book of Joshua, where Joshua ordered the sun to stand still in the sky (Josh. 10:12). This proved to the leaders of the Church that the earth was the static center of the universe around which the sun moved each day. The Bible, every word of it, had been invested with ultimate and literal truth. Therefore anything contrary to the Bible was, by definition, false. Galileo did recant in order to save his life, and the Church presumed that a great victory had been won. However, no external authority can ultimately repress truth, and Galileo was exonerated as his ideas gained ascendancy. Finally, in 1991, the Vatican admitted that Galileo had been correct and the Church and the Bible had been wrong. This confession of error on the part of the Church was 350 years too late. By that time Galileo hardly cared, and the credibility of the Church was as poorly served by that arrogant confession as it had been by its original closed-minded ignorance. Besides that, the Church, even in its admission of guilt, hardly dealt with the major threat to its power: namely, that if Galileo was correct, what happens to the whole context in which the Bible was written? It had been immediately rendered all but unbelievable by the sea change in thought inaugurated by Galileo. Perhaps the religious hierarchy assumed that no one would raise this question.

Within a century of Galileo, an English physicist named Isaac Newton applied Galileo's insights to create his vision of a mathematically precise universe operating according to fixed physical laws. When Newton had completed his work, the realm in which miracle and magic had once been thought to operate had all but vanished from our sight.

Yet the story of the Bible was written to validate an intervening deity who performed miracles and magic with regularity. This God was said to have turned the Nile River into blood and to have sent various other plagues on the recalcitrant Egyptians (Exod. 8–11). This God had called to Moses out of a burning bush that was not consumed (Exod. 3:1–6) and had equipped Moses with magical tricks, such as providing Aaron with a staff that would turn into a serpent when thrown to the ground. This feat supposedly gave credibility to Moses' demands for his people's freedom (Exod. 7:10 ff.). When the pharaoh's magicians were able to accomplish the same trick, God's power was further demonstrated in that the serpent that belonged to Moses and Aaron simply ate up the serpents belonging to the magicians!

These qualities of miracle and magic permeated the entire biblical story. Elijah was fed by ravens (1 Kings 17:4–6) and by angels (1 Kings 19:4–8). He called down fire from heaven to burn up his (and presumably God's) enemies (1 Kings 1:9–12). He expanded a widow's bread and oil supply so that it was never exhausted (1 Kings 17:8–16), and he even restored the widow's son to life after he had died (1 Kings 17:17–24).

Elisha did many of these same things but was also said to have had other magical powers. When the iron head of a borrowed ax fell into the river Jordan, Elisha made the iron ax head float so that it could be recovered (1 Kings 6:1–7). The biblical world apparently was not governed exclusively by the laws of physics about which Newton wrote.

The Jesus story was also told in terms of this world of miracle and magic that Newton in large measure laid to rest. Jesus walked on water (Matt. 14:23), expanded food supplies (Mark 6:38 ff.), and violated the laws of gravity by rising from this earth to ascend into God's heavenly presence (Luke 24:51, Acts 1:9).

After the writings of Isaac Newton, it became much more difficult to answer "yes" to the question, "Did it really happen?" which we had been taught was the only proper question that people of faith could ask of the stories in the gospel tradition.

The intellectual revolution of the modern world after Copernicus, Galileo, and Newton continued to chip away at the assumptions made by the biblical writers. Charles Darwin not only destroyed the objective truth of the literalized story of creation, but he also forced the world to question whether or not human life was a special creation made in the image of God. Perhaps, Darwin suggested, human beings were but an accident of the evolutionary process.

Darwin also presented us with a vision of a universe that was still evolving and was thus unfinished and therefore incomplete. After Darwin, human beings began to recognize that, in contradistinction to the popular Christian assumptions, there has never been a human perfection from which we have fallen away. There has been rather only the evolution of a higher consciousness that has occurred over billions of years and in which *Homo sapiens* are still participating. So it becomes meaningless for theologians to talk about the Fall or even about original sin. There can be no fall from a perfect creation in the garden of Eden if there has never been a perfect creation.

Suddenly, it began to dawn on us that portraying Jesus as the divine rescuer who came to save human beings and the rest of the fallen creation and to restore us and our world to the perfection that God had intended in creation was no longer a translatable concept. If life was still evolving, restoration was not the proper idea. All of the atonement theories and the atonement stories, especially those that speak of Jesus as the sacrifice or ransom, began, in the light of Darwin's thought, to be nonsensical. For that reason the thought of Charles Darwin represented a radical threat to religious folk and to religious leaders.

The Christian Church in the nineteenth century did not have the power to force Darwin to recant as it had once forced Galileo to do. But that did not mean that Christian leaders did not open up a ferocious attack on the writings of Charles Darwin. In the United Kingdom, that attack was led by the Anglican bishop of Oxford, Samuel Wilberforce, who debated with Darwin's advocate, Thomas Huxley, throughout the realm. Because of his oratorical proclivities, Bishop Wilberforce acquired the nickname "Soapy Sam." By and large, however, the Wilberforce attacks amounted to little more than an uninformed ridicule and the exaggeration of some complete misconceptions found in Darwin's thought. Today few people are aware of Samuel Wilberforce, but all the world still knows the name of Charles Darwin.

Once again, this intellectual giant left the Christian traditions built on the literal biblical record in tatters. For the Bible was both written and understood in terms of a worldview that, after Darwin, was no longer believed to exist. The clash between Darwin and the Bible came to public attention in Dayton, Tennessee, in 1925, at the trial of a high school teacher named John T. Scopes. He was charged with teaching evolution, which was specifically against the law in Bible-believing Tennessee. Like Galileo, Scopes was found guilty of violating the truth of holy scripture. He was fined a nominal sum and removed from his teaching post.

Galileo's sentence was imposed in Catholic Europe, so an official apology could come from the Vatican centuries later. Scopes was found guilty in Protestant America, so no central authority exists that could speak the word of apology to him. But the fact remains that the whole social order has long ago overturned the guilty verdict against Mr. Scopes in a thousand ways. Despite the fact that an occasional southern or rural community in the United States still seeks to establish in the local school curriculum an alternative to evolution called "creation science," it is nonetheless true that the whole field of biology and medicine today assumes that the principles of Charles Darwin are true, and school textbooks for six-, seven-, and eight-year-olds across the world have incorporated these principles into their content. This is even true for Tennessee. Once more, a portion of the Bible, like the story of a seven-day creation, a couple named Adam and Eve, a serpent, and the tempting fruit of a tree had been demonstrated not to be literally true. So when the question, "Did it really happen?" continued to be asked, the answer "no" began to be heard with increasing frequency. However, the pressure against viewing the Bible as literal truth did not stop with these identified onslaughts against its perceived inerrancy.

Sigmund Freud rose in the early years of the twentieth century to challenge and probably even to destroy those naive religious assumptions that had portrayed God as either a rewarding or a punishing parent figure. Freud suggested that all religious systems represented an infantile neurosis from which human beings would someday emerge as mature adults. He exposed the power needs that organized religion had developed in which to hide from truth. He also laid bare the religious defensiveness that lies hidden underneath those peculiar religious claims to be the true faith or to worship the true God or to possess the only true revelation, and thus to be the only authorized spokesperson for that revelation. Freud made such claims inoperative.

Yet these were the very claims that echoed throughout the biblical story. These claims also had been enveloped by the hierarchy of the Church into a body of doctrine and dogma that some parts of the Church have insisted must be believed on pain of the loss of salvation. But now, in the light of this intellectual revolution, it became increasingly obvious that the primary theological structures of the Church, including its doctrines and dogmas, depended on that literal view of scripture, which was no longer intellectually defensible. The Church was thus in a battle for its very life.

For most of its history, the Church had approached its scriptures through no other lens except the question, "Did this really happen?" and assumed that the answer to that question was a resounding "yes!" Now that same Church began to face the fact that this "yes" answer was increasingly without credibility. Of course the "no" answer, which seemed to be the only alternative, would mean the end of Christianity. If these things did not really happen, then Christianity was suspect at best, perhaps fraudulent at worst. That was not a viable notion for Christians to entertain. So the answer "yes" was surrendered slowly and begrudgingly. Biblical foundations once thought to be invincible no longer appeared to be so. Indeed they appeared to many to be no longer even credible. For the leadership of the Church, the writings of Sigmund Freud represented a devastating challenge. So he was vilified and resisted as long as possible. That seemed to the Church leaders the only choice available, but penetrating truth can finally be neither ignored nor resisted.

Before Freud's challenge was fully admitted, to say nothing of being entertained or even absorbed by the religious public, Albert Einstein had arisen to destroy any remaining credibility that might have existed after Galileo to the biblical notion that this planet was the center of the universe. Einstein also put nails into the coffin of the concept that human life was the purpose of creation. This great physicist even rendered our traditional concepts of both time and space to be less than objective categories, and he demonstrated the relativity of all articulated truth. Yet, once again, these were the very foundations upon which the Christian faith had been built. These were the assumptions upon which the Christian story had always been told. The ability of a modern person to continue to view the Bible literally had all but disappeared. If there was no other way to read the Bible than literally, then the sunset of Christianity had entered the Western world. This challenge was so basic and so severe that it is no wonder that denial was destined to be the primary way in which Christians dealt with this crisis. For it was fast becoming inescapably obvious that people living in the modern world could no longer answer the question "Did this really happen?" with a convincing "yes." But those who believed themselves to be Christians were also not willing to admit that their faith tradition was in fact built on a hoax or on ignorance or on a total misconception. Yet, in the expansion of knowledge and in the insatiable human search for truth, such a defensive religious system could not be expected to endure. These are the realities and the tensions that now haunt the ranks of organized religion.

I see three primary responses emanating from those ranks today that seek to deal with this crisis in the integrity of our faith. One is the response of the monolithic Roman Catholic hierarchy. The other two are the responses of conservative and liberal Protestant Christianity respectively. None of these responses, in my opinion, offers any hope for the future.

The Roman Catholic response is basically built on the perpetuation of that previous denial. This was an easier approach for the Roman Catholics than it would have been for Protestants because scripture has never been a major source of Catholic authority. Critical biblical scholarship did not invade Catholic consciousness until the twentieth century. It is a bit easier to ignore the erosion of biblical authority if you have historically downplayed the Bible. Authority for Rome had been located in the Church's official teaching, residing in the magisterium and operating underneath the infallibility vested in the papal office.

However, far more than even Rome might imagine, their original doctrinal positions, which the magisterium has defended so vehemently, were built on a very literal use of the Bible by the fathers of the early Church. If one examined the formation of Christian doctrine in the first few centuries of the Christian era, one would discover that it was totally dependent on a literal understanding of biblical texts. Great efforts were made by the fathers to harmonize biblical contradictions if they could not be simply ignored. It is also fair to say that during the fourth and fifth centuries of the Christian era, when such doctrines as the Incarnation and the Trinity were being formulated, it was the literalized words of the Fourth Gospel, above all others, that buttressed their arguments. To base theology on the literal words of John is to erect the most fragile of structures. The first cause for suspicion is that there is hardly a word attributed to Jesus in the Fourth Gospel that was recorded in any of the earlier Gospels. So the Johannine words are quite late and thus clearly are not original. More and more scholars acknowledge that most of the words attributed to Jesus in the Fourth Gospel were actually shaped by the conflicts in the ninth and tenth decades of the Christian era.

The Jesus Seminar, a group of American biblical scholars, both Catholic and Protestant, who have met for more than a decade seeking to determine the authenticity of Jesus' words in the various gospel traditions, faced this issue squarely. They concluded that none of the words of the Fourth Gospel were in what they called the red letter category, which they defined as accurately reflecting the voice of Jesus. One saying (John 4:43) was in their pink category, which meant that Jesus probably said something like this, but it is not a literal word from Jesus. Only one saying did they place into their gray category (John 13:20), which meant Jesus did not say this, but it contained some ideas that might have been close to his own.[1] Every other "word of Jesus" in the Fourth Gospel this group of scholars marked black. That is, it was their conviction that Jesus did not and could not have said these words. The words attributed to Jesus represented rather the content of the Church fighting battles at a much later time. If the insights of this group of eminent biblical scholars are correct, then the doctrinal superstructure of classical Catholic Christianity has been built on a wobbly foundation indeed.

Beyond the theological claims made for Jesus based on John's gospel, most of the fathers of the Church accepted the miracle stories of the Gospels as the literal accounts of Jesus' power and signs of his supernatural status. The Son of God in human form certainly had the capacity to do wondrous things, it was asserted.

As this Catholic tradition developed, its theology was separated from the scriptural basis that undergirded it and it became communicated simply as "the Church's teaching." Doctrines were added to that teaching based on the claim that the hierarchy of the Church interpreting the Church's faith could also interpret accurately the continuing revelation of God. So traditions like the Immaculate Conception of Mary, the infallibility of the pope, and the Bodily Assumption of the Blessed Virgin were raised into the status of the dogma of the Church. None of these new theological developments even claimed to be based on the authority of scripture, nor was that essential to Roman thought.

When Roman Catholic scholars in this century did finally turn their attention to an exploration of biblical truth, they broke quickly into two quite distinct types. The first group recognized that their pursuit of truth did in fact call the traditional doctrines of the Church into question. Hence, if they confined their scholarship to erudite tomes that would never reach the reading public, they were simply ignored. But if they wrote for a popular audience or gained some public notoriety, they were quickly marginalized, harassed, or removed from their positions of authority. This group includes such people as Hans Küng, Charles Curran, Edward Schillebeeckx, Rosemary Ruether, Matthew Fox, Elisabeth Schüssler Fiorenza, Leonardo Boff, John Dominic Crossan, and Uta Ranke-Heinemann. These scholars are barely able to keep their noses under the tent of the Roman Church.

The second type of Roman Catholic scholars is those whose primary agenda is to serve the needs of the ecclesiastical institution rather than simply to seek the truth. They believe, as loyal servants of Rome, that the institution always possesses the truth. This list includes Raymond Brown, John Meier, and Joseph Fitzmyer. Each of these men is a brilliant researcher, but none of them will draw the conclusions to which their research clearly leads them if it violates the official teachings of the church they serve. As such, their credibility in the world of biblical scholarship is somewhat compromised. Nonetheless, let me quickly say that I have learned much from the likes of Raymond Brown, John Meier, and Joseph Fitzmyer, and I am deeply in their debt even if I do not admire what I regard as their lack of intellectual courage.

But the point remains that Catholic theology totters today because at its heart and base it still assumes a literalism that was imposed on the scriptures by the early fathers, who radically misunderstood and prejudicially suppressed the Jewish origins of the Gospels in a total and significant way. As such, the day will come when that superstructure will collapse of its own weight. When that day arrives, all of the pope's horses and all of the pope's men will not be able to put the doctrinal superstructure back together again. That day is coming sooner than most people think, for that which the hierarchy of the Church likes to refer to as the "authority of the Church" has not escaped the intellectual revolution that renders its presuppositions invalid. An educated laity is not likely to accept blindly and to salute obediently that which they cannot embrace intellectually.

The Protestant understanding of Christianity was always more specifically centered in the scriptures. At first, Protestants defended the inerrancy of "the Word" with vehemence. Those who continue in this tradition are today called the literalists or fundamentalists. "Yes," they assert, "it happened just as the Bible says!" A bumper sticker on the car of such a fundamentalist stated, "God wrote it! I believe it! That does it!"

In periods of great social turmoil, this mentality—in all of its irrationality—emerges anew from the shadows and exerts its power on church and society alike. It places a cover of religious respectability on behavior that reveals enormous and overt hostility. This kind of angry religion usually becomes so extreme and excessive that it burns itself out. If that does not occur, it creates a balancing backlash that forces its recession back into the shadows until the anxiety of the masses once more invites it to return.

In the midst of these churning forces, and not quite so obvious to the social order as to the various religious movements, are those less shrill Christian voices who think they abhor the fundamentalist mentality but who have themselves become selective literalists. Their history is that they defend the literal truth of parts of the Christian story while expressing a willingness to surrender other parts, thus creating an illusion of openness. It is a strategy that works for a while, but ultimately it is doomed to failure also. Perhaps, they suggest, some minor parts of the gospel tradition did not literally occur. Perhaps Jesus did not really transfer the demons from their human host to a whole herd of swine, causing them to stampede to their deaths by drowning in a lake (Mark 5:11 ff.). Perhaps a coin was not found in the mouth of a fish with which taxes might be paid (Matt. 17:27). Perhaps, at Jesus' death, the graves near Jerusalem were not opened and the dead did not arise to walk around the city to be seen by many (Matt. 27:52–53). These more bizarre gospel references can be sacrificed, they argue, so long as the essential truths contained in the Bible are held intact literally. So the retreat from literalism has begun by those who occupy this stance, but it is to be done quite slowly and with lots of aggressive rear-guard action designed to make that retreat seem orderly and rational.

But the fact remains that the first separation in Protestant Christianity from the literalism of the past has been between the thoroughgoing fundamentalists and the selective literalists. In time, the selective literalists themselves divided into two camps, known generally as the conservatives and the liberals. The conservatives are those who want to surrender very little of their literalistic security system. The liberals are those who are willing to part with much more. It is always fascinating to see what is not on the table for discussion much less for surrender. Key parts of the tradition, such as the virgin birth, the reality of miracles, and the physical resurrection, are well down in the list of those things thought to be discussible. So the Protestant divide is over what point the insistence "that this event really happened" is to be ultimately fought.

For years, I identified myself as one of the liberals. Some, who knew little or nothing of the true academic liberals, even assigned to me the label of the ultimate liberal. The very conservative folks wondered out loud whether I believed enough of the Christian story to remain in this household of faith. It might come as a surprise to them to hear me say that I think this liberal approach to scripture and its objective truth is as empty, vapid, and meaningless as the conservative approach to scripture is uninformed, unquestioning, and ignorant. I do not believe that Christianity will be saved or even well served by what has come to be called the liberal approach to the Bible. That approach seems to me rather to remove from the Christian faith all of its power and authenticity by looking for natural explanations for apparently supernatural events.

Does this mean that I have experienced a late-life conversion and am now prepared to return to a conservative understanding of traditional Christianity? Am I now ready to defend the literal truth of the gospel tradition? No. That approach also offers me no hope for the future. No matter how hard I try, I cannot bend my mind into a first-century pretzel. I cannot turn my postmodern mind into a premodern shape. I cannot believe in my heart something that my mind rejects.

What I do mean by this analysis is that I am convinced that Christianity can be made a viable option for future generations, but only if we develop an entirely new approach to the Gospels that will avoid the literal/nonliteral dichotomy or the conservative/liberal split. This cannot be done, however, until we remove from the Bible the traditional interpretive mind-set of the Western world. For it is that mind-set that produced the peculiar battles that today mark Catholic doctrinal theology. It is also that mind-set that has given Protestant Christianity its literal versus nonliteral divisions first, and which then divided the nonliteral camp into its present conservative versus liberal factions. While these various groups battle to rearrange the deck chairs on the *Titanic,* the Christian faith looks more and more like that sinking ship. There is, in my opinion, a bankruptcy attached to each of those approaches.

The fact that we must recover is that Christianity was not born as a Western religion. A Western mentality has been imposed on this Middle Eastern understanding or revelation of God. The Bible is a Jewish book. It was written by people who thought as Jews, embraced the world as Jews, and understood reality as Jews. Does this Jewish perspective offer a new possibility? Can it provide us with a new angle of vision or with new insights into the wonder and mystery of God? Can it open the Bible to a meaning that we will think is new, but which has, in all probability, simply been lost? I contend that it might, and that an exploration into this perspective can be a worthy enterprise. At least it might broaden the scope of the present religious debate so that the options do not seem so dead-end.

The Western mentality concentrates on an external world. It is a mentality anchored in time and space and objectivity. It always seeks to answer the historic questions: Is this real? Is this objectively true? Did this really happen? With these questions to guide us, the Western mind has always had trouble embracing the truth found in myth, legend, intuition, or poetry. That was for dreamers, for visionaries, and perhaps for irrelevant mystics. But these questions will determine the shape of the answers that can be given, and thus the perception of reality that determines the boundaries on truth. The Western questions—Did this really happen? Is this real?—always require a "yes" or "no" answer. Only begrudgingly will the Western mentality admit to a hedging "yes" answer, but little more. But when the Bible in all its miraculous magic, its chosen people, its three-tiered universe populated with demons and angels is the subject of the inquiry, a "yes" answer is such nonsense that it requires a surrender of all intellectual faculties; a hedging "yes" answer is a compromise with both honesty and courage and only postpones the inevitable; and a "no" answer removes the realm of spirit, mystery, and meaning from any objective consideration. That is where we are in the post-Christian contemporary world. In today's world, the "yes" answer produces the passion of the religious right; the hedging "yes" answer produces the conservative to liberal, but still dying, mainline religious approach; and the "no" answer produces the secular humanists, who want to be done with all things religious. There is little hope and little future for the Christian faith, in my opinion, in any of these alternatives.

But having reached that conclusion is far from entering some kind of godless religious despair for me. The fact is that I am more deeply persuaded of and moved by the truth I find in Christianity at this moment than I have ever been before. That persuasion, however, has not come from arriving at the ultimate and irreducible bottom line of faith that the erstwhile liberal always seeks. It has come rather by stepping out of my Western mentality altogether and seeking to absorb the Jewish origins and the Middle Eastern nuances of my faith story. I am no longer concerned about discovering whether certain biblical events actually occurred. I am far more interested in entering the experience that lies behind the description that found expression in the biblical text. I no longer ask, "Did it really happen?" or, "Is it true?" Rather, I ask, "What does it mean? Why was this image chosen to convey this insight?" The Jewish originators of my gospel tradition, I now see, wrapped around their descriptions of Jesus' words and deeds the narratives of their own religious past. When they confronted what they believed was the presence of God in a contemporary moment, they interpreted this moment by applying to it similar moments in their sacred story when they were convinced the presence of God had also been real to their forebears in faith. They wrote, therefore, in the timelessness of valid religious experiences. So the Gospels were not descriptions of what happened or what Jesus said or did; they were interpretations of who Jesus was based on their ancient and sacred heritage. That was the only way they could understand and process the God presence they found in Jesus that was so powerful. That is also why they located their hopes for salvation in him. Through this Jesus they believed themselves drawn into the wonder of both God and that mystical sense of oneness with the divine that they found in him.

With my life reordered by this insight, and my quest for truth delivered from a yes-or-no approach to the things of the spirit, I have begun to sink my life into the Jewishness of the Gospels. My witness is that the power of these books and the compelling nature of the Jesus experience glow for me today with a new intensity and compel me with an uncharacteristic evangelical fervor to share these insights so that other Christians might also escape the dead-end struggles in which I perceive so much of the contemporary religious energy is dissipated.

I do not today regard the details of the gospel tradition as possessing literal truth in any primary way. I do not believe that the Gospels offer us either reliable eyewitness memory or realistic objective history. I do believe that the Gospels are Jewish attempts to interpret in a Jewish way the life of a Jewish man in whom the transcendence of God was believed to have been experienced in a fresh and powerful encounter. I do believe that the God met in Jesus is real, and that by approaching the scriptures through a Jewish lens, saving reality can be illumined and—even more important—can still be entered.

I write, therefore, with the passion of a believer. I yearn to share with others this truth by which I now live, and I invite you into this odyssey with two caveats: First, you may have to surrender, not just some, but all of those aspects of the familiar religious security system of your Christian past, for this approach will be far more radical than most Christians have ever before considered. It will require a totally new perspective. Second, I offer you something that I have come to believe is better than the religious security system of the past. I offer the exhilarating insecurity of a journey without boundaries or goals. I offer the radical nature of honesty and the intense humanity that is found in seeking truth freely apart from the authoritative pronouncements of yesterday. I find the God I meet in the midst of this risky adventure to be powerful, life-giving, and real, and this is the God I have found in Jesus of Nazareth when I learned to approach him from within the traditions of the Jewish world that produced him. So place on your eyes a Jewish lens and open your mind and heart to Jewish understandings of that which is real, and come with me as I seek to enter anew that Jewish book that the world has traditionally called the New Testament.

2

The Gospels Are Jewish Books

When I was a child growing up in an evangelical part of the Christian Church in the United States, I was convinced that Jesus must have been a Swede or at least an Englishman. Every picture I saw of him, and there were many, portrayed him with fair skin, blonde hair, and blue eyes. He had the angular look of a northern European. In my region of America, there was little ethnic diversity. Most of the people I knew in my monolithic but tiny world were of English, Scottish, or Welsh backgrounds, but they basically defined themselves as the "true" Americans as opposed to those they still thought to be foreigners. The occasional German or French family that lived in my small world was readily identifiable, for names like Schmidt or Haas and Carpentier or Jousset stood out amid the Johnsons, Browns, Wilsons, Griffiths, Smiths, and Joneses. Of course, there were also African Americans in this region of my nation; but they had been victimized by racial prejudice for so long that, in this period of history, they appeared almost to accept the prevailing conviction that they did not quite belong to this land. They even seemed to accept the conclusion that Jesus must have been a northern European.

If someone with a sense of both history and objectivity had said to me at that time, "Do you not realize that Jesus was a Jew?" I suppose I would have been shocked by the possibility. Everything I knew about this Jesus, presumably from the Bible, would have screamed out in opposition to such a thought. Jesus was clearly defined for me as something good. Jews were clearly defined for me in church, in Sunday school, and through what I had been taught was in the Bible itself, as something evil. To say that Jesus was a Jew would have been, to my limited mind, almost an oxymoron, and certainly a contradiction in terms. It is amazing how ignorance and prejudice can distort history.

Yet, Jewish Jesus was. The continent of his birth was Asia, not Europe. His citizenship was in a part of the world known as Palestine, and called the Holy Land. In the years of my childhood, the state of Israel simply did not exist. I saw lots of pictures of Palestinians as a child, since this troubled part of the world even then was frequently in the media, which for me meant newspapers, magazines, and the Movietone news at the cinema on Saturday morning. People who lived in Palestine, I observed, were dark-skinned with black hair. They were lean, not fat, and possessed distinctive Middle Eastern features. In the segregated world of my upbringing, Palestinians, including the Jews of Palestine, and thus Jesus of Nazareth, would have been denied access to public accommodations. They would not have been welcomed in the restaurants, hotels, parks, and libraries of my youth, not even in those facilities paid for and supported by the public treasury of tax-paying citizens, which included everyone who earned money. It was beyond my imagination to think that Jesus could have looked like a member of the segregated underclass of that evil social order.

From where did such a distorted view of reality arise? How was it that one whose name was Yeshuah or Joshua of Nazareth, whose mother's name was Miriam, could come to be thought of in history as anything but a Jew? He was, we are told in the biblical story, circumcised on the eighth day of his life, presented in the Temple on the fortieth day, and (perhaps in some kind of puberty rite that later developed into a bar mitzvah) taken to the Temple in Jerusalem at age twelve for a great celebration (Luke 2).

The life of Jesus was lived almost entirely within the boundaries of his small country. He may have touched the non-Jewish world in an episodic way from time to time, but it was only in those places where that world impinged on the world of the Jews. Perhaps he scandalized that Jewish world by his contact with the Syro-Phoenician woman (Mark 7:26) and the gentile centurion named Jairus (Mark 5:22), or when he crossed the Sea of Galilee and walked into the gentile region of the Gerasenes (Luke 8:26).

His life appears to have been made aware of the emotional and physical divisions between Jews and non-Jews (Mark 10:42, Matt. 5:47). His religious system suggested to him that this division was as deep as the one between those who were ritually clean and those who were ritually unclean. Gentiles, lepers, and menstruating women all fell into that definition of uncleanness, hardly creating the kind of category which the gentiles of northern Europe had ever used to categorize themselves.

Not only did I not understand that Jesus was Jewish, but it never occurred to me to assume that his disciples were Jewish either. I could not imagine Peter, James, John, and Andrew as Jews, to say nothing of Mary Magdalene and Paul. Strangely enough, however, I did assume that one of the chosen twelve was a Jew. Judas Iscariot was his name, and the prejudice of my region painted this disciple as dark, sinister, and evil. Those were the characteristics that, not coincidentally, I had been taught were typical of the Jews. Yet they were also the characteristics that I could never have attributed to Jesus, or to his mother, Mary, or to the chosen apostles—who, I assumed, after the defection of Judas, had numbered only eleven until Matthias was elected to take Judas's place and thus to restore wholeness to the number twelve (Acts 1:15–26).

My Sunday school classes had clearly taught me that Jesus and his disciples were the good people in the biblical drama. Judas and such clearly identified Jews as Annas, Caiaphas, the scribes, the Pharisees, and the Sadducees were the bad people. They were Jesus' enemies. They were constantly plotting against him. They tried to entrap him with trick questions of petty sophistry (Luke 20:2, Matt. 22:28). I had been convinced by this educational process that it was the Jews who betrayed him, arrested him, tortured him, and saw to it that he was put to death. I did learn from the Bible that the actual crucifixion of Jesus had been done by the Roman authorities, but the Imperial Roman Empire appeared to me to have been represented by benignly passive leaders who simply carried out the will of the hostile Jewish hierarchy. I have now discovered that I also had been seduced by that prejudiced twisting of history that had enabled one named Pontius Pilate to be exonerated for the execution of Jesus. He had ordered the dastardly act of crucifixion against both his own desires and his better judgment just to satisfy the bloodthirsty Jews, I was told. I accepted as literal truth that picture of Pilate washing his hands and claiming to be innocent of the blood of this Jesus (Matt. 27:24). The phrase in the creed that seemed to deny that Jesus was actually crucified "by" Pontius Pilate, and said that this only happened "under" Pontius Pilate, added fuel to this conclusion.

This Jewish hostility toward Jesus did not cease even with his execution, I was told. The chief priests and the Pharisees, I learned, went to Pilate and demanded that a guard of Roman soldiers be placed around the tomb of this Jesus to prevent his disciples from stealing his body and putting out rumors that he had risen from the dead. Pilate, who seemed to grow nicer and more "Christian" as the days went by, had declined this request; but he did suggest that the Jews had Temple guards of their own who might perform this chore, and he urged that solution upon them (Matt. 27:62–66). So it was Jewish soldiers who were assigned to the tomb of Jesus to guard it against the possibility of an Easter resurrection, at least according to Matthew. When this Jewish guard proved ineffective even in this assignment, I was told that "the Jews" then put out the word that what the Christians called the resurrection was in fact the very fraud that the Jews anticipated and feared. The disciples had stolen Jesus' body (Matt. 28:13). Easter was a lie concocted by the Christians. Such hostile explanations were easy for me to accept because they fitted neatly into the stereotype that I was learning. This stereotype suggested that Jews were evil people who did terrible things and who clearly were not to be trusted.

When my Sunday school education got to Paul and his exciting missionary journeys, this prejudiced stereotype was constantly reinforced. Since no one had ever suggested to me that Paul might have been a Jew, I read about his life with the assumption that he was not Jewish. Whenever Paul preached the gospel, the Book of Acts informed me, he was attacked and persecuted by the Jews. In Lystra, Derbe, Iconium, Corinth, Ephesus, and Philippi, Paul preached first in synagogues; but because he created there such divisions among the Jews, he was forced to turn to the gentiles to deliver his message. Paul, I learned, would have himself been put to death by the Jews had it not been for the fact that he was a Roman citizen. Only by appealing to that citizenship did he escape execution. Instead, he was sent off on his final hazardous voyage to Rome to be tried in the courts of the Caesar, which was the privilege of that citizenship (Acts 25:11). The story of Paul's fascinating adventures, told to us in the Book of Acts, closed before Paul's death (Acts 28). For this reason we read nowhere in the Bible about the tradition that Paul met his death in Rome at the hands of the Roman emperor named Nero. Nonetheless, that was clearly the consensus of the early Christian understanding. Such a narrative, if it had been included in the Bible, might have helped to counter the searing anti-Jewish prejudice that was rampant in that generation of Christian believers. Unfortunately, however, it was omitted from the pages of holy scripture.

These negative stereotypes of the Jews were so extensive that, as I look back on the way I had been introduced to what we Christians still pejoratively call the "Old" Testament, I discover them operating in a distorting way even there. How, for example, can one study the ancient Hebrew scriptures and not recognize that this was the sacred story of the Jewish people? Yet we managed to do it in the Christian church of my youth. To distort history that completely takes a real stretch, but prejudice is capable of accomplishing rather remarkable things.

As the sacred scriptures of the Jews entered my young Christian consciousness, there was a clear distinction drawn between the heroes of the biblical story and the ordinary people. Ever so subtly we budding Christians learned to identify ourselves with the heroes and, perhaps not coincidentally, to recognize the rebellious people in these stories as the real Jews.

Noah was righteous, I learned, but the people were evil, so God had to destroy them in the great flood (Gen. 6:11 ff.). Such a view of God did not terrify me, for I had so clearly identified myself and those I knew with the righteous Noah as to be not fearful of such a god. Abraham had the courage to separate himself first from Ur of the Chaldees (Gen. 12:1 ff.) and second from his not so noble nephew, Lot (Gen. 13:8–13). So Abraham, the hero, was not seen as part of the Jewish people from whom he had stepped away. Jacob, despite being a cheat and a dissembler, became the one who stood in the line of righteousness instead of his clumsy and roguish twin brother, Esau (Gen. 25:29). Joseph was the wronged and righteous member of his band of twelve brothers. This noble figure even acted to save those evil brothers who plotted to take his life (Gen. 37–50). One of those evil brothers was Judah, the father of the Jewish nation (Gen. 37:26). Moses, who gave his all to free the Jewish people from slavery, nonetheless suffered incredible abuse, rebellion, and shameless behavior at the hands of these same people in the wilderness years (Exod. 32, Num. 12:1–16). Somehow, in my mind it was these rebellious people who were the Jews, while the heroes of this story—Noah, Abraham, Jacob, Joseph, and Moses—were not. Imagine a prejudice so deep that it enabled people to make non-Jewish heroes out of the likes of Moses and Abraham. Yet that is what occurred in my life as I came into an awareness of the content of the Bible as the Christians of my world taught it. I would like to think that such a twisted view of both history and reality was perhaps unique to me and to my upbringing. Unfortunately, I fear that this prejudiced stereotypical approach to the Jews of the Bible has been the daily bread of the Christian church for most of the 2,000 years of Christian history.

So the Jewishness of Jesus, the Jewishness of Mary, his mother, the Jewishness of the Apostles, the Jewishness of Paul, and even the Jewishness of the heroes of the Hebrew past was at worst systematically denied and at best subtly understated. It is thus easy for me to understand today that few people in the Christian West have been able to think of the Bible, including both testaments, as a Jewish book. If one cannot even embrace emotionally the Jewishness of Jesus, then why would one study the sacred scriptures of the Jewish people as the primary means of knowing and understanding this Jesus? How aware are people today, for example, of the fact that every author in the entire Bible was Jewish by birth or conversion and that there was only one convert? How often has the interpretive task of the Christian expositors of the Gospels begun with the suggestion that, since the books we call Gospels were written by Jewish authors, we might want to study just how it was that Jewish people wrote sacred narratives so that we might understand even the Gospels? Has it not occurred to anyone to ask, "How can a Jewish work be understood if one ignores the Jewish context, the Jewish mind-set, the Jewish frame of reference, the Jewish vocabulary, and even the Jewish history that shaped and formed the writer?" But that has been the reality of the Christian West for most of our history.

Even when we begin to deal with Luke, who was the Bible's single gentile-by-birth author, we are still not escaping the Jewish worldview. For the evidence is overwhelming that the author of Luke was a gentile proselyte to Judaism. That is, he was one of those gentiles who had been deeply drawn to the worship of the Jewish God and to the practices of the Jewish religion. Proselytes were attracted to the theological concept of ethical monotheism that marked Judaism. Judaism thus appealed to many a gentile mind, especially when the ancient traditions that focused on the gods of the Olympus began to die. Luke and most gentile proselytes, however, were not particularly drawn to the cultic side of the Jewish religion. These proselytes tended to avoid such ritual practices and observances as the Sabbath-day requirement, the kosher dietary laws, and the rite of circumcision. As regular attendees at synagogue worship, however, they did hear the ancient scriptures being read, and they began to allow this sacred story of the Jewish people to wash over their minds and to infiltrate their lives. The great prophets in Jewish history, such as Amos and Hosea, spoke powerfully about justice. The ethical aspects of the Ten Commandments and the dawning universalism that can be found in Elijah, Moses, Isaiah, and even Malachi, were appealing to these gentiles, who were seeking an authentic worship experience. Gentile proselytes were also drawn to those tremendous words of the prophet Micah, who in response to the question, "What does the Lord require of you?" answered, "To do justice, to love kindness, and to walk humbly with your God" (Mic. 6:8). Such words were warmly received in gentile ears. So even Luke, the single gentile writer in the Christian Bible, was a convert, a proselyte who had been steeped in Jewish thoughts and who gave ready expression to Jewish concerns and Jewish values. Hence Luke's gospel must also be read inside the Jewish context. It was written by a Jewish convert. Indeed, one will never understand any of the Gospels, I am now convinced, unless and until one can embrace their essential Jewishness. This is a radical claim that may, for lack of understanding or sensitivity, not be recognized as being quite as radical as I am suggesting. People who think that they understand the Jewishness of the Gospels will tend to trivialize my words and to suggest that I am proposing nothing new. They will misunderstand my message badly.

I do not mean to say for a moment that Christians, either in the first generation or today, did not recognize certain Jewish antecedents that are present in the gospel tradition. They certainly did. But I do mean to suggest that after the deaths of the first generation of Christians, the vast majority of whom were Jewish, the second and third generations of Christians, who tended to be gentiles, would read these Jewish antecedents in the gospel story with a deeply prejudiced anti-Jewish bias that distorted their understanding. I do also mean to suggest that this bias was challenged less and less as the years rolled by, until this attitude became viewed, not as a prejudiced distortion, but as an unchallenged kind of orthodoxy. That created finally the long period of history in which the Gospels were cut away from their essential Jewishness and were interpreted as if they were primarily gentile books. We are just now beginning to emerge from this mentality. During this period of history, the Jewishness of the Gospels was actually lost. Furthermore, I mean to suggest that this gentile reading of the Gospels has distorted the message of these books, creating a situation in which many earnest and well-meaning Christians today read what they think is the clear message of the Bible and do not recognize how destructively prejudiced is their understanding of biblical or gospel truth.

The outline of this Christian negativity toward things Jewish is seen in the way Christians use the Old Testament even to this day. The primary value the Hebrew sacred story has had for most Christians lies in the prejudiced assumption that the meaning of the Old Testament is exhausted once its task of pointing to and being fulfilled by the New Testament has been accomplished. The prophets were thought to be something like fortune-tellers who served as the divine predictors of future events. One noted American televangelist has said that the divinity of Jesus can be proved in that his life fulfilled a number of specific predictions of things to come found in the prophets.[1] In the Bible from which I read as a child, little stars were placed beside the verses in the Old Testament that were assumed to be biblical predictions that had been fulfilled by Jesus. The first one appeared as early as the Book of Genesis, where God was portrayed as actually speaking to a serpent: "I will put enmity between you and the woman and between your seed and her seed; he will bruise your head and you shall bruise his heel" (Gen. 3:15). It was never quite clear to me exactly how this was a prediction of the life of Jesus, but since it came near the beginning of the Bible, it was thought to indicate that the entire sacred text was a unified story revolving around Jesus. I discovered later that this particular verse was involved in the whole theology of the atonement, which did not develop instantaneously even in the earliest interpretations of the life of Jesus. So there was a great deal of after-the-fact searching for supportive proof texts that led expositors to these words in Genesis.

Many of the literal details chronicled in the story of the cross, I was told, were graphically spelled out centuries earlier in the psalms and the prophets. When I read these sources with my prejudiced Christian eyes, there was in fact a stunning similarity that seemed to buttress that argument. All of this fitted together so well with my limited knowledge and constituted a persuasive argument in my youth.

There was also about this view of the Gospels a sense that the stories of Jesus, as we have them, were told in a chronological time sequence. The Gospels appear to start at the beginning of Jesus' life, with his birth or his baptism, and then to proceed to the conclusion of his life with his death and resurrection. So it was easy to think of them as both biographical and based on eyewitness accounts. We seem to have a movement from Jesus' origins in Galilee to his climactic experience in Jerusalem. This concept tended to divide the Gospels into the presumed three phases of Jesus' public ministry: his time in Galilee, the journey to Jerusalem, and the climax of his life in Jerusalem. It fitted neatly into our preconceived linear framework of time. Hence, when one studied the Gospels, the tendency was to assume that the authors wrote under the authority of linear time and biographical history. Such a framework also enabled the reader to ignore those places where the data simply did not fit this preconception. For example, was Jesus' public ministry one year or three years? Did Jesus make one or three journeys to Jerusalem? When the Gospels are read as history, that detail is not clear. Other anomalies abound. Why does the journey from Galilee to Jerusalem that culminates in the Palm Sunday procession (outlined especially in Mark, Matthew, and Luke) seem to back and fill aimlessly before it finally arrives? Why does Luke have Jesus weep over Jerusalem when he is still seventy miles away? What does one do when gospel writers disagree about when a particular episode occurred? (Compare John 2:13–22 with Mark 11:15–19.) The time sequence also appears frequently to be confused. Does "three days" mean seventy-two hours of linear time? If so, then why is that time frame, "three days," so inconsistent in the biblical text? Sometimes the preposition "on" is connected to the symbol of the third day, sometimes it is the preposition "after" that is used. They are quite different. "On the third day" and "after three days" would not refer to the same moment in time. On one occasion the text actually uses the phrase "three days and three nights" (Matt. 12:40), which is different still. Yet the actual time between Good Friday and Easter in the gospel story is only thirty-six hours, a day and a half at most. How does that time inconsistency get interpreted? What was going on in Luke's gospel when Jesus was portrayed as returning to Nazareth and the people said to him, "Do here also in your hometown the things that we heard you did at Capernaum" (Luke 4:23)? The primary trouble with that text is that, according to Luke, Jesus had not yet been to Capernaum! Again, the assumed time frame in which we have thought the Gospels were written becomes elusive.

Is it therefore possible that we have inappropriately imposed a Western understanding of time on a Jewish tradition? Since we are beginning to recognize the Gospels as Jewish books, would it not be well to determine what time meant in Jewish sacred traditions? Are we aware that the rabbis argued that the sacred texts of scripture were timeless, possessing no before or after qualities? Or perhaps we should inquire as to the way in which the gospel stories developed originally. Was it biographical, so that the memories created the Gospels? Or was there a quite different Jewish context that might be probed for hidden clues?

Finally, there are stories in the Gospels that are so deeply reminiscent of stories in the Old Testament that one might inquire as to the reason for their similarity. Was that accidental or coincidental? Or does it point to something we might have missed? The confusion of tongues at Babel (Gen. 11:1–9) is surely related in some way to the overcoming of that confusion of tongues at Pentecost (Acts 2). The story of Pharaoh seeking to kill the Jewish boy babies in Egypt (Exod. 1:22 ff.) is surely connected to the story of Herod seeking to kill the Jewish boy babies in Bethlehem (Matt. 2:16–18). The story of Moses, who, after meeting God on the mountain, had his face shine so brightly that it had to be covered (Exod. 34:29 ff.), is surely related to the story of Jesus being transfigured so that he too shone with an unearthly radiance (Mark 9:2–8, Matt. 17:1–8, Luke 9:28–36). The account of the Palm Sunday procession (Mark 11:2–10, Matt. 21:1–9, Luke 19:28–38) is surely related to the story in Zechariah (9:9–11) where the king came to Jerusalem, lowly and riding on a donkey. These and countless other illustrations seem to cry out for a Jewish knowledge that might help us unlock the treasures hidden in these Jewish books we Christians call the Gospels.

As long as the Gospels were read and interpreted only by gentile people, however, either these ancient Hebrew connections were unknown or it was assumed that these were nothing but Old Testament foreshadowings of the life of Christ. To believe that these texts are actual anticipations of Jesus meant that Christians had to believe that these verses had been placed into the texts of antiquity by the holy God so that hundreds of years later people would see in Jesus' literal fulfillment of these expectations proof of his divine nature. If that was to be the way that God worked, we need to recognize that God has had to run some enormous literary risks, to have been constantly vigilant and significantly invasive, for such a scheme to work. Suppose there had been miscopying by scribes, or mistranslations by translators? Suppose that these sacred writings had, through the centuries, been inadequately protected from enemies and so had been destroyed. Would not God's plan have been thwarted? The Dead Sea Scrolls, many of which date from the centuries just before the birth of Christ, were hidden in jars for 2,000 or more years. Many of them were destroyed by their Bedouin discoverers before they recognized their worth. A similar fate could have befallen the writings of the prophets. I suppose that this literal-minded tradition would have to assume that the God who planted those clues in the ancient texts would also have guarded the passage of these texts through the perils of copyists, translators, and any possible destruction at the hands of enemies. It would, however, be a rather unusual concept of God that so fragile a method of revelation had to be employed. Is it possible that when we stare into the absurdity of some of our common assumptions about the Bible, we might begin to suspect that we have imposed on these sacred texts a strange and foreign agenda? Would it not have seemed obvious to someone ever to ask whether this was the way that the Jewish people wrote or interpreted their sacred stories? Few gentiles there were, however, who, in the arrogance of their power and in the dominance of their religious certainty, ever stopped to consider this or any other possibility that might challenge the deeply imposed version of Christian wisdom. So it was that this distorting, prejudiced, unquestioning anti-Jewish attitude that created this gentile captivity of the Gospels went on unchallenged for centuries. The price that Christians paid because of this captivity was the loss of the essential meaning of the Gospels. For the truth found in the Gospels could be revealed only by reading these texts through a Jewish lens. That Jewish lens, however, remained hidden from Christian eyes for centuries.

The same anti-Jewish mentality was also busily occupied in the task of the erosion of the Jewishness of these Gospels. By the early years of the second century, the Christian church had become an almost exclusively gentile church. This meant that from that day until this generation, only gentiles have read and only gentiles have interpreted the Christian scriptures. These gentile interpreters did not know—nor were they even aware that they did not know—the Jewish background. Ignorance joined hands with prejudice first to distort truth and understanding and then finally to lose the original meaning of the Gospels altogether.

Lastly, this ignorance imposed a non-Jewish literalness on the gospel texts that the Jewish authors, I am convinced, would never have understood or appreciated. Somewhere around the year 140 C.E., the status of the Gospels as Jewish books descended so low that a man named Marcion actually sought to remove the Hebrew God and the Hebrew scriptures from the Christian Bible. He failed officially. Far more than Christians recognized then or later, however, he succeeded unofficially. As a result of that unofficial success, the Gospels were for centuries covered with a blinding negativity to all things Jewish. This negativity is only now beginning to lift, and it is my thesis that, because it is lifting, a new way to approach the Gospels is finally emerging.

In a deep and significant way, we are now able to see that all of the Gospels are Jewish books, profoundly Jewish books. Recognizing this, we begin to face the realization that we will never understand the Gospels until we learn how to read them as Jewish books. They are written, to a greater or lesser degree, in the *midrashic* style of the Jewish sacred storyteller, a style that most of us do not begin even now to comprehend. This style is not concerned with historic accuracy. It is concerned with meaning and understanding. The Jewish writers of antiquity interpreted God's presence to be with Joshua after the death of Moses by repeating the parting of the waters story (Josh. 3). At the Red Sea that was the sign that God was with Moses (Exod. 14). When Joshua was said to have parted the waters of the Jordan River, it was not recounted as a literal event of history; rather it was the *midrashic* attempt to relate Joshua to Moses and thus demonstrate the presence of God with his successor. The same pattern operated later when both Elijah (2 Kings 2:8) and Elisha (2 Kings 2:14) were said to have parted the waters of the Jordan River and to have walked across on dry land. When the story of Jesus' baptism was told, the gospel writers asserted that Jesus parted not the Jordan River, but the heavens. This Moses theme was thus being struck yet again (Mark 1:9 ff.), and indeed, for a similar purpose. The heavens, according to the Jewish creation story, were nothing but the firmament that separated the waters above from the waters below (Gen. 1:6–8). To portray Jesus as splitting the heavenly waters was a Jewish way of suggesting that the holy God encountered in Jesus went even beyond the God presence that had been met in Moses, Joshua, Elijah, and Elisha. That is the way the *midrashic* principle worked. Stories about heroes of the Jewish past were heightened and retold again and again about heroes of the present moment, not because those same events actually occurred, but because the reality of God revealed in those moments was like the reality of God known in the past. As this journey through the Gospels progresses, we will watch this *midrashic* principle operating time after time.

We are not reading history when we read the Gospels. We are listening to the experience of Jewish people, processing in a Jewish way what they believed was a new experience with the God of Israel. Jews filtered every new experience through the corporate remembered history of their people, as that history had been recorded in the Hebrew scriptures of the past.

If we are to recover the power present in the scriptures for our time, then this clue to their original meaning must be recovered and understood. Ascribing to the Gospels historic accuracy in the style of later historians, or demanding that the narratives of the Gospels be taken literally, or trying to recreate the historical context surrounding each specific event narrated in the Gospels—these are the methods of people who do not realize that they are reading a Jewish book.

But before we can fully address this issue and begin to read the Gospels as Jewish books, we must cast our gaze on the early history of the Christian movement to seek to understand where things went wrong. What were the forces of history that collaborated to tear the Christian church away from its Jewish origins? If we are ever to find our way back to the Jewish perspective that produced our Gospels, then we must understand how that perspective was first broken, then denied, and then lost. It was not an accident. To that story we now turn.

3

How These Jewish Books
Became Gentile Captives

In the seventieth year of the common era, the city of Jerusalem was destroyed by the Roman army. That destruction represented the climax, if not the end, of a war waged by Rome against the Jews that began in 66 c.e. It formed one of those pregnant moments that changed the face of human history far more dramatically than historians have yet imagined. One result of that war was that the Jewish nation disappeared from the maps of the world, and it was destined not to reappear on those maps for almost 1,900 years—indeed, until the Balfour declaration of the League of Nations in 1917 was finally implemented by the United Nations in 1948.[1] This meant that from the year 70 to 1948, Jewish people possessed no homeland and thus no protection. Another direct result of this war was that the

Christian faith, which had originally been a Jewish movement, began the shift that was destined to redefine Christianity as a bitterly anti-Semitic and anti-Jewish movement. This war quite literally cut the taproot that connected Christianity to its Jewish past. Still another result of this pivotal year 70 C.E. was that every book later to be incorporated into the New Testament either reflected the tensions that produced that war or was written against the background of that Jewish defeat and destruction. Indeed, one cannot understand the books of the New Testament unless one understands the violent history of that part of the world in which the Christian movement was first born and against which it was defined.

Since Paul died in 64 C.E., we need to recognize that all of Paul's authentic letters were written prior to this crucial seventieth year. This means that the epistles known as 1 and 2 Thessalonians, Galatians, 1 and 2 Corinthians, Romans, Philippians, and Philemon are for certain placed prior to 70 C.E. Colossians and Ephesians, which are debated as Pauline originals, could also be placed on the far side of 70, even if their actual Pauline authorship is finally denied. This dating, however, would not be universally saluted.

The only gospel in existence prior to 70 is believed to be Mark. It is generally dated in a range from 64 to 72, with consensus falling in the year 69 or 70, or just prior to the cataclysmic events of that seventieth year.

There is a strong, but neither universally recognized nor even an in-the-majority, tradition that the epistle to the Hebrews might also be a pre-70 literary work; but if so, that would complete the list of New Testament writings that arguably could be placed on the calendar prior to the year 70 C.E. The other three Gospels (Matthew, Luke, and John), the pseudo Pauline epistles (1 and 2 Timothy and Titus), the General Epistles (1 and 2 Peter, 1, 2, and 3 John, Jude, and James), the Book of Acts, and the Book of Revelation are all quite clearly post-70 literary works. Each of these books in some way reveals, however, that it was written under the impact of the events of that crucial year.

This dramatic and catastrophic year affected both Jews and Christians so profoundly that it must be lifted out of antiquity and placed squarely before our awakened consciousness.

The kind of conflict represented by that war, the kind that produces oceans of human bitterness, is never born in a single moment or as the result of the events of a single instant. The conflict between the Romans and the Jews had been building in intensity for decades in the history of this region. We can find hints of these early tensions even in the Church's memory of Jesus, as that memory came to be recorded in the writing of the Gospels. The little Jewish nation had been conquered by the forces of the Roman empire in 63 B.C.E. Jesus was born, according to our best estimates, somewhere between 8 B.C.E. and 4 B.C.E., and his earthly life came to its conclusion somewhere between 27 and 33 C.E. (For my purposes in this book, and simply for the sake of the convenience of an even number, I will take the year 30 as the year of the crucifixion event/resurrection experience.) So the entire life of this Jesus was lived among a people who were citizens of a conquered nation. The sacred soil of the Jews had been polluted by the occupying military forces who served the victorious Roman empire. In that conquest much of the land that had historically provided a living for its Jewish citizens had been confiscated. The resulting poverty and displacement of those who formerly had been the tillers of this soil was readily apparent. The dignity of this proud people was regularly insulted; and, as is so often the case in military occupation, Jewish women were frequently victimized for sexual sport by the army of occupation. The power equation between the Roman empire and the Jewish nation was such as to provide no realistic reasons for hope that some day this occupation would come to an end or that freedom would ever be restored.

The response of the conquered Jews to their plight ran the gamut that normally marks a defeated people. First, there were those who cooperated with their conquerors in order to cut a deal for themselves that would ease their burdens. Next, there were those who simply endured their conquered status, surviving as best they could within the very narrow options available. Finally, there were the defiant ones who refused to accept conquest and who vowed to make the life of their conquerors as difficult and as expensive as possible. Defiance sometimes took the form of sabotage. When the saboteurs were caught, execution was normally swift and cruel. As a control tactic, ofttimes the circle of those executed would be expanded by the Romans to include relatives, friends, and even those merely suspected of being the acquaintances of the guilty one. So many an innocent victim paid with his or her life for this activity of defiance. Because crucifixion was the Roman way of doing capital punishment, crosses with their dying victims attached were not an uncommon sight in this land of the Jews under this oppressive conqueror.

A second activity of defiance that found expression in the population at this time was guerrilla warfare. In the hills of Galilee, bands of Jewish "freedom fighters," as the Jews might have called them, or Jewish "terrorists," as the Romans probably referred to them, could roam in relative safety. And roam they did. In the manner typical of guerrilla fighters everywhere, these Jewish vigilantes would engage in hit-and-run attacks. Roman casualties were not normally very large, but they were bothersome. In the euphemistic way that we use words today to hide from the horror of war, we might refer to this casualty rate as "tolerable" or as "within the bounds of acceptability." But the casualties were constant; they were disruptive to Roman order and they fed a constant morale problem, with which Rome finally had to deal.

Some of these Jewish guerrilla fighters were known as the Zealots. The fact that Luke, both in the gospel (Luke 6:15) and in the Book of Acts (1:13), referred to one of Jesus' twelve disciples as "Simon the Zealot" may either be an anachronistic reading back into the time of Jesus of the events of this later development in Jewish history, or these references may reflect the fact that this Zealot movement had been in existence for as long as fifty years. It may even point to a largely denied possibility among Christians that Jesus and his Galilean band of twelve might have been far more closely identified with the Jewish guerrilla movement than most religious people are comfortable admitting.[2] Surveying the biblical references that appear to indicate that the disciple band was armed with swords also suggests this possibility rather overtly (Matt. 10:34, 26:5 ff.; Mark 14:47; Luke 22:36, 22:49; John 18:10, 11). It is to be noted, however, that both Mark and Matthew, who wrote prior to Luke, refer to this Simon not as the Zealot, but as the Canaanean (Mark 3:18, Matt. 10:4).[3] So this point is certainly not established. It is only hinted.

In any event, the Jewish province called Galilee was all but unconquerable as far as the Romans were concerned. So it was that this region itself became a synonym for the hostility that Romans had for Jews. Galilee was a land of rugged terrain inhabited by fierce, fearless, and warlike people against whom Rome was required to keep constant vigilance.

This subterranean hostility between the Galilean Jews and the Roman army finally grew so strong and so organized that, in the year 66 C.E., it broke out into full-scale warfare. Rome could no longer ignore the situation or continue to treat it as a minor irritation. So the armed might of the Roman empire began to move against the Galilean hideouts and the Zealots were flushed out of their mountain strongholds, one pocket after another. It was a costly and laborious task that took longer than military officials could anticipate. In the process, hostilities between Jews and Romans reached a fever pitch of negativity. During this time, as is true to the reality of warfare, the propaganda machine of the Roman empire began to turn out increasingly shrill, anti-Jewish sentiments. Jews were portrayed by the Romans as subhuman, uncivilized, base, and evil. In this political climate, anyone who had any grievances against the Jews found it politically correct to express that negativity publicly. When the mutilated body of a Roman soldier was discovered, other Roman soldiers were often forced to view the remains. As a result, they became emboldened by their own sense of the barbaric nature of their enemy. This heightened hostility only served to mold the

Roman soldiers into a better fighting force. As each side avenged itself against the other, the cruelty factor in this war increased, as it tends to do in every war.

Finally, the Roman army, commanded first by Vespasian and later by his son Titus, decided that in order to bring this bloody Galilean rebellion to an end, they must conquer not only the extremities, but also the head and heart of the Jews. Strategically, this meant that Jerusalem had to be destroyed. So the military leadership of Rome moved its army into siege positions around the holy city of the Jews.

That siege was ultimately successful. In that fateful seventieth year of this common era, the walls of this city were toppled and Jerusalem finally fell to its conquerors. The Temple, thought of as the dwelling place for the Holy God, was razed to the ground, leaving only one wall standing. At this wall the Jews have mourned and wailed ever since. The buildings of Jerusalem were reduced to rubble. It became a devastated, destroyed, dead city; and with that death the Jewish nation, for all practical purposes, came to an end.

We need now to become aware of, to understand and to embrace, the trauma that entered Jewish life in this kairotic[4] moment of its history. In this defeat these Jewish people had lost their nation, their holy city, their Temple, and their priesthood. They had also lost their ordered social and worship life, which the Jewish leadership people of Jerusalem had established. Because their very identity was tied into these things, it is fair to say that in this moment the Jews had all but lost their identity.

The war did drag on for a short time beyond the year 70, so that this loss did not have to be processed all at once. The ragtag army of Jewish soldiers who escaped the Jerusalem debacle retreated to a place called Masada, where resistance continued until the year 73, when the war ended—not with a Jewish surrender, but with a massive Jewish act of suicide. With food and supplies spent, the last defenders at Masada chose to die rather than to submit to what would surely have been public execution. Whatever sacred documents they had been able to spirit out of Jerusalem in their retreat had been hidden in the desert.

Some of them were destined to be lost until this century, when they emerged as the Dead Sea Scrolls of the Qumran caves.[5]

This collapse of the Jewish nation and the loss of any national identity for the people of this land meant that generations of Jews were destined to be homeless people, exiled wanderers on the face of the earth. As powerless people who seemed to belong nowhere, the Jews would be victimized, oppressed, ghettoized, persecuted, tortured, and killed. All of the values by which the Jewish people lived, all of the gifts with which they had once enriched the world, were now dependent on the single goal of survival. So it was that survival, nothing else—just survival—became the highest value and the driving force among the Jews in this long period of homelessness. The only possession the Jews had that was not destroyed in this disaster was their sacred story, their scriptures, which included the Torah, the writings, and the prophets. If they were to lose their scriptures, then they would no longer know who they were and no power on this earth could have preserved their national identity. Many a nation has, in fact, ceased to exist as a recognizable people in human history when its homeland was conquered. Adaptation and intermarriage have usually marked the survivors. That was the fate of such ancient people as the Hittites, the Moabites, the Edomites, the Ammonites, and, a bit later, even the mighty Assyrians and Babylonians. It was not an unusual fate in the ancient world.

So, following that defeat in the year 70, we find that every other value of the Jewish people was sublimated or put into the service of survival. Survival became the overwhelming and primary agenda of the Jewish people. The sacred scriptures of the Jews became not just their only possession of note but also their chief weapon in their quest to achieve this goal of survival. In such a struggle, it was inevitable that people would defend their chief weapon with a vehemence unknown and unheard of before in the history of these sacred writings. That, in fact, is what happened among the Jews, especially the Jews of Judea and Jerusalem. It was in the process of turning their sacred scriptures into a weapon with which to fight for survival that enormous ramifications lay for the future of the Jews and, indeed, for the Christians.

Prior to this fateful year 70, Judaism had been able to tolerate varieties of opinions within its household of faith. Pluralism is always a byproduct of security. But when the survival of this faith tradition—their single claim to a future—was at stake, their level of toleration began to dissipate perceptibly. Within the synagogues of the Jewish people from the year 30 to the year 70 resided some of their brothers and sisters who had come to believe that God had acted in Jewish history in a new way in Jesus of Nazareth. These people were not yet called Christians. They were rather called the "followers of the way." Prior to the year 70, within the synagogues, they were at best an enriching new tradition and at worst a minor irritation. But on the other side of that fateful year, these "followers of the way" began to find themselves classified as a threat to Jewish survival. The fact that many followers of Jesus throughout the empire, both Jewish and gentile, had begun to interpret the fall of Jerusalem and the loss of the Temple as God's punishment of the Jerusalem Jews for their rejection of Jesus did not ingratiate the Jewish Christians to the surviving staunchly traditional worshipers of Jerusalem. Beyond that, the presence in the synagogues of Jewish people who acknowledged Jesus as Lord and Messiah had the effect of relativizing the claims that rigidly orthodox Jews were beginning to make for their scriptures. The "liberalizing" Jewish Christians did not cling tightly to that single-minded understanding of the Jewish source of revealed truth. Their very presence meant that the fragile hold of orthodox Jews on the possession to which they clung for their very identity was intolerably weakened. Thus the stage was set for hostility to erupt, and erupt it did.

The Jewish authorities were certainly aware that these Jewish people, who were embryonic Christians, had for some forty years interpreted their experience of Jesus in terms of the sacred stories of the Jewish past. Paul had suggested around 56 C.E. to 58 C.E. that the story of Jesus had been acted out according to the scriptures (1 Cor. 15:1–6). At that time there were no Christian scriptures, so this was a clear reference to the Jewish sacred story of the past. Before the fall of Jerusalem, it was quite clear that Jesus was in the process of being incorporated by Jewish people into the Jewish faith story as a new and dramatic chapter. Following the defeat of the Jews and the fall of Jerusalem, however, that process of incorporation began to destabilize this sacred tradition as a source of "unchanging authority." For if a new chapter was capable of being added to a traditional faith system, the message became clear that at least some believers did not regard this particular faith system as having been whole and complete before. Revelation would thus be understood to be progressive and, by implication, still changing. When relativity was introduced into this religious system, insecurity was enhanced. Throughout the history of the world, that is a predictable reality. Relativity, one must understand, gnaws away at those certainty claims that rigid religious systems always require if they are to thrive. Thus relativity and open-endedness can be tolerated only in times of religious security. When the very survival of a particular religious system is at stake, however, that spirit of toleration becomes anathema! Relativity and open-mindedness are transformed from tolerable virtues into being life-threatening daggers aimed at the heart of the claims of religious certainty. So, following the fall of Jerusalem, acrimony grew—with almost textbook inevitability—between Jews committed to Jesus and Jews committed to the concept that in their sacred scriptures they possessed the ultimate truth of God in a final and complete form. These traditional Jews who claimed orthodoxy for their convictions were tied increasingly to the belief that the God they worshiped could be found only in the unchanging completeness of the Torah. This shift into a survival mentality set the stage for a heightened negativity to develop.

Orthodoxy in Judea had, by this time, already endured the threat and the challenge to its life and boundaries brought about by the gentile mission of the Jewish Christians in the 50s and 60s. This mission of inclusiveness was led by such hellenized Jewish figures as Paul, Silas, Barnabas, and John Mark. At least that was the Church's memory as it was related in the Book of

Acts, written almost half a century after the fact. Even though this gentile mission was still under Jewish control, as illustrated by Paul's felt need to confer with more conservative Jerusalem leaders regularly, it nonetheless had the effect of opening the sacred customs and values of Jewish people to new stresses and interpretations.

This gentile mission actually began in the synagogues of the Jews who were dispersed across the Mediterranean by both the accidents of war and the search for economic opportunity. It created conflict almost instantly because the ones who responded to Paul's preaching tended to be first the gentile proselytes, who lived on the edges of the synagogues, and second those Jewish members of the synagogue community who had become weary of the burden of Jewish cultic practices that impeded their abilities to live in their gentile world profitably and comfortably. So the primary effect of the gentile mission of Jews like Paul and others was to siphon off from the synagogues both the pool of potential gentile converts to Judaism and the more liberal elements of their own Jewish community. The message of Jesus, as interpreted by Paul, was primarily the message of God's unflagging and unconditional love. To the ears of survival-oriented Jews, this message seemed to remove the demand for total obedience as the ultimate requirement of the Torah. Hence this growing liberal religious system was viewed by the more conservative Jews as an open invitation to moral anarchy. Perhaps even more dangerous, they saw in the Christian movement a willingness to blur the essential line of division that kept the Jew separate and distinct from the non-Jew and therefore capable of maintaining Jewish identity in a hostile and non-Jewish world. Survival could not easily tolerate that blurring.

We are told both by Paul in Galatians (2:1–10) and by Luke a bit later in the Book of Acts (15:1–29) that this conflict was solved, or at least ameliorated, in a compromising manner. Basically, the Jews were to remain faithful to the law and the gentiles were to be faithful to certain moral principles of the law, while seeking not to offend those to whom the cultic practices were of paramount importance. The settlement also seemed to recognize that Christianity was to have a Jewish mission and a gentile mission, with standards differing according to who was being missionized.[6] In all probability this was a victory for the followers of Paul, or the liberalizers, but it did not impinge significantly on the lives of the more traditional Jewish communities in Judea and in Jerusalem, who mixed very little with those who had left the homeland. Because they could do so, the rigid survival-oriented Jews tended to ignore the religious experimentation that took place in the provinces. They could even tolerate a minority movement of Christians within the ranks of Judaism at home, as long as it remained relatively weak and the ancient traditions were kept relatively strong.

But that tolerance of deviation in the provinces, based on distance, and of pluralism at home, based on its minority status, was not capable of being extended once Jewish survival became the ultimate issue. That is what occurred when Jerusalem fell to the Romans in the seventieth year of the common era. So the fall of Jerusalem, the destruction of the Temple with its attendant priesthood, and the resultant loss of a Jewish national identity created a crisis of significant proportions among the most traditional adherents of the religion of Moses and the prophets. This meant inevitably that the tension between Jewish Christians and the more orthodox Jewish faith tradition increased dramatically. Jewish Christians were first marginalized, then made to feel unwelcome. Between the years 70 and 100, Christianity became more gentile in the provinces; and even in Judea the Christians began slowly but surely to separate themselves, not necessarily in a voluntary manner, from the Jewish womb that gave the Christians their birth.

A second motive also began to develop following the defeat of Jerusalem in this war. As the identification of a rigid understanding of the Torah with saving truth became the definition for orthodoxy among the Jews centered in Judea and Jerusalem, so these Jews came to be looked upon with great negativity by the Romans. As hostility toward all things Jewish pervaded the empire, it became extremely wise politically for Jewish Christians to make public political distinctions between the rigid

49

orthodoxy of the traditional Jews and themselves. So Jewish Christians, following the example of the Jewish Paul, began to talk openly of their own difficulties with Jewish authorities. The idea that even Jesus himself had been a victim of the Jews began to be enhanced. The role played by the Roman governor, Pontius Pilate, in the death of Jesus began to be softened, his blame lessened or transferred to the Temple priesthood. The dark portrait of the traitor named Judas began to grow. Christian Jews began to suggest that God had created a new Israel based on the twelve apostles, designed to replace the old Israel based on the twelve sons of Jacob, who had become in Jewish mythology the fathers of twelve tribes of Israel. The way in which Jesus' death had first been interpreted by Jews in terms of Jewish ritual sacrifice was now carried to new heights. "He died for our sins," said Paul (1 Cor. 15:3). He was, said Mark (10:45), "a ransom for many," an idea echoed in the pseudo Pauline writings (1 Tim. 2:6). He was the sacrificial lamb (John 1:29; 1 Cor. 5:7; 1 Pet. 1:19; Heb. 5:3, 10:12, 10:36, 11:4), whose perfect sacrifice made all other sacrifices unnecessary, and therefore the destroyed Temple was rendered redundant as a place for continuous sacrifices to be offered. It began to be said of Jesus that he was himself the eternal and great high priest, who by entering the temple in heaven had put away forever the need even to have an earthly high priest (Heb. 4:4). These ideas, all of which find expression in the early Christian tradition, had the effect of moving Jewish Christians and their gentile proselyte allies into the post-Jewish world. But they had also drastically exacerbated the threat and the growing hostility that existed among those who claimed to be the true defenders of traditional Jewish orthodoxy who felt that their survival as a people required that protective layers be built around their sacred scriptures. The Jewish hold on the very things of God that they believed to be eternal had to be protected by guarding their literal scriptures from erosion. These survival-oriented Jews could not allow their single surviving Jewish asset to be used in such a way as to suggest that the defining limits which they had placed around their scriptures were not real.

The more this kind of rigid orthodoxy gained in favor, the more the traditional Jews sought to protect their sacred scriptures from what they regarded as an improper use of these scriptures by the Jewish Christians. That in turn caused these Jewish Christians to respond with an answering hostility. Each group thus claimed ownership of the Jewish scriptures, and each group used those scriptures as a lethal weapon against the other. It was not to be the last time that a sacred book, thought of by its adherents as a book of life, came to be used as an instrument of death.

The Christians, even those of Jewish background, began to suggest that if they were not welcome in the synagogues, they would leave—but the sacred scriptures of the Jews would go with them. They argued, to the consternation of these orthodox traditional Jews, that the Hebrew scriptures found their only fulfillment in the Messiah Jesus, and that apart from him there was no value in that rich sacred past. Proof texts abounded as each side sought to capture God for its version of truth.

The Jewish Christians began to build anthologies by which they identified the shadows of Jesus everywhere in the ancient sacred story of the Jews. In time these anthologies were employed by the compilers of the post-70 Gospels writers—Matthew, Luke, and John—when the oral traditions of their faith communities were transformed into written documents through which the Jesus story could be heard on a regular basis. We see these Jesus stories following in their written forms the liturgical tradition of the synagogues in which surely the Jesus story was first preached. We discover now and again the license that every preacher takes in the way the stories of the past were used to shape the stories of Jesus. Their concern was to show how Jesus was foreshadowed in the Jewish scriptures of yesterday and, indeed, how the life of Jesus was illumined by those scriptures. So echoes from the heroes of the Jewish past were woven, orally at first, into the story of Jesus. It was not dishonest. It was the ancient tradition of the Jews being employed by the Christians, most of whom were still Jews, to tell their story of Jesus.

That is the way Jewish people had always expanded their sacred story. The Gospels were created by the need to put into writing the oral tradition in which Jesus had been defined inside the synagogue worship life, either by a Jewish community or by the mixed community where gentile proselytes had found welcome alongside their hellenized Jewish neighbors. So the Gospels were born—not as chronological biographies describing literal events of history, but rather as collections of expository teaching or preaching that had been created in the same way that the rabbis would create what came to be called the *midrash rabbah*.[7] They pored over their sacred texts of the past to discover new meanings by which they might understand and interpret experiences that were occurring in their present.

Difficult as it is to pour new wine into an old wineskin, this process was accomplished without great upheaval so long as the stress level among the Jewish majority was tolerable. When that stress level reached crisis proportions, however, this Christian use of Jewish sacred material was viscerally resented.

It was the fall of Jerusalem, with its resulting destruction of the Temple and the priesthood, that raised the price of that uneasy accommodation to such painful levels that fracture was inevitable. The intolerable quality of this event did not appear all at once. Rather its intensity grew from the moment of Jerusalem's defeat over the next twenty years, until the separation was so total and so hostile that finally the Jewish Christians were literally expelled from the synagogues. As this tension built toward its climax, both Christian hostility toward the orthodox Jewish traditions and Jewish hostility toward heterodox Jewish Christians expanded. Echoes of this rising hostility can be found quite overtly in the Gospels. As the rhetoric heightened, the lines around what Jews could tolerate inside Judaism tightened considerably and those heterodox Jewish Christians, offended by this increasing hostility, began to move more and more into gentile circles.

So as the years rolled by, fewer and fewer Christians wanted to identify with the rigidly orthodox survival mentality that Judaism had become, and fewer and fewer Jews wanted to see any aspect of this Jesus tradition left inside their faith traditions. The final fracture occurred in the late 80s, when these orthodox Jewish leaders revised their regular worship traditions to include "anathemas" against all who deviated from strict orthodox standards and all who relativized the ultimate truth of the Torah. This was the last straw in the rising tension, and it resulted in the excommunication of the Jewish Christians from synagogue life and ultimately from Judaism. The Fourth Gospel was the work written after this expulsion, and its blatant negativity toward orthodox Jews (John 8:44) and its descriptions of being put out of the synagogues reflect that final fracture in the relationship between Jews and Jewish Christians (John 9:22, 12, 42). For Christians to distance themselves from all things Jewish became the modus operandi of the Christian Church between 70 and 100. The expelled Jewish Christians soon faded into increasingly hellenized and gentile circles. In a generation of both association and intermarriage, the Jewish Christians ceased even to think of themselves as Jews, while those who claimed the Jewish identity moved sharply to the right in quest of survival and became more and more firmly entrenched in their tradition. The common ground between Jews and Christians, once so powerful, became nonexistent. This hostile negativity toward Jews and all things Jewish has remained dominant in the Christian Church from that day to this.

This was the attitude that gave birth to that Christian refusal to see Jesus as Jewish, or to see the Gospels as Jewish books. It was this attitude that blinded Christians even to considering the possibility that the Gospels were written in a Jewish style by people who understood Jewish traditions. Finally, it was this attitude that imposed on our Gospels a gentile captivity that led us to ascribe to these books an accuracy about historical facts and a literalness about the events being described that none of the Jewish authors of the New Testament had ever intended. The Jewish authors of the Gospels were attempting to relate and to interpret meaning that was real. But their works, under gentile interpretation, came to be thought of as books that had captured not an experience of reality, but reality itself. Gentile interpreters of the Gospels began to claim that both objectivity and objective truth were present in the words of these texts. These Christians, torn loose from their Jewish moorings, began to see the Gospels as narratives through which the living word of God had been captured. A rigid Christian orthodoxy was on the way to being born. No longer were these texts read with that Jewish hope that these sacred words might draw the reader into the power of the God experience that the author was describing in his very Jewish way. Increasingly, the words of the Gospels were literalized as God's very words. The events described were thought to be literal events that took place inside literal history that were thus believed to be objectively true. A tradition arose in which three of the Gospels—Mark, Matthew, and Luke—were actually called "synoptics." Their authors would have been aghast at the suggestion that their narratives were objective enough to be identified as "eyewitness" accounts.

These were all the results of that crisis that occurred in 70 C.E. It was because of the forces of history that Jewish books that we call Gospels written in a Jewish style came to be read exclusively by gentile people who knew not the ways of the Jews. More importantly, those Jewish books came to be interpreted exclusively by gentiles without any regard to their original Jewish style or meaning. It was, furthermore, on the basis of these gentile interpretations that the creeds, theological systems, and ecclesiastical superstructures of the Church were erected.

These creeds served us well for centuries. But no human constructs are eternal. Unchanging concepts always become inadequate in time. At that moment the structures of the past built on those concepts will begin first to lose their power, next to crumble, and finally to collapse. We have suggested already that this was exactly what occurred in the Christian West.

We Christians are today, in a fascinating way, living with the very same issues of survival that marked the life of the Jews after 70 C.E. Like our forbears in faith, many Christians today have made survival their primary agenda. We have in some parts of Christianity decided that pluralism is impossible and so we seek to purge nonconforming views from our midst. Other Christians, having become embarrassed by the strict rigidity of the

Christian right, have voted with their feet and walked away from organized religion altogether.

We are thus ready, indeed eager, to find some new approach that will deliver us from what appear to us to be lifeless choices.

Perhaps we are even ready to approach the Gospels with Jewish eyes.

Part Two

◇◇◇

Examining the Gospel Texts from a Jewish Perspective

4

The Jewish Calendar and the Jewish Liturgical Year

Before we can begin to be aware of the way in which Jewish traditions shaped the Gospels, we must understand how the worship life of first-century Jewish people was organized.

I think it is fair to say that most Westerners have at least heard of Passover and Hanukkah. These two holy days permeate our consciousness, if only because they have gotten caught up in the cultural celebrations of Easter and Christmas. If we have Jewish friends or Jewish business associates, or if we live near a synagogue, we might also be aware of Yom Kippur, the Day of Atonement, and even Rosh Hashanah, the Jewish New Year. However, these sacred days are never anticipated outside Jewish circles, and our awareness of them is quickened only when co-workers are absent or when we see heavy traffic patterns around synagogues. We have almost no sense of such Jewish festivals as Pentecost or Tabernacles, to say nothing of minor observances such as the Ninth of Ab or Purim.

How these various holy days and feast days relate to one another or to the sacred history of the Jewish people is also not common knowledge among Christians and post-Christians. We might assume that Rosh Hashanah, the Jewish New Year, marks the beginning of the Jewish liturgical year. That would, however, be a misconception, at least for that period of Jewish history in which Christianity was being formed within the Jewish womb.

After the Babylonian Exile—which began in the first years of the sixth century B.C.E.[1] and lasted for some Jews fifty to sixty years, and for other parts of the Jewish family became a permanent Diaspora—the tradition arose of starting the new year in the spring, after the custom of the Babylonians. This date also appealed to those patriotic and nationalistic feelings of the Jewish people, for their major spring holiday, known as the Passover, celebrated the birth of their nation and constituted a fitting place for commencing the year. So the Jews reordered their worship life during that Exile and began their liturgical year on the first day of Nisan, a month that corresponds roughly to mid-March/early April. The Feast of Passover was incorporated into a festival of unleavened bread that lasted eight days. When the Passover celebration developed liturgically, the day on which the paschal lamb was slaughtered and the ritual meal eaten became the focus of the festival. It became the time for the telling and retelling of the account of Israel's birth as a nation. This meant that the first and second Sabbaths of Nisan were Sabbaths of preparation for the Passover, a kind of Jewish Advent, if you will.

Another post-Exile requirement of the Jewish people also affected their worship life dramatically. From that time on, the Jews felt compelled to complete the reading of the entire Torah over a one-year period. The Torah, also known as the books of Moses, included Genesis, Exodus, Leviticus, Numbers, and Deuteronomy. This one-year liturgical cycle of Torah readings also began on the first Sabbath of Nisan. To complete the reading of the Torah over the fifty to fifty-one Sabbaths in the Jewish year would require the reading of a passage of approximately five of our present chapters per Sabbath. Since the Torah was written on large, heavy, and cumbersome scrolls, the only way to read it was in order, beginning each Sabbath at the point where the reading ceased the previous Sabbath. The Jewish year, we need to note, was constructed on a lunar model, not on the present Julian calendar. Since twelve new moons do not make 365¼ days, the Jewish people would have had to add a month periodically to keep their calendar from falling too far behind. This meant that the Jewish calendar, and therefore the liturgical pattern based on it, had to have some flexibility or adaptability.

One of the themes of the major Nisan festival, known as the Feast of Passover, was the anticipated dawning of the Kingdom of God. Since the Nisan reading of the Torah began with Genesis, the assignment on the second Sabbath of the Jewish liturgical year, or the Sabbath before the Passover, would be the Noah story about the world being destroyed for its evil by God only to start anew after the flood. This reading conspired to make that Sabbath come to be dominated by the theme of the end of the world, and was to have interesting implications for the Gospels, as we shall see.

Genesis would normally be read over twelve Sabbaths, which would include the four Sabbaths of Nisan, the four Sabbaths of Iyyar, and four of the five Sabbaths of Sivan. A second major Jewish festival, namely the Festival of Pentecost, or Shavuot, would occur within that time of Genesis readings. Pentecost occurred on the fiftieth day after Passover. This festival originally marked the early harvest of the ancient Canaanites, but the Jews had taken that over and superimposed on it a celebration of God's gift of the Torah and its reception by Moses on Mt. Sinai. So Pentecost marked a major moment in Israel's history and was celebrated with a vigil service covering twenty-four hours.

The Book of Exodus normally began to be read on the fifth Sabbath of Sivan and generally consumed a total of eleven

Sabbaths, which would also include the four Sabbaths of Tammuz, the four Sabbaths of Ab, and two Sabbaths of the month of Elul. Falling within this Exodus cycle would be the observance of the Ninth of Ab, a penitential day that remembered the fateful occasion in Jewish history when the city of Jerusalem fell to the Babylonians in the sixth century B.C.E.

The Book of Leviticus began to be read on or about the third Sabbath of Elul and normally continued for eight Sabbaths, including three in Elul, four in Tishri, and one in the month of Cheshvan. It was during this Leviticus cycle that three major Jewish observances came in quick succession.

The first day of Tishri (roughly mid-September to early October) was the Jewish New Year, Rosh Hashanah. Between the second and third Sabbaths of Tishri (or in early to mid-October) came Yom Kippur, the solemn Day of Atonement. Normally, between the third and fourth Sabbaths of Tishri, the major harvest festival of Tabernacles, or Sukkot, was observed. This was an eight-day celebration set in Jerusalem. It was probably the best-loved, the most fun, the least somber, and the most anticipated festival of the Jews. The Jewish people built temporary dwellings or booths for this celebration, to recall to consciousness their homeless days of wandering in the wilderness. Tabernacles was marked by processions, chants, and the waving of branches of greenery called a *lulab*. Tishri was a busy liturgical month for the Jews.

The Book of Numbers was normally read over the remaining four Sabbaths of Cheshvan and the five Sabbaths of Kislev and concluded on the first Sabbath of Tebeth. The major festival that fell within the Numbers cycle was the Feast of Dedication, or Hanukkah. It was not a Torah festival, for it got its contemporary focus well after the Torah was formed, during the period of the Maccabees in the middle of the second century B.C.E. This celebration marked the restoration of the Temple to Jewish worship when Judas Maccabeus defeated the Syrians. So it was observed by the lighting of the *menorah* so that the light of God could be visibly restored to the Temple. Dedication also came in the dead of winter in the northern hemisphere, and thus it captured that ancient prehistoric observance of the moment when the sun ceased its retreat into darkness and began its return to longer days.

The Book of Deuteronomy normally began to be read on the second Sabbath of Tebeth and was read over the remaining three Sabbaths of that month, the four Sabbaths of Shebat, and the four Sabbaths of Adar. The minor festival of Purim occurred during the Deuteronomy cycle. This holy day marked the deliverance of the Jews from danger and death during the time when they lived under the rule of the Persians. With the completion of the reading of Deuteronomy, the Jewish community finished both the annual cycle of the Torah and the liturgical year of the Jews; the worshipers stood ready to enter the month of Nisan, when the whole cycle began anew. Because proselytes and converts were normally taken into Judaism in time for Passover, the cycle of Sabbaths during which Deuteronomy was read was also used to instruct the prospective new converts.

It is quite difficult to keep in mind a full calendar that is strange and different. It is also difficult to remember either the order or the content of the festivals and fasts of the Jewish liturgical year, especially when those holy days do not mark the events of one's own history or experience. For this reason I have appended a brief outline of the Jewish year to the end of this chapter. What we need to remember, however, is that this was the liturgical year familiar to the people of Galilee and Judea in the first century of the common era, so this was the calendar that organized both the worship and the daily life of Jesus of Nazareth. This was also the calendar that those Jewish people who were the first Christians continued to follow. Therefore it was against this calendar and in terms of these festivals that I will contend the Gospels of Mark, Matthew, and Luke were written. Only if this organizing principle is understood will my attempt to show how Mark, Matthew, Luke, and perhaps the Book of Acts were all shaped by these liturgical customs and practices make sense. Perhaps we shall even discover that the

Gospel of John is more deeply connected to the liturgical year of the Jews than most of us have ever guessed. So this calendar becomes important to both our reading and our understanding of the Gospels. We cannot find a new way to approach the Gospels until we can see and comprehend the background, the worship context, and the setting in which they were written. Therefore this brief chapter of mundane and seemingly unimportant data becomes crucial to the task of reading the Gospels with Jewish eyes, and we shall return to this liturgical year of the Jews again and again as we walk through the synoptic Gospels.

The Order of the Months of the Jewish Year Followed in the First Century:

1. Nisan	5. Ab	9. Kislev
2. Iyyar	6. Elul	10. Tebeth
3. Sivan	7. Tishri	11. Shebat
4. Tammuz	8. Cheshvan	12. Adar

The Prominent Festivals, Fasts, and Holy Days of the Jewish Year in the First Century:

1. Passover	14–15 Nisan. A special day that inaugurated an eight-day celebration to mark the birth of their nation and their escape from slavery in Egypt.
2. Pentecost (Shavuot)	The fiftieth day after Passover, during the month of Sivan, observed with a twenty-four-hour vigil to celebrate the giving of the Torah to Moses at Mt. Sinai.
3. Ninth of Ab	A day of mourning to recall the fall of Jerusalem to the Babylonians, celebrated literally on the ninth day of the month of Ab. The Book of Lamentations would be read on this day.

4. New Year (Rosh Hashanah)	First day of Tishri. Originally, in pre-Exilic days, the start of the Jewish year. It became the day on which to proclaim the coming of the Kingdom of God.
5. Atonement (Yom Kippur)	Normally between the second and third Sabbaths of Tishri. A day of penitence marked by the offering of the perfect animal sacrifice and the loading of the sins of the people onto the back of a scapegoat.
6. Tabernacles (Sukkot)	Normally between the third and fourth Sabbaths of Tishri. An eight-day celebration of the harvest. Used to recall the wilderness years of Jewish history.
7. Dedication (Hanukkah)	Normally between the third and fourth Sabbaths of Kislev. An eight-day celebration of the return of God's light to the Temple.
8. Purim	Normally between the second and third Sabbaths of Adar. Celebrated the delivery of the Jews from peril during the reign of the Persians. The Book of Esther was written for this celebration.

NOTES TO TABLE

1. After the Christian octave of Easter developed, there were two Sabbaths/Sundays of Easter that would cause the Gospels to start on the fifth Sabbath of the Jewish year instead of the fourth.
2. The Jewish year had fifty to fifty-one Sabbaths. It followed a lunar calendar, not a Julian calendar. In seven out of nineteen years an additional month 2 Adar would be added to the year to keep from

getting too far behind. This makes an exact lectionary all but impossible to create.

3. The Jewish festivals required by the Torah were Passover, Pentecost, New Year, Yom Kippur, and Tabernacles. Dedication (Hanukkah) was added with the Maccabees. The Ninth of Ab was post-Exilic. Purim was added to celebrate an episode of deliverance of the Jews during the Persian period, following the Exile. It could have been as late as the Maccabees.

4. The Jewish New Year, Rosh Hashanah, was not where the liturgical year began in post-Exilic Jewish history. It was observed on the first day of Tishri. Normally, this was before any Sabbath. The Torah said that Rosh Hashanah was the first day of the seventh month.

5. Passover began as part of an eight-day observance of unleavened bread. The "most holy night" of Passover was the opening of that observance.

6. Jewish Pentecost (Shavuot) was a twenty-four-hour vigil divided into eight three-hour segments.

7. Genesis generally took twelve Sabbaths, Exodus eleven, Leviticus eight, Numbers nine, and Deuteronomy eleven. This represents the best guess of contemporary scholars, but the vagaries of the Jewish calendar always mean that this is generally true rather than precisely true.

8. The textual divisions in the Torah mentioned here are also approximations, but I believe them to be generally accurate.

9. Nisan corresponds roughly to late March or early April. Tishri would be mid-September to mid-October. Kislev would come generally in December.

10. Tabernacles could come before the second Sabbath of Tishri, but most often it came after the second Sabbath and embraced the third Sabbath in its octave of eight days.

5

Mark

The Story of Jesus from Rosh Hashanah to Passover

The Gospels came into being relatively late in Christian history, some thirty-five to seventy years after the earthly life of Jesus of Nazareth had been concluded. When they did first appear, none of them was in the Aramaic language that Jesus spoke, but in the Greek language that he, in all probability, did not speak.[1] Through the centuries numerous theories have been offered to account for their origins. Some of these theories are rather filled with the concepts of magic. Others have served primarily to undergird the theological agenda of those proposing them. Some can be dismissed quickly. It is certainly fair to state categorically that the Gospels did not drop from heaven fully written as a divine message from God. Nor did God dictate their content to a faithful scribe. These and various other concepts of verbal inspiration fail to account, not only for the origins of the Gospels, but also for the particular and peculiar slant that each gospel takes—to say nothing of the contradictions and additions that each gospel reveals. The suggestion that the Gospels were written by eyewitnesses also confronts the difficulty that Mark, Matthew, and Luke do not claim that their accounts are based on their own eyewitness memories. John was the only gospel to suggest that the material was based on a personal eyewitness contact with Jesus (John 21:24). That assertion, however, is simply not supportable with facts. The most obvious fact is that John was the last gospel to be written, which means that if that eyewitness claim were accurate, its author would have been almost 100 years old when he wrote—hardly a possibility in the first century. I know of no reputable scholar in the world today who would support the accuracy of the claim that this gospel was the work of that "beloved disciple." There are others, of course, who would propose a totally secular cause that produced the Gospels, or even a sinister motive to propagandize or to distort deliberately.

It is my conviction that the only way to address the question of the origins of the Gospels is to look internally at each individual gospel itself to find its own clues and seek to draw conclusions from those. I will begin this task by turning to the gospel that is all but universally agreed to be the earliest, the one we call Mark. It is also the shortest of the Gospels, which I believe is a more significant clue to its origin than has yet been fully appreciated.

A casual reading of Mark's gospel reveals its major units. It begins with the story of Jesus' baptism and then describes, in a wide variety of rapid incidents, both the initial impact and the rising conflict that marked his life in Galilee. This covers Mark's content from chapter 1 to the story of the transfiguration in chapter 9.

The second unit is the story of Jesus' journey with his disciples from Galilee to Jerusalem. It is characterized as a time for Jesus to instruct his disciples for their role in the life of the Christian community. It is marked by one teaching episode after another: on humility, on divisions within the fellowship, on marriage and divorce, on the care and treatment of children, on wealth. It concludes with the story of Jesus' entry into Jerusalem in chapter 11.

Once Jesus is in Jerusalem, Mark's story moves on to the account of the cleansing of the Temple, and then to more teaching material, supposedly given in Jerusalem, on such subjects as forgiveness, prayer, life after death, the summary of the law, and generosity. Then the strange chapter 13 appears in the text. Scholars call this chapter "the Little Apocalypse" because it is reminiscent of the apocalyptic writing style present elsewhere in the Bible, by which they mean writing about the signs that will accompany the end of the world. Chapter 13 speaks of wars and rumors of wars, earthquakes, famines, persecutions, a darkened sun and moon, and the coming of the Son of Man on the clouds of heaven. This chapter ends with the repeated admonition to be alert, to watch.

Chapters 14 and 15 contain the story of Jesus' passion. This section begins with the time reference that it was two days before the Passover, and it contains such episodes as the anointing of Jesus' feet by a woman in Bethany and the first contact of Judas Iscariot with the chief priests. Both episodes serve to set the stage for the account of Jesus' passion. Then this passion story unfurls with dramatic intensity, culminating in the crucifixion and the death and burial of Jesus. Next the narrative pauses for the Sabbath and then concludes with the brief story of the resurrection, which it asserts occurred on the first day of the week. That is the basic outline of Mark, the first written gospel. So into that text we must now go, looking for clues that will illumine its origin.

It is the suggestion of some scholars that the story of Jesus' passion was the first part of Mark's gospel tradition to achieve written form. It is the only part of this gospel that has a compelling story line—stretching from the last supper to the betrayal, to the arrest, to the interrogation and mocking torture, to the crucifixion, to the burial, and finally, to the story of Easter.

Also, this dramatic account of Jesus' last days was likely the core of the original Christian message, and hence the part to be written first. It is therefore appropriate that we begin with that narrative and work from back to front in this gospel, seeking the origin of each segment and then of the whole.

The passion narrative seems to contain an interior time schedule that is revealing. It chronicles in an orderly fashion activities from 6:00 P.M. on what we now call Maundy Thursday to 6:00 P.M. on what we now call Good Friday. Mark noted at the beginning of this story that it was evening when the disciples gathered with Jesus to eat the Passover meal. That means that the drama began about 6:00 P.M. on a Thursday night in late March or early April. In a nonelectrified world, outside activity ceased when the sun went down. At this Passover meal, we are told, Jesus predicted his betrayal, interpreted the bread and wine of that meal as his body and blood, and instructed the disciples about the relationship of this meal to the Kingdom of God. This meal concluded, we are told, with the singing of a hymn and so did this first section of Mark's passion story. Then Jesus and the disciples went out to the Mount of Olives. The tradition of the times would suggest that it was now around 9:00 P.M., or the end of the first watch of the night.

On this journey there was more conversation about betrayal and apostolic abandonment, and most particularly the prediction of Peter's denial before the crowing of the cock. Then they arrived at a place that Mark and Matthew called Gethsemane. Luke called it simply a place on the Mount of Olives (Luke 22:39–40). Only John has called it a garden (John 18:1).

Once there, Jesus instructed the disciples to remain on guard, as it were, while he went to pray. Taking Peter, James, and John with him, he moved more deeply into Gethsemane. Then, leaving the three who constituted the inner circle, he went alone a bit further to his place of prayer. After a period of time, he returned to find the three sleeping. "Could you not watch with me one hour?" he asked. The same question, we are told, he asked after a second and a third time of prayer. The disciples could not watch one, two, or three hours! After the third of the hourly inquiries, they all left the garden. My presumption is that it was now 12:00 A.M. The second watch of the night was complete.

Next came the story of the betrayal and the arrest, followed by the account of apostolic desertion. This narrative was placed in the liturgical watch from midnight to 3:00 A.M. The darkest deed in human history was thus made to have occurred in the darkest portion of that darkest of all nights. Jesus was then led away to the chief priests, the elders, and the scribes.

The watch of the night from 3:00 A.M. to 6:00 A.M. was called cockcrow. It marked the period of time that saw the end of the darkness. It got its name from the fact that the crowing of the cock heralded the return of the morning light. In this portion of the gospel tradition, the accusations against Jesus are made by the high priest, while witnesses were sought to seal the case against Jesus. Then the story of Peter's denial is dramatically related. This session ended, we are told, by the second crowing of the cock. I suspect, however, that the name of the watch itself was literalized in that detail, and that it had far more to do with marking the time of the liturgical drama than it did with the literal crowing of literal roosters. In any event, the official charges, plus Peter's threefold denial, would carry us to 6:00 A.M.

Mark took note of this in the beginning of chapter 15 with the words "as soon as it was morning" (Mark 15:1). So at 6:00 A.M. Mark suggested that after the whole council had held a consultation, Jesus was led away to Pilate, the governor. That, together with the story of Pilate's release of Barabbas and the torture of the soldiers, filled the fourth watch, or carried the story up to 9:00 A.M. Mark announced this by saying, "And it was the third hour when they crucified him" (Mark 15:25).

The details of his time on the cross were then related, taking us to midday, which the text confirmed by stating "When the sixth hour had come" (that is, at 12:00 noon), "there was darkness covering the whole land until the ninth hour" (that is, until 3:00 P.M) (Mark 15:33).

Then the text noted that at that ninth hour, Jesus uttered the cry of dereliction, "My God, my God, why have you forsaken me?" Then he breathed his last, said Mark. That dramatic moment was accompanied, Mark continued, by a series of symbolic actions that he asserted occurred at the time of Jesus' death. The veil separating the Holy Place from the Holy of Holies in the Temple was split from top to bottom, and a gentile centurion pronounced Jesus to be "the Son of God."

Then, as evening was approaching (that is, between 3:00 P.M. and 6:00 P.M.), so as not to violate the Sabbath (which began at sundown on Friday), Jesus was taken down from the cross and buried, and the story of Joseph of Arimathea entered the narrative. After the burial this passion narrative came to an end. The Jewish Sabbath was at hand. A concluding chapter was to be added to bring that passion story to the climax of Easter. That story was the account of the empty tomb being discovered at dawn on the first day of the week by a group of women.

It becomes obvious as we journey through this section of Mark that what we have in the passion story is the outline of a twenty-four-hour period. It is marked in seven instances by specific time references that signal the beginning or ending of a segment of time. In our search for origins, this analysis leads us to ask the question, "Was there anything in the worship pattern of the Jews that might throw light on the time scheme revealed in Mark's schedule that organized his passion story?" The answer is: "Indeed there was!"

Recall that the Jews observed the most holy night of their Passover by liturgically bringing to memory the story of their origins. This solemn night was the focus of the people's worship during this season. Christians developed this night into a full vigil. In all the earliest lectionaries of both the Jerusalem and Byzantine traditions, the twenty-four-hour vigil from Maundy Thursday night through sundown on Good Friday was enjoined upon the Christians. They were to fast when the Jews slaughtered the paschal lamb to begin the Passover celebration.[2]

When we examine the order in which Mark has told the story of the passion of Jesus, it begins to be clear that the events that brought the Christian people into existence as the people of God have been recounted in a liturgical pattern quite similar to the one used by the Jews on the day of Passover. The passion story was the Christian Passover story. Jesus was the new paschal lamb. What we are reading in Mark's text is a liturgical recreation of the final moments in Jesus' life designed for use in worship. This story of Jesus' death was never intended to be an eyewitness account of objective history. If this developed passion narrative marked the beginning of the written gospel tradition, it becomes clear that the written gospel tradition was initiated for and by the liturgical needs of the early Christian community.

The writing of the Gospels thus had little to do with those earlier explanations offered to account for their origins. The first explanation centered around the deaths of the primary disciples, Peter and Paul, and the need to transform the words of Jesus that they remembered, and the experience of or with Jesus that they had known, into written records. The second explanation focused on the growing awareness that the second coming of Jesus, and thus the end of the world, was not imminent, as they had once believed. With this reality facing them, the need for written records for the long haul became apparent. But the liturgical shape of the passion story, illumined by the Jewish practice at Passover, points to a different conclusion, namely, that the first segment of gospel material to achieve written form did so not to create content to be read for its own sake but to create content to be used in services of worship for people whose lives were still lived inside the patterns of the synagogue. The need for a Christian version of the Jewish observance of Passover was the first cause of gospel writing.

If that is true, as I am convinced it is, then we come to the next question: How did the rest of the Gospel of Mark, which has been described as a passion story introduced with a long preamble, come into being? I would suggest, and will seek to document, that it had a similar origin, but to do so I need to demonstrate that the writing of this first gospel developed exactly backward from the way we now read this gospel, and that it was this fact that has kept us from seeing the liturgical connection at the heart of the gospel tradition before. So we focus now on the section of Mark's gospel that comes just prior to the story of the passion. That would be the account of Jesus' journey from Galilee to Jerusalem.

When the Christian Church was first born, new converts appear to have been incorporated into the faith community at the moment of their conversion. They were baptized on the spot, if you will. The Book of Acts described that as the early situation when Peter preached his first sermon and 3,000 people were immediately baptized (Acts 2:41). That also seemed to be the case when the Ethiopian eunuch, responding to the words of Philip, was quoted as saying, "See, here is water. What is to prevent my being baptized?"(Acts 8:36–37).

However, as the Church became a more settled and organized movement, new habits and new liturgical patterns were developed. Once more, these habits and patterns were borrowed quite specifically from the Jewish tradition. As we noted in the previous chapter, the Jews followed the practice of instructing their proselytes and converts during the latter part of their liturgical year—that is, immediately prior to the celebration of the Passover. This would mean that the proselytes would complete their instruction, be circumcised, have sufficient time to allow healing to occur, and then proceed to the ceremonial cleansing bath. All of this would be done in a time sequence that would enable them to join the Jewish faith community in the Passover meal as the first act of the incorporated convert.

It was not a coincidence, therefore, that since these proselytes were being instructed during the last part of the liturgical year, their instruction would be dominated by the book of the Torah that was being read in the synagogues at that time. That would be the Book of Deuteronomy, the last book of the Torah, which was read in the synagogues during the last eleven to twelve Sabbaths of the liturgical year.

The title of this book, Deuteronomy, literally means "the second giving of the law."[3] It was a book that summarized Jewish history. If the Jews could be said to have a catechism, it would be the Book of Deuteronomy. This book rehearsed the law and the history of the Jews and commended it to the next generation. So the custom developed of using Deuteronomy to prepare converts;

and, since the new liturgical year of the Jews began with a preparation for and a celebration of the Passover, it made that service the proper service for incorporating the new converts.

I would suggest that the Christians, who were overwhelmingly Jewish at this time in history, also followed this example of the Jews. Christians began to observe baptism, their rite of passage, on Easter eve. Baptism was adapted from the ceremonial postcircumcision cleansing bath of the Jews. The Christians, having done away with circumcision, simply kept the ceremonial bath and developed a liturgy around it. This meant that, again following the custom of the Jews, the first act of the newly baptized would be to participate in the Christian meal that reenacted the story of Christian beginnings in the passion and resurrection of Jesus.

So the Christians, like the Jews, also had a need to develop a similar period of instruction, during which time converts, called the catechumenate, might learn about what it meant to be a Christian prior to their baptisms. This instruction, therefore, would also need to be accomplished in the period of time prior to the observance of Passover/Easter. The Christians, however, could hardly use the Book of Deuteronomy as the content of their catechetical text for instructing converts. So a new text had to be created for that purpose. As we walk backward through Mark, that appears to have been the primary purpose of the next section of Mark's gospel to be written, the section that purports to be the account of Jesus instructing his disciples on their final journey from Galilee to Jerusalem. What better format could be conceived in which to assemble in a proper form the material to prepare the catechumenate? This was the teaching of the Lord, the material he shared with his disciples prior to his departure; and so the journey section of the Gospel of Mark came into being to serve as the Christian Deuteronomy, if you will. The journey section included one teaching vignette after another, and the echoes of what later came to be called "the way of the cross" began to be heard.

So it was that on the Sabbaths prior to Passover and Easter, the liturgical emphasis within the Christian community was on instructing new disciples in preparation for their incorporation into the body of Christ. The season of Lent has its origins in this custom. To help us embrace what I am suggesting, and to undergird this theory, we need to know that in one of the earliest texts of Mark's gospel that we have, a text known as Codex Alexandrinus,[4] the Gospel of Mark is divided into forty-nine separate lections for use in worship. One lection in this Codex was used for Easter on the Sunday after Passover. Next that same Codex Alexandrinus designated the eight units of the passion story as the Christian units to form a Christianized and expanded version of Passover. With these points of connection between Christian and Jewish liturgical usage established, and following the outline of Marcan lections in Codex Alexandrinus, we can now begin to stretch the Gospel of Mark back one lection per Sabbath against the background of the Jewish liturgical year. When we do that, we find that the journey section of Mark's gospel is exactly the length needed to cover the number of Sabbaths on which Deuteronomy was read in the synagogues. So once again the intimation arises from the text that the journey section of the Gospel of Mark was composed with the same motive that the passion story was composed: to meet the early Christian Church's liturgical needs to Christianize a prevailing synagogue practice—and, in the process, to provide authoritative teaching from the Lord to serve as the basis for the instruction for the catechumenate who were seeking baptism.

When we begin this backward walk in Mark, segment by segment, to arrive at the beginning of this journey portion of the gospel, we discover another delightful liturgical surprise that adds weight to this theory. The Sabbath immediately before Passover would be Nisan II, the second Sabbath of the post-Exilic Jewish liturgical year. On that Sabbath the Jews, in the anticipation expressed by the prayer that the Passover would be celebrated "next year in Jerusalem," came both to hope and to give liturgical form to the expectation that the Kingdom of God would dawn at the upcoming Passover. So the Jews began to fill the Sabbath prior to the Passover with the theme of the end of the world and the promise of things to come.

As we noted previously, the annual reading of the Torah had begun anew on the first Sabbath of Nisan with the Book of Genesis, so the Torah lesson for that Sabbath would be the early Genesis story of Noah and the flood. There the theme being expressed was that of God's judgment on the wickedness of human life. It was a total judgment, reminiscent of Armageddon, when all the world would be destroyed. This Torah reading on that Sabbath was supplemented, at least in the earliest Jewish lectionaries that we can locate, with a reading from the early portion of the Jewish scriptures known as the former prophets, namely, the story of Joshua crossing the Jordan river. In that text the Kingdom of God was about to dawn for the desert-wandering Jews. They were entering the Promised Land. Again, following the earliest known lectionaries, the lesson for that Sabbath, taken from the prophetic cycle of Isaiah, was about the coming of the day of the Lord at the end of time. So, from a variety of angles, the theme among the Jews of this pre-Passover Sabbath was the end of the world.

So what would be the section of Mark's gospel that would fall on that Sunday if we stretched Mark back across the Jewish liturgical calendar? It would be that strange chapter 13, the chapter that I suggested was known as "the Little Apocalypse." This was Mark's story of Jesus talking about the end of the world. We discover yet again that the first gospel was written under the domination and influence of the Jewish liturgical calendar. This pattern seemed to stick in the later Gospels, for similar apocalyptic material precedes the passion narrative, not only in Mark, but also in Matthew and Luke.

Continuing this backward walk through the Jewish liturgical year and moving just beyond the period of instruction for the catechumenate, we come face-to-face with the Jewish Feast of Dedication, or Hanukkah. The lection in Mark's gospel that would fall on that day would be the story of Jesus' transfiguration.

The Feast of Dedication, we noted, was a late-developing holy day among the Jews—at least as a separate liturgical celebration. Because it was not found in the Torah, it tended to draw much of its content from other Jewish celebrations. When, under the impact of the victory of the Maccabees and the rededication of the Temple in 164 B.C.E., the return of the light of God to the Temple became its primary theme, the Feast of Dedication developed a character quite its own. Then, in typical *midrashic* style, the Jews began to weave around this festival details out of their sacred history that demonstrated that the light of God always came to rest on that place where heaven and earth seemed to come together; namely, the place where sacrifices that ascended into the very presence of God were offered. These were the themes that conspired to produce the Feast of Dedication.

So how better could the Christians transform that tradition of the Jews than to portray Jesus standing as the new Temple and having the body of this Jesus embraced by the heavenly light of God? Let me simply note first that the story of the transfiguration suddenly begins to make sense as a Christian attempt to wrap around Jesus the themes of the Jewish Feast of Dedication.

But understanding the story of the transfiguration is even more involved than this. This narrative was filled with many Jewish images from the past. We pause to call them to remembrance. Two people appeared with Jesus in this unusual tale. They were Moses and Elijah. A search of the Jewish scriptures will reveal that both of these Jewish heroes had unusual deaths. Moses, said the Book of Deuteronomy, died alone and was buried by God and no one knew the place of that grave (Deut. 34). In Jewish thought that mystery was explained by suggesting that Moses had not really died at all, that God had taken him directly into the Divine Presence as a reward for his extraordinary life. Such a fate was not unknown in Jewish circles. A man named Enoch, the father of Methuselah, was said to have "walked with God" so closely that God took him into the heavenly realm without his having to go through the gateway of death (Gen. 5:24). So it was that Moses was also accorded this status in the tradition.

Later in Jewish history the same fate, but a bit more elaborately drawn, was said to have been the destiny of Elijah. At the time of Elijah's departure from this world, a fiery chariot drawn by fiery horses was said to have come out of heaven to fetch Elijah and to take him directly into God's presence (2 Kings 2:11–12). So in Jewish folklore three people—Enoch, Moses, and Elijah—were thought to be dwellers with God in heaven.

In the second century before the birth of Jesus, one of these figures, Enoch, was said to have written a book from this heavenly perspective that chronicled his vision of things to come. This Book of Enoch was very popular and exercised great influence on Jewish thought from that time through the life of Jesus.

The remaining two heroic figures who were thought in some way to have defeated death were thus available to become part of the transfiguration story. So it was that Moses and Elijah were pictured as talking together with Jesus on the mountaintop. The three of them were believed to have had in common the conviction that each had conquered death. So the story of the transfiguration incorporated this part of the Jewish tradition of the past and spoke of Jesus in this new way. But that is not all that this story reveals.

Next we are told that the quality of a translucent brilliance came upon Jesus. This phenomenon was also not unknown in the Hebrew scriptures. In the Book of Exodus (24:1 ff.), Moses was said to have gone up the sacred mountain with three disciples, Aaron, Nadab, and Abihu, except that Moses also took with him in addition seventy elders. There was a cloud in this Moses story also. Moses entered this cloud of God on top of the mountain. He stayed for forty days, during which time the covenant was formed. Later, when he returned, the text stated that "the skin of his face shone" (Exod. 34:30). Moses, after appearing with God, was transfigured.

Other Hebrew texts point to this same transforming reality. Aaron's clothes were on one occasion transformed into a radiant glory (Exod. 28:1 ff.). On another occasion the priest, Joshua, had his "filthy garments" taken away and was then reclothed in God's splendor (Zech. 3:3–6).

When these notes are added to the tradition that God's holy light had always connected the people of Israel to God's presence, the *midrashic* elements in the story of Jesus' transfiguration become even more obvious. This tradition of being connected to God's light began in the wilderness, when the pillar of fire guided Israel by night and the pillar of cloud guided Israel by day. Both the fire and the cloud were symbols of the divine connecting light.

Later, while still wandering in the wilderness, the Jews were told to designate a particular holy spot in their camp as their sacred space and to call that spot "the Tent of Meeting" (Exod. 40).

After that sacred space had been marked off and properly prepared according to God's specific directions, it was dedicated. In that dedication the light of God, which was called the Shekinah, was said to have descended upon that Tent of Meeting (Exod. 40:34). Later, this same Shekinah was thought to have continuously marked the dwelling place of God by coming to the Temple in each of its successive manifestations. Finally, when Judas Maccabeus, in the second century before Jesus, defeated the Syrians and restored the light of God to the Temple, all of these themes flowed together to give liturgical shape to the festival that came to be called Dedication or Hanukkah.

When Christians came to believe that the life of Jesus was nothing less than the new dwelling place of God, and that Jesus had himself become the ultimate and final sacrifice that rendered additional Temple sacrifices irrelevant, they began to suggest that Jesus had replaced the Temple. This theme grew in intensity when the Temple was destroyed in 70 C.E. So the idea that the light of God had actually come to rest in Jesus expanded in the tradition. This was the background and origin of the story of the transfiguration, and into this story all of these elements were skillfully added. Jesus, like Moses, went up the mountain with three named associates. He, like Moses, entered the cloud of God. The Shekinah, or light of God, then came and rested on him. He was transformed, his clothes were translucent, and suddenly the Jewish Feast of Dedication had a Christian emphasis. This was not a literal story about a literal moment in the life of Jesus. This was a skillful *midrashic* and homiletic attempt to interpret the power of Jesus in terms of well-known Jewish symbols. So it was that Mark told the story of Jesus' transfiguration at the time of Dedication. Matthew and Luke not only kept Mark's designation, but actually expanded these Hanukkah themes. But as long as we read this story with no understanding of the Jewish liturgical year that organized the gospel narratives, we will never see this connection.

We have now walked backward through two-thirds of the first Gospel, and so far it appears to have been constructed under the influence of the Jewish liturgical calendar—the episodes in Jesus' life correlated with the celebrations and the Sabbaths of that Jewish year. If this theory is to be complete, we must now ask: What created the opening segment of Mark's gospel? If we are suggesting that this gospel came into being backward—with the passion story and its Easter climax being formed first, and with the journey section being created next to serve as the basis for instructing the catechumenate, and that just beyond the journey was the Feast of Dedication, for which the transfiguration story was created—then what were the forces that operated to carry the narrative back to the opening segment of Mark that described the Galilean origins of Jesus?

First of all, it was necessary for the gospel writers to originate the story of Jesus in Galilee for several reasons. Each had to deal with the widely recognized realization that Jesus' life had had its beginning in Galilee. Jesus was known as "the Galilean." His embarrassing roots in Nazareth of Galilee could not be suppressed, for remember people said, "Can anything good come out of Nazareth?"(John 1:46).

Also, the journey phase of Jesus' life assumed that the trip carried Jesus and his followers from Galilee to Jerusalem, so the gospel tradition was compelled to account for this earlier phase of his life. Was there then a natural starting place in the Jewish liturgical calendar that invited Mark to add the Galilean phase of Jesus' life to his story in order to bring that story liturgically to that proper Jewish place of beginning? Indeed there was!

In pre-Exilic Judaism, the Jewish New Year, called Rosh Hashanah, came in the fall of the year, a couple of months before the Feast of the Dedication. Would not this traditional Jewish New Year be a fit place for Mark to begin his gospel, so that his narrative would carry the Church from Rosh Hashanah to Passover? If that is plausible, then we should expect the early part of the story of Jesus' life, as Mark related it, to be told in terms of the Jewish lections between the Jewish New Year and Dedication. That would inevitably require the gospel writer to deal with both the fall festivals and with the major fall fast of the Jewish people. Working backward from Dedication, that would mean that one must journey through the Festival of Tabernacles to Yom Kippur, the Day of the Atonement, in order for the worshiper to arrive at Rosh Hashanah, the Jewish New Year. Following once more the divisions of Mark, as outlined by Codex Alexandrinus, which broke the text at natural points, one would discover that the celebration of Jewish New Year and the observance of the Day of the Atonement would overlap with Mark 1 and 2,[5] and that the festival of Tabernacles would involve us with the third and fourth chapters of Mark.[6] This would still leave a reading for the intervening Sabbaths that connected Tabernacles with Dedication in the Jewish liturgical year. So we examine these possibilities to see if there can be found a liturgical connection between the Gospel of Mark and these Jewish worship traditions. Does the theory that Mark was written to illumine the Jewish calendar with the story of Jesus fit yet again?

Because we are walking backward, we start first with Tabernacles or Booths. This eight-day fall festival was primarily related to the harvest, but this celebration also featured the note of the coming of God's messiah and it spoke of a gathering of the nations of the world in Jerusalem. In the Tabernacles tradition, these foreigners were thought first to have gathered as enemies in warfare. They were destined, however, to be defeated by God's messiah, and so, in defeat, they remained to worship the Lord of Hosts. They also expected to be the recipients of endless water, which would be a sign that the Kingdom of God had come. This permanent living water, in time, came to be identified with the spirit of the living God, the presence of which was also a sign that the Kingdom of God had come. Finally, Tabernacles called all Jews to remember the wilderness years of Jewish history, when the Jews dwelt in temporary shelters or booths. From this part of the tradition, the festival derived its name.

The lessons from Mark that would fall during this festival show an interrelatedness to the themes of such a celebration. The Marcan segments reveal first that massive crowds of people had gathered around Jesus in his ministry. Next these crowds, like the crowds at Tabernacles, began to be internationalized. Mark said that the Galilean followers were joined by residents from Judea, Jerusalem, and Idumea, from beyond the Jordan, and from Tyre and Sidon. In the section of the Torah that described the celebration of Tabernacles (Lev. 21–24), the people were encamped at the foot of Sinai, while Moses went up the mountain to receive the Lord's statutes. Moses took with him the names of the twelve tribes. Later, Moses would send twelve men to go spy out the Promised Land. One of them was named Joshua, which was simply the Hebrew way of spelling Jesus. So Mark, in the lections that would be read during this festival, had Jesus go up the mountain and call to himself twelve disciples. These disciples would then be sent out to preach and to have power over demons. Jesus had replaced Moses in Mark's story just as Joshua had replaced him in the Hebrew scriptures, but the themes of Tabernacles were still obvious. This cannot be coincidental! This episode was followed in the Leviticus lesson used at Tabernacles by the Jews with Moses' teaching on blasphemy. So Mark told a story about Jesus' teaching on true blasphemy, which was defined as a refusal to acknowledge the action of the Holy Spirit in Jesus' healings. Once again, this placement defies the claim of being a coincidence.

With these notes of Tabernacles set, Mark then moved to pick up the harvest aspect of this fall festival, and so we have such narratives as the parable of the sower (Mark 4:1–9); then the interpretation of the parable of the sower (Mark 4:10–20); the parable of the seed growing secretly (Mark 4:26–29); and the parable of the mustard seed (Mark 4:30–32). And finally, he concluded this harvest segment of Jesus' teaching with a narrative about the power of Jesus over nature—the story of the stilling of the storm. So far, every major Jewish festival in our backward trek through Mark has been reflected in this gospel, and it has come in exactly the right place and in exactly the right order to match the Jewish calendar. But the test continues.

If Mark's gospel was designed to carry the Christian worshiper liturgically from Jewish New Year to Passover, then Mark must first open his gospel with narratives appropriate to Jewish New Year and then he must move quickly thereafter to deal with Yom Kippur, the Day of Atonement.

The Jewish New Year was a call to repentance. It was marked by the blowing of the *shofar,* the ceremonial ram's horn used to call the worshipers to the liturgy. The *shofar* was thought to announce the coming reign of God. The New Year was also perceived as a time of judgment and even as a time of divine vengeance. As that judgment dawned, the tradition of the Jews was that eyes were opened, ears were unstopped, and a highway was prepared on which God might travel. This highway began in the desert, which was thought of as the abode of unclean animals, like the camel (Lev. 11:4) or the satyr or the "scapegoat" that was driven into the wilderness with the people's sins on its back (Lev. 17:7). The wilderness also was populated by one called the night hag, written *daimon* in Greek (Isa. 34:14). Those were the notes of the Jewish celebration of Rosh Hashanah or Jewish New Year.

So what do we have in Mark? Mark opened his gospel with John the Baptist, a voice crying in the wilderness, like a human *shofar.* His task was to prepare in this desert the highway for the Lord. John was clothed with the skin of a camel, an animal unclean for eating and therefore a sign of the wilderness. The camel was a desert animal whose ability to store water made it fit to walk a desert highway. John preached the Jewish New Year message of repentance. When Jesus came to him and was baptized, a heavenly voice affirmed him as God's son and sent him immediately into the desert to battle the daimon named Satan. So the first chapter of Mark is filled with the themes of the Jewish New Year.

As the calendar moved quickly from the Jewish New Year to the Day of Atonement, the Torah from Leviticus (12–13) about clean and unclean things was being read according to the Jewish custom. In that passage attached to Yom Kippur, God was teaching Moses and Aaron to distinguish between the common and the holy. Laws about clean and unclean foods followed. There we read about a woman's uncleanness in conception, about human uncleanness through leprosy, and about uncleaness through sexual discharge. Aaron, the priest, was to make atonement for the uncleanness of the people of Israel.

Now, what do we find in Mark that would be read by the Christians against the background of the Day of Atonement? In the balance of Mark 1 and deep into Mark 2, we find stories where Jesus was the source of forgiveness, where forgiveness was understood as healing in the episode of Peter's mother-in-law (Mark 1:29–31); in the story of those possessed of demons (Mark 1:32–35); in the account of the unclean leper (Mark 1:40–45); and in the restoring of the paralytic. In each of these narratives, the miracle was accomplished quite specifically by Jesus pronouncing forgiveness on the sick, the distorted, and the unclean. Next, we read of Jesus calling into discipleship a man named Levi, the tax collector, who was associated with and who worked for the hated and unclean gentiles (Mark 2:14). Finally, we read the account of Jesus sitting at table with the unclean tax collectors (Mark 2:15–17). The message of Yom Kippur, the act of atonement, was being lived out by Jesus in this section of Mark. It was once again a powerful connector between the form of the Gospel of Mark and the organizing principle of the Jewish liturgical year.

So—lining up first Mark's story of the passion with the Jewish celebration of Passover, and then stretching Mark backward Sabbath by Sabbath and Jewish festival by Jewish festival, as his story came to be compiled—we discover that Mark's gospel would begin with the Jewish New Year, and it would cover six and a half months of the liturgical calendar culminating in the celebration of Passover, to which Mark has added his Easter climax and conclusion. However, the various portions of Mark's gospel that tell the Jesus story appear designed to be read during the Jewish observances of New Year,

Atonement, Tabernacles, Dedication, and Passover, and each would fall in order in the proper place in the narrative story line that Mark was developing.

This biblical analysis reveals quite clearly to me that the gospel tradition, in addition to being a *midrashic* retelling of the Jesus story based on the Hebrew scriptures, was also organized around the liturgical year of the Jews under whose influence the Christian story was born.

This means that Mark's gospel is neither biography nor history so much as it is a corporate memory, informed and affected by the Hebrew scriptures and organized according to Jewish worship practices. If we can read this gospel with Jewish eyes, we become aware that we do not have in this narrative much of what Jesus actually said and did nearly so much as we have a chronicle of the impact of what he said and did, funneled by Mark through the sacred story of the Jews. The content of this gospel appears to have existed first as Christian preaching on the lections of the synagogue and as the Christian attempt to interpret Jesus in terms of the great festivals of the Jewish liturgical year. Indeed, when one becomes aware of this organizing principle, one wonders how one could possibly read the Gospel of Mark except through Jewish eyes and hope to understand anything that it says.

These are the insights into the origins of the gospel tradition in Mark, the first gospel to be written. These are in the insights that drive me as a Christian more and more deeply into that faith of Abraham and Sarah. But if this was the pattern of the first gospel, would it not be proper to see if the later gospels followed this pattern? This would be especially so, since it is clear that the second and third gospels to be written, Matthew and Luke, made extensive use of Mark. So for further data to illumine the Jewishness of the Gospels, we turn next to Matthew.

6

Matthew

Setting Matthew into a Jewish Framework

In a book by B. W. Bacon published in 1931, entitled *Studies in Matthew*, the author identified five teaching discourses in Matthew's gospel, each of which was concluded with a consistent formula.[1] This formula appeared to link the five units together in some way or at least to seal them off as distinct units in Matthew's corpus:

1. The first discourse was Matthew 5–7, readily identified as the Sermon on the Mount. It concluded with these words: "When Jesus had finished all these sayings, the crowds were astonished at his teaching for he taught them as one who had authority and not as their scribes" (Matt. 7:28).

2. The second block of teaching material (Matt. 10:5–11:1) was made up of instructions given to the twelve when they were first sent out on a mission to proclaim that "the Kingdom of God is at hand." This unit concluded with the words "and when Jesus had finished instructing the twelve disciples, he went on from there to teach and preach in their cities" (Matt. 11:1).

3. The third identifiable block of teaching material (Matt. 13:1–53) was tied together by the common theme of the harvest. It included, among other things, the parable of the sower together with the elaborate interpretation of the parable of the sower. This unit was brought to conclusion with these words: "And when Jesus had finished all of these parables, he went away from there" (Matt. 13:53).

4. The fourth block of Matthean teaching material (Matt. 18:1–19:1) began after the story of the transfiguration and represented once again instructions given to the disciples preparing them for the time when Jesus would no longer be with them. This unit concluded with the words: "Now when Jesus had finished these sayings, he went away from Galilee and entered the region of Judea beyond the Jordan" (Matt. 19:1).

5. Finally, there was the long discourse that began with what is called the "apocalyptic" chapter 24 and stretched into chapter 25, with parables about being ready when the Bridegroom comes or when the Master returns or when the Son of Man arrives on the day of judgment to separate the sheep from the goats. This unit was brought to a conclusion with the words: "Now when Jesus had finished all of these sayings, he said to his disciples, 'You know that after two days the Passover is coming and the Son of Man will be delivered up to be crucified'" (Matt. 26:1–2).

A search of the entire Gospel of Matthew would reveal that the phrase "when Jesus had finished" was used by this author five times and five times only, and each instance brought one of the five Matthean teaching blocks to a conclusion. It was clearly a formula of some significance to this gospel writer.

In no other gospel are these units of teaching material quite so identifiable. Matthew has more than doubled the teaching words of Jesus that he found in Mark. Luke, on the other hand, seemed to have no need for concentrated blocks of teaching material, so he broke up Matthew's long discourses into more manageable segments. In the edition of the Bible familiar to me as a young evangelical growing up in the southern part of the United States, all of the words of Jesus were printed in red. This meant that the naked eye could discern these five blocks of teaching material in Matthew with the immediacy of a single glance as one simply leafed through the pages of this gospel text.

B. W. Bacon recognized the uniqueness of these units and was aware of the long-acknowledged Jewishness of Matthew's gospel. He offered the suggestion that Matthew had deliberately punctuated his gospel with five blocks of teaching material in order to suggest that this book was to be a kind of Christian Torah. He was contending that Matthew's gospel was written to parallel in some way the five sacred books of the Jewish law—Genesis, Exodus, Leviticus, Numbers, and Deuteronomy. It was an attractive theory at first sight, and it quickly made its way into the theological seminaries of the English-speaking world. It was still alive and well, even if undocumented, when I did my theological training in the early 1950s. This insight also added to the growing conclusion, arrived at on the basis of other data, that the author of this gospel was in fact a Jewish scribe.

But while Professor Bacon established recognition of the reality of these five units, his theory attempting to interpret that reality did not stand the test of time very well. On deeper analysis the "Matthew as the Christian Torah" suggestion raised more questions than it answered. For example, the first teaching discourse in Matthew, the Sermon on the Mount, bore no discernible relationship to the Book of Genesis, which was the first volume of the Torah. It rather had a strong connection with the Book of Exodus. It cast Jesus in the role of a new Moses, giving a new interpretation of the law from a new Mt. Sinai. It contrasted the teaching of Jesus directly with some of the Ten Commandments from Exodus 20: "You have heard it said . . . but I say to you" (5:21–22, 5:27–28, 5:31–32, 5:33–34, 5:38–39, 5:43–44). Nonetheless, the world of biblical scholarship was still intrigued by this theory and so the scholars began to play with it in a wide variety of ways, trying to force a fit and thus to crack the hidden interpretive code of this gospel.

Austin Farrer added to the debate in a 1954 contribution to D. E. Nineham's *Studies in the Gospels*,[2] by suggesting that the genealogy chapter of Matthew 1 was actually designed by the author to parallel the Book of Genesis. He noted that it began, "The book of the genealogy (or genesis) of Jesus Christ, the Son of David, the Son of Abraham," and went on to chronicle Jesus' ancestry. This meant, however, that Farrer now had six units instead of the five set pieces identified by Bacon, and thus he violated the Torah theory. The Torah was, after all, called the Pentateuch, which meant five books, not six. Since Farrer needed a sixth book to make things come out evenly, he added the next book in the Hebrew scriptures, the Book of Joshua, to his scheme and then he correlated his now six Matthean blocks with the Torah, plus Joshua. It was an ingenious attempt to make the Bacon premise work. By making the genealogy of Matthew's chapter 1 serve as his Genesis, Farrer could now correlate the Sermon on the Mount with the giving of the law in Exodus. Then he saw a connection between the commissioning of the twelve in Matthew's chapter 10 with the Book of Leviticus by suggesting that the twelve were chosen to serve as the priests of the new Israel. The harvest notes of Matthew 13 were then likened by Farrer to the gathering of the people into the Church and thus patterned with the Book of Numbers, which got its name from the story in which Moses ordered the counting of the people of the former Israel. Next, Farrer pointed out that chapter 18 of Matthew contained a number of references to Deuteronomy. Finally, this great New Testament scholar suggested that the teaching segment of Matthew that introduced the Passover was designed to present Jesus as the new Joshua. Farrer capped his argument with the note that, just as Joshua crossed the Jordan River to enter the Promised Land of Canaan, so Jesus crossed the barrier of death to enter the Promised Land of the Kingdom of God. Both thus opened a promised land to a whole people—the old Israel in Joshua's case, the new Israel in Jesus' case.

Farrer's suggestion intrigued the world of New Testament scholarship and titillated the imagination. But Farrer's connections to the Torah plus Joshua were quite thin and at times seemed deliberately contrived, once he got past the Sermon on the Mount. Yet, in the study of Matthew's gospel, it was a step in the right direction. Its failure lay in its continued attempt to relate the blocks of Matthew's teaching material to the Torah. That theory simply would not fit, no matter how hard the scholars tried.

It was Michael Goulder, a student of Austin Farrer, who broke the log jam by applying his mentor's insights to a different background.[3] The five teaching blocks in Matthew were not related to the Torah, said Goulder, as attractive as that theory had once seemed. They were related rather, he argued, to the five great celebratory festivals in the Jewish liturgical year. Those festivals were Pentecost (Shavuot), New Year (Rosh Hashanah), Tabernacles (Sukkot), Dedication (Hanukkah), and Passover.[4] Note that in this order, Passover has been moved into the position that Christians imposed on it, namely, from first to last. Driven by this insight, Goulder began to develop a startling new principle through which one might begin to understand the inner structure of all of those works that came to be called the Gospels. The Gospels were not, Goulder asserted, written as "a literary genre" at all. "A gospel is a liturgical genre," he asserted. The Gospels, at least the synoptics of Mark, Matthew, and Luke, were designed, he argued, to be lectionary books. That is, they were developed to be a series of Christian lections (or gospels) designed to be read in public worship week by week *"in lectio continua."*[5] Every liturgical church still today has a book of "gospels" that is carried in possession, elevated, and read section by section in each Sunday's worship service. We have already suggested the possibility that the Jewish lectionary was the organizing principle behind the gospel of Mark. It is worth noting, however, that for Goulder it was the study of

Matthew's gospel that was the critical breakthrough in developing his lectionary theory of gospel development, and only later
did he apply it to Mark.

When this possibility dawned on Goulder, he quickly set out
to recreate the Jewish liturgical calendar and to determine the
actual readings from the Torah, the Former Prophets, and the
Latter Prophets that were assigned to each Sabbath in the synagogue of antiquity and to each feast and fast in the Jewish annual cycle of liturgical worship. This task not only fueled his
work on Matthew, but it also shaped his later work on the other
gospels, published in a book entitled *The Evangelist's Calendar*.[6]
However, this total reconstruction of the Jewish lectionary
proved to be an overly ambitious project because adequate ancient records are not available. Undaunted by this lack of data,
Goulder attempted to fill in his Jewish liturgical calendar with
much informed guesswork and rigorous attempts to cover the
historic blanks. It was a brilliant and imaginative effort, but
Goulder's total lectionary recreations have not won the field. As
is so typical of the vested interests of the recognized scholars of
the world, his weaknesses apparent in the recreated Jewish lectionary were attacked vigorously while the magnitude of the insight he was offering was not adequately appreciated: namely,
that at least the synoptic Gospels were developed against the
background of a Jewish liturgical year rather than as biography,
history, or any other kind of literary writing process. That insight has not to this day been discredited, nor is it likely to be.
While many of the details in the reconstructed lectionary theory
proved insupportable, the theory itself still remains both illu-
mining and potent. But the ability to entertain this theory properly requires a far deeper immersion into Jewish thought than
most New Testament scholars, or most ordinary Christians,
seem capable of achieving. Such an immersion, however, provides the insight that opens the gospel material to fresh and dy-
namic new possibilities.

Goulder contended that the Gospel of Matthew emphasized
the Jewish festal calendar, and for this reason Matthew provided
blocks of Christian teaching material to be used in preparation

for or during the five great celebratory Jewish festivals of the year. There was also in the Matthean text, Goulder argued, appropriate material at the appropriate places for the great penitential Jewish fast, Yom Kippur, the Day of Atonement, and the minor penitential observance of the Ninth of Ab. Armed with this organizing principle discovered in Matthew, Goulder then was able to see Mark also as a lectionary book and still later to see Luke as a lectionary book but adapted to a far more hellenized world. This remarkable insight into the formation of the Gospels remains as Goulder's great contribution to New Testament study. Slowly but surely, Goulder's work is gaining a hearing in New Testament circles. It should because it solves many of the mysteries that have haunted scholars for centuries.

Furthermore, this lectionary theory of how the synoptic Gospels came to be formed grounds these gospels deeply and dramatically in the worship life of the Jewish people. It illumines many gospel passages in dramatic new ways. It reveals the way in which the *midrashic* elements, and the overt references to ancient Hebrew texts, so pervasive in the Gospels, came to be suggested in the first place. It strikes a mortal blow at the literalistic view that the Gospels were written as literary pieces by eyewitnesses to capture the objective reality of Jesus and his teaching. For these reasons, Goulder's theory, which offers a new starting place, demands consideration.

What happens to the way we view the Gospels if we begin to suppose, as I did in the chapter on Mark, that the various episodes in the Gospels were first sermons preached in the synagogues on the texts of the Jewish lections for that Sabbath? Would this not be an exquisite way in which to validate the conclusion so popular among the earliest Christians that everything written about Jesus in the Hebrew scriptures had been fulfilled? Under the homiletic genius of the early Christian preachers, Paul's words that "Christ died for our sins *in accordance with the scriptures*" and that "he was raised on the third day *in accordance with the scriptures*," came to be given very specific content. In time these sermons, relating the story of Jesus to the Jewish lections, came to be put together by gifted members of specific worshiping communities in serial form to create gospels and to provide a Christian reading to accompany the regular Sabbath synagogue readings from the Torah and the other sacred writings of the Jews. By adding a lection from the gospel to their synagogue tradition, some Jewish communities moved in the early decades of Christian history to incorporate Jesus specifically into the worship life of the Jewish people. When these Jewish Christians were finally banished from the synagogues late in the ninth decade, they simply took the Gospels with them. Luke wrote Acts, I believe, to be a second Christian reading to be used in worship, a companion piece to his gospel in that newly separated Christian community.[7] Then, as the Church moved more and more into a gentile direction, the original Jewish context of these gospels was lost. When finally Sabbath worship was completely replaced by Sunday worship, Christians and Jews were separated. When the Church entered the more hellenized and gentile world, the original synagogue readings from the Jewish scriptures were more and more deemphasized or replaced by readings from the Gospels, the Acts, and the Epistles.[8] So it was that in this evolving historical set of circumstances, the Jewish liturgical connection that first shaped the gospel content was not only lost, it was also forgotten. It was the discovery of these five blocks of teaching material in the Gospel of Matthew that provided the clue to Goulder and later to others that the lectionary theory of gospel formation was in fact the missing link that neither Bacon nor Farrer had been able to grasp.

A hint of how the Gospels developed against the lectionary of the Jews can be found in the Book of Acts when we know what it is for which we are looking. Paul and his companions, we are told, "passed on from Perga and came to Antioch of Pisidia. And on the Sabbath day, they went into the synagogue and sat down. After the reading of the law [that is, the Torah] and the prophets, the rulers of the synagogue sent to them saying, 'Brethren, if you have any words of exhortation for the people, say it.' So Paul stood up and motioning with his hand said. . . ." (Acts 13:14 ff.). Then the Book of Acts records a version of a sermon Paul might have delivered on that occasion (Acts 13: 16–42). This passage from the Book of Acts has preserved the liturgical context of Christian preaching in the synagogues of antiquity.

Paul's sermon in the Book of Acts was filled with biblical references. It began "Men of Israel." Women were not always welcomed in the synagogue, until the church moved out of its strict Jewish context.[9] References to the scriptures of the Jews were sprinkled throughout the sermon. Paul referred to the seven nations that the Jews had supplanted (Deut. 7:1, Josh. 14:1). He recited the call of David, quoting both from the Psalms (89:20) and from the first Book of Samuel (13:14). He then referred to Psalm 2 (verse 7) in his attempt to show that Jesus was the son of David. He added a reference to the servant figure from Isaiah (55:3) to bring that connection into consciousness. He returned to the Psalms to find a reference to undergird the three-day tradition (Ps. 16:10) and to demonstrate that the deceased body of Jesus did not ever begin the process of decay. He concluded with a quotation from Habakkuk (1:5) about those who cannot believe no matter who tells them. It was a sermon crafted by Luke in the style of Luke's day. It revealed how the Jewish mind worked as it employed the scriptures of antiquity. If that is the way the content of the Gospels was born, then other insights flow quickly out of this hypothesis; for suddenly we begin to read the Gospels from a new perspective.

Through the ages Christians, treating the Gospels as historical accounts, have drawn some rather interesting literal conclusions from these texts. They assumed, for example, that the public ministry of Jesus was but one year in duration because they did not recognize that the ordering principle of the synoptic Gospels was not the life of Jesus, but the liturgical year of the Jews, which covered that life on an annual cycle. They assumed that Jesus journeyed only once to Jerusalem, and that was for the climactic moments of his life. They assumed that the outline of Jesus' life was covered by the story of the Galilean phase, culminating in the journey and concluding in Jerusalem. It is of interest to note that John countered each of these assumptions in his gospel. The great benefit to us of the lectionary theory of gospel formation today is that we gain new insights when we begin to look at the life of Jesus through this ancient liturgical pattern. More, our imaginations are freed when we begin to read the Gospels outside the imposed literalistic straitjackets of the past.

In the previous chapter on Mark, we noted that the first day of the Passover watch was transformed by Christians into the passion watch, culminating in the story of the crucifixion. In this process Jesus was identified with the paschal lamb that was slain at the origination of the first Passover celebration. In the Passover tradition, the blood of that first paschal lamb was said to have been placed on the doorposts of the Hebrew homes to protect them from the angel of death, who was sent by God to be the final plague imposed upon the Egyptians; the plagues were designed to motivate the pharaoh to free the people of Israel from slavery in Egypt (Exod. 12). That angel of death was to slay the firstborn of every household in the land whose doorposts were not protected by the blood of the paschal lamb. Now we can see how, in quick succession under the pressure of the liturgical and homiletical needs of the early Church, Jesus came to be thought of as the lamb slain. The cross became the doorposts of the world on which the blood of the lamb of God was sprinkled to save people from death. Salvation came by way of one known as the firstborn of God, who was now seen as the perfect offering. The angel of death in time became Satan, whose power was broken by the cross. The resurrection, when added by the Christians to the passion story as its climax, became the new expression of the triumph and victory that the Jews had experienced: first, when they miraculously navigated the Red Sea to enter the freedom of the wilderness; and second, when they followed the earlier Joshua/Jesus into the Promised Land called Canaan. Now the new Promised Land became the realm of heaven, which had been entered by the new Joshua/Jesus in his resurrection and was offered and opened to all who would be his disciples. In the synagogues that included the Jewish people who were also Christians, and on the Sabbath following the Passover, the story of Easter was read. Over the years the Easter story gradually expanded as the celebration of Easter became an eight-day festival. At that time a second Easter lesson was added to the lectionary to cover the second Sabbath of that octave. To get this order correct, recall once again that the liturgical year of the post-Exilic Jews began with the month of Nisan. Passover was celebrated on the fourteenth and fifteenth of Nisan, and thus the first two Sabbaths of the year were preparation for Passover. This would mean that the Passover observance came between the second and third Sabbaths. Therefore the Christians made the third Sabbath of the year their Easter. Later, when the eight-day octave was placed around this major festival, they made the fourth Sabbath of Nisan their octave Sabbath. Thus the Christians had to complete their passion-Easter observance before they could start the story of Jesus' beginnings. Consequently the Jewish liturgical year began on the first Sabbath of Nisan, while the Christian liturgical year began on the fourth Sabbath of Nisan and later even one Sabbath beyond that. So, in the Christian year, Passover came at the end and not at the beginning and was thus listed last, not first, by the Christians. These dating procedures become instrumental in helping us unravel the order first of Matthew and later of Luke. This strange starting place, the fourth (and sometimes the fifth) Sabbath of the Jewish liturgical year, obscured for centuries the connection between the Jewish lectionary and the formation of the Gospels. For it meant that the Christian liturgical year that produced the Gospels normally started on at least the second Sabbath/Sunday after the Passover, or on at least the fourth Sabbath of the Jewish year.[10]

When this lectionary theory was introduced in the previous chapter on Mark, we noted that the first gospel developed in reverse order from the way we now read it, in order to meet the emerging liturgical needs of the Christian community. It began when the passion story of Jesus was related to the Passover story of the Jews. Then, just as the Jews had a significant period of preparation for their converts who were incorporated at Passover and welcomed at the Passover meal as Jews, so the Christians felt they needed a period of instruction and preparation for their converts before they were baptized on Easter eve and then welcomed to the Christian meal, the Eucharist. The journey section was developed in Mark's gospel to provide teaching "from the Lord" to meet this need. So, from Passover/Easter, the liturgical year of the Christians began its backward journey into its formation.

Next we noted that Mark wrote the Galilean section of his story to carry the Christian lections back to what he deemed to be a proper liturgical starting point at Rosh Hashanah, the old traditional Jewish New Year that had been replaced in the Exile. This meant, however, that although Mark, the first liturgical account of Jesus' life and teaching, was enormously popular, it nonetheless provided the Christians with liturgical readings for only six and a half months of the calendar year as they continued to worship in the synagogues. It was that sense of incompleteness that inspired first Matthew and later Luke to expand Mark so that gospel readings were available for every Sabbath/Sunday of the year. It is for this reason alone that Matthew and Luke are both roughly twice as long as Mark.

Before chronicling that development, may I first suggest that the sense of Marcan incompleteness is still present in the Christian liturgical calendars of the twentieth century. The order is a little different, but the fact remains that from its beginning with the season of Advent in late November to early December, to Whitsunday or Pentecost in late spring, May or June, the Church year is still only six and a half months long. In the older liturgical calendars, the Church filled up the balance of the Sundays with a season called the Sundays after Trinity or the Sundays of the Trinity Season. In the later liturgical calendars, this was changed to the Sundays after Pentecost or the Sundays in the life of the Church. But those Sundays simply completed the liturgical reliving of the life of Jesus so that the whole calendar year could be covered with readings in worship.

It was, however, this very frustration of incompleteness that drove Christian communities to feel the necessity of expanding

Mark. Both Matthew and Luke responded to Mark's incompleteness. So we turn first to the scribe we call Matthew, living in Syria, who was deeply in touch not only with the scriptures of the Hebrew people but also with the great festivals of the Jewish liturgical year, to understand how he rewrote Mark's gospel to be more adequate for the liturgical use of the Jewish Christians he served.

7

Matthew

Reading Matthew Through a Jewish Lens

There is no question about the fact that the author of Matthew knew the Gospel of Mark intimately and well. Of the 664 verses in Mark, Matthew incorporated in some way some 606 of those verses into his gospel.[1] Sometimes these verses were incorporated verbatim, removing any doubt that this Jewish scribe had Mark in front of him when he worked. Sometimes, however, he changed Mark to suit his personal or theological tastes. It is in the study of these changes that the author of Matthew emerges out of the shadows.

The gospel called Matthew was written well after the fall of Jerusalem in 70 C.E. had become part of Jewish reality. But this gospel was also written in Jewish circles well before the final tearing away of Jewish Christians from their participation in synagogue worship that occurred around the year 88 C.E. That would tend to anchor the date for this gospel in the years between 75 C.E. and 85 C.E., with the range of 80 C.E. to 82 C.E. being the best guess of most scholars.

The first striking change that Matthew makes in Mark is in the way he blunts Mark's criticism of the scribes. There were in Mark's gospel twenty-one references to the scribes. Nineteen of these references were hostile. Of these nineteen hostile references, Matthew kept only six (9:3, 15:1, 16:21, 20:18, 26:5–7, 27:41), seven were dropped completely, and six were glossed in such a way as to lessen or to remove the negativity. Sometimes this glossing was accomplished by contrasting "their" scribes with "our" scribes so as to focus the negativity on improper actions rather than on the mere fact of being a scribe. Matthew then suggested that Christian scribes were subject to persecution by their Pharisaic counterparts. These facts are part of the reason that scholars assume that the break with Judaism had not yet occurred and that the author of this gospel was himself a scribe.

The role of a provincial scribe in this era was twofold. He not only led a synagogue as a *sophar,* that is, a worship leader, but he also served as a provincial schoolmaster for Jewish children in his Syrian town. The primary task of a scribe who headed the synagogue was to teach the scriptures to the adults who gathered to worship and, in the process, to relate one text to another in *midrashic* fashion. This served to illumine events occurring in the present with specific appeals to the people and the events that made up the sacred past of the Jews—which is, of course, the principle of Jewish *midrash.*

When the scribe was serving as the provincial schoolmaster, his primary task was to introduce the children to the scriptures and to enable them to take their places inside the sacred traditions of their people. Some scholars even suggest that Matthew, the Christian scribe, placed an autobiographical note in the narrative of his gospel when he wrote that "every scribe who has been trained for the Kingdom of Heaven is like a householder who brings out of his treasure what is new and what is old" (Matt. 13:52). In the scribal tradition, the new insight did not replace the old, it merely expanded it. That appears to be Matthew's understanding of what he was doing to the Gospel of Mark. As a scribe dedicated to the things that are "old," Matthew had a profound and lifelong respect for the traditions of his people and, most especially, for the Torah. As a follower of Jesus, whom he acknowledged as the Christ, he had a passionate desire to show this Jesus primarily as the one who had fulfilled the law and the prophets. In this dual role, Matthew also appeared to have been embarrassed by some of the radical positions taken toward the law by Mark. So his next task, after repairing the reputation of the scribes, was to proceed to soften the negative Marcan attitude toward the law.

Mark, for example, had told the story of the disciples of Jesus plucking grain on the Sabbath in a clear violation of the law (Mark 1:23–28). Matthew eased this implied violation by adding to his story the suggestion that the disciples "were hungry" (Matt. 12:1–8). This cut the blatant disregard that Mark appeared to show for the Sabbath. Matthew then sought in a typically rabbinic way to show that even priests in an emergency could set aside the law when human need requires it. He concluded this narrative by insisting that it was "lawful to do good on the Sabbath" (Matt. 12:12). On another occasion Mark had proclaimed that the Sabbath was made for man, not man for the Sabbath (Mark 2:27), and he also had Jesus declare all foods clean (Mark 7:19). Matthew simply omitted both of these anti-Torah verses from his text. Omission happened so rarely that when it did, it was telling and insightful. It had to be purposeful.

Matthew's respect for the law of the Jews was profound. To Mark's text he added the words that not "one iota or a dot"[2] shall perish from the law "until all is accomplished" (Matt. 5:18). It was this fulfillment of the scriptures that was of the greatest value to Matthew. The Christ he acknowledged came not to abolish but to fulfill the law. Jesus had come in Matthew's mind to put into action that which had been pointed to for centuries in the sacred writings of the Jews. For Matthew the law pointed to Christ, and it was his task to hold these two sacred sources of revelation together in proper tension.

Matthew clearly was familiar with the traditions of his people. His book revealed a knowledge of the Targum, an Aramaic translation of interpretive material. He alone referred to such Jewish things as phylacteries and tassels or fringes (Matt. 23:5). He was knowledgeable about proper cleaning of the plates and cups so that they would be kosher (Matt. 23:25). He was even aware of sackcloth and ashes (Matt. 11:21). Finally, he used scripture in a typically rabbinic fashion. He taught "the Book" to the children of his provincial school. He read from the law and the prophets and expounded the content of "the Book" to the adult worshipers each Sabbath/Sunday. One cannot comprehend this gospel until one has a sense of the way it was originally used and what the values were that led its author to craft it in the way that he did.

Other biographical features of Matthew are revealed as we examine in depth the way he used the Marcan material.

Time and again, Matthew filled in Mark's blanks. He would not leave unanswered questions lying around. This was especially true in the resurrection narratives. Mark's women, for example, came to the tomb on the first day of the week, wondering how they could remove the stone. Upon arrival, they found it already removed, but no explanation was given (Mark 16:1–8). Matthew explained that mystery in great detail: An angel did it. This angel came to earth on the wings of an earthquake, put the soldiers to sleep, rolled back the stone, and sat on it (Matt. 28:2–4). Matthew's account was quite vivid, but since we know that his source was Mark, we can readily identify the Matthean elaborations.

Mark had the Easter messenger promise that Jesus would have a Galilean rendezvous with the disciples, but Mark never related that rendezvous (Mark 16:1–8). So the promise was left hanging and unfulfilled in Mark. Characteristically, Matthew also filled in this blank. It did take place, he stated, in Galilee on top of a mountain. Matthew even created the dialogue and had the risen Christ exhort the Church to world mission and to Trinitarian baptism (Matt. 28:15–20).

There were also times when Matthew seemed embarrassed at anomalies in Mark, and so he rectified them. Mark, for example, had Jesus say to one questioner, "Why do you call me good? No one is good but God alone" (Mark 10:17, 18). Matthew appeared offended at that language, and so he changed it to read, "Why do you ask me about what is good? One there is who is good!" (Matt. 19:17 ff.). Mark had the women in their Easter morning visit to the garden flee in fear and say nothing to anyone when the messenger of the resurrection confronted them (Mark 16:1–8). Matthew, unwilling to portray the women so negatively, once more changed Mark. So the women in Matthew hear the resurrection message and then go at once and tell the disciples (Matt. 28:8). By isolating the variety of ways in which Matthew changed, edited, and used Mark, we see the outlines of Matthew's personality and begin to sense the values that marked his life.

The scribe who composed this gospel was also responsible for the worship life of the synagogue. As we have already noted, the typical Sabbath service in the synagogue consisted of lections read from the law, the Former Prophets,[3] and the Latter Prophets.[4] Of these, the law was most important. That is why only the Torah was required to be read in its entirety once a year. In these services there might also be a recitation from the Targum by memory and a sermon delivered by the scribe expounding on the lections. These readings and preachings were interspersed with prayers and psalms to complete the worship experience. The schoolteacher and scribe would prepare the readers of the scriptures week by week and would ordinarily deliver the sermon. Mark's gospel must have been a godsend to assist such a person with this weekly homiletical task. It presented him with the most complete story of Jesus that was available. It gave him a base from which to write a fuller, more complete lectionary version of a gospel, and most especially a way to highlight and to celebrate the holy days of his Jewish liturgical life.

There is also reason to believe that Matthew had some or all of the writings of Paul at his disposal. Paul, however, related almost no biographical details of Jesus' life. Since Mark, in the mind of Matthew, lacked adequate teaching, Matthew could and did turn to Paul for teaching material. However, since Paul lacked biographical details, Matthew would turn to Mark for that. Neither source, however, provided sufficient material for Christians to celebrate the great Jewish festivals. Then there was that primary Marcan inadequacy. This gospel only provided lections from Rosh Hashanah to Passover.

These were the experienced Marcan shortcomings that caused the Christian scribe we call Matthew to undertake a massive *midrashic* rewriting of Mark. In this process Matthew would revise, expand, and transform Mark into a document almost twice its size, and he would also make it far more suitable for use in a relatively strict and theologically conservative Jewish Christian world. He would create a gospel narrative that was capable of providing a lection from Christian writings to be read on every Sabbath worship occasion of the year. He would also provide the teaching material that would transform the great Jewish festivals into Christian celebrations. These were the ambitions and realities that brought the Gospel of Matthew into being.

There are two primary ways by which we can check and validate the suggestion that Matthew expanded on Mark's lectionary basis to form the gospel tradition found in this second Gospel to be written. The first would be to examine the way Matthew dealt with the only major festival of the Jewish year that Mark had omitted. That would be the festival of Pentecost, which came in the late spring to early summer—long before Mark's starting place at Rosh Hashanah. The second would be to compare Matthew with Mark to see if and how Matthew front-end loaded Mark's narrative. For Matthew needed to provide lections that would begin after Easter and carry the worshiper forward to the Jewish New Year in the fall, which was the period of time that Mark had not covered. An examination of the corpus of Matthew's gospel reveals quite clearly that this author has met both of those tests. He also met them in a rather obvious way once his readers and interpreters know that for which they are searching.

To address the second test first, we discover that Matthew in chapters 13 through 28 has followed the Marcan order very closely (Mark 3:31–16:8), even while expanding the story line rather dramatically. This recognition has caused some scholars to suggest that Matthew is nothing but a rewritten version of Mark with a greatly lengthened beginning. When we see the way the material has been expanded, once again we see the *midrashic* style of the Jewish tradition at work. In chapters 1 through 12, however, Matthew has rearranged Mark's order and material freely (Mark 1:1–3:30) and has added large chunks of new material, among which are the genealogy, the story of Jesus' birth, the elaboration of the account of the temptation experience in the wilderness, the content of the Sermon on the Mount, and significant blocks of other teaching material. In the latter part of Matthew (13–28), where Mark was followed much more closely, Matthew's style was generally to insert new material into Mark's order. So the front-end loading of Mark by Matthew is readily apparent.

An analysis of the details of that front end also enables us to see some surprising changes. For example, in his gospel Matthew has placed the content of the preaching of Jesus, found at the beginning of Mark's gospel, into the mouth of John the Baptist! In Mark it was Jesus who said, "The time is fulfilled and the Kingdom of God is at hand; repent and believe the gospel" (Mark 1:15). In Matthew, however, where a more elaborate story of Jesus' preparation for his adult life has been told, it was John the Baptist who burst on the scene with the words, "Repent, for the kingdom of heaven is at hand" (Matt. 3:2). The question always arises as to where this new material originated. Did Matthew have other sources? Was there a Q document that he used to supplement Mark, or did Matthew create the material himself from his known twin sources of Paul and Mark? Increasingly, my study has led me to the conviction that an analysis of the material itself will point us to the latter conclusion. Q is, in my opinion, a Matthean creation.[5]

As a major source to supply Matthew's need for expanded material, we note that Matthew has added elaborate parables to

Mark's corpus. We need to be aware that parables were in the rabbinic style of teaching and they were the means whereby one rabbi would keep current the teaching of a former rabbi. A rabbi with a storytelling gift would take a point in the teaching of a well-known rabbi of the past and develop it into a parable, which would then be attributed to that revered rabbi of the past. That was not, for the Jews, a dishonest practice but a way of honoring the gifts found in their heritage. Four of Mark's parables Matthew appears simply to have transcribed as he found them in Mark. Other parables, however, such as the ones we call the parable of the seed growing secretly and the parable of the doorkeeper, Matthew appears to have expanded significantly from their original Marcan nucleus. Still others Matthew appears to have himself created based on as little as a single line in Mark or a reference in Paul or a place in the ancient Hebrew texts. For example, Matthew seems to have taken a line of Jesus' teaching in Mark (2:19), "Can the wedding guests fast while the bridegroom is with them?" and turned it into the parable of the wise and foolish virgins (Matt. 25:1–13). Another single line of Mark attributed to the teaching of Jesus, "For to him who has will more be given, and from him who has not, even what he has will be taken away" (Mark 4:25), was expanded to become the text that simply concluded Matthew's parable of the talents (Matt. 25:14–29). Still other parables unique to Matthew seem to have great affinity with ancient Hebrew narratives. The parable of the good shepherd who seeks out the single lost lamb for example, is clearly related to a story in the Book of Ezekiel (34:1–16, but especially verses 11–16). The parable of the final judgment when the sheep were divided from the goats likewise appears to lean heavily on Ezekiel (16:17 ff.), where God was said to have judged between "the sheep and the sheep, rams and he goats."

To illustrate the need Matthew felt for more teaching material, one has only to note that in Mark there are 240 teaching verses while in Matthew there are 620.

For some other parts of this expanded teaching, Matthew actually seems to have leaned on Paul. That conclusion surprises people, since Paul and Matthew are not generally thought of together. Yet words written in the Pauline corpus as Paul's teaching appear to show up in Matthew's gospel as the teaching of Jesus. A closer look at the Gospels reveals that Matthew did not originate this practice, for Mark appears to have used Paul in this manner as well. For example, Paul said in Romans (13:7), "Pay all of them their dues, taxes to taxes are due," while Mark had Jesus say, "Render to Caesar the things that are Caesar's." Again, Paul declared in Romans (14:14) that "nothing is unclean in itself," while Mark had Jesus say, "Thus he declared all foods clean" (Mark 7:19).

Matthew chose from Mark only those teaching bits that fitted his agenda, such as the line about rendering "to Caesar the things that are Caesar's." He omitted from his gospel, however, those teaching bits that simply violated his Jewish sensitivities. This author, who insisted that Jesus came to fulfill, not to destroy, the law was not eager to quote Jesus as doing away with the kosher dietary rules of Leviticus, for example. But Matthew, however, also went to his Pauline source for other bits of teaching, which he reconstructed and then placed on the lips of Jesus. Paul, for example, said in Romans, "I would have you wise as to what is good and guileless as to what is evil" (Rom. 16:19). Matthew, who loved to employ animal and farm images,[6] transformed this Pauline saying into Jesus' words, "Behold, I send you out as sheep in the midst of wolves; so be as wise as serpents and innocent [guileless] as doves" (Matt. 10:16).

In Corinthians Paul argued that the laborer was worthy of his food, and even attributed this principle to the command of the Lord (1 Cor. 9:14). So Jesus in Matthew was made to state that "the laborer deserves his food" (Matt. 10:10). Earlier in this same epistle, Paul had said, "When you are assembled . . . my spirit is present with the power of our Lord Jesus" (1 Cor. 5:4), while Matthew had Jesus say, "For where two or three are gathered [assembled] in my name, there am I in the midst of them" (Matt. 18:20).

Paul likened the coming of the day of the Lord to a thief in the night (1 Thess. 5:2), while Matthew had Jesus say, "If the householder had known in what part of the night the thief was coming, he would have watched and would not have let his house be broken into" (Matt. 24:43–44).

I cite all of these illustrations to indicate the rabbinic and *midrashic* methods in which this scribe known to us as Matthew took his basic sources of Mark, Paul, and the Hebrew scriptures and adapted them to fit his liturgical purposes. Since his task was to expand Mark to cover the entire liturgical year of the Jews, and to provide special teaching materials for the major festivals of that Jewish year, he was in need of much more material than Mark provided for him. So, based on his sources, he created that material. That is one of the reasons that I see no need for postulating some special source from which Matthew drew primary material.

Turning now to the second test of the lectionary theory, we examine the question of whether or not Matthew provided adequately for the festival of Pentecost, which Mark's shortened calendar would have omitted. Like all Jewish festivals, it was rooted in both the Canaanite agricultural past and the Jewish sacred history. From the Canaanite background, it was the first wheat harvest of the year. For the Jews it was the time when the giving of the Torah to Moses and the people of Israel at Mount Sinai was recalled and celebrated.

When we place the Gospel of Matthew against the background of the Jewish liturgical year, we begin to see connections that we have never seen before. First we need to be aware that in ancient manuscripts of Matthew, such as Codex Alexandrinus, to which we have referred before, we discover that Matthew's gospel was divided into sixty-eight units in addition to chapter 1, which served as a preface, making sixty-nine units in all. Since there is good reason to believe that Codex Alexandrinus reflected a far earlier tradition, I will use it to lay Matthew's gospel out against the Jewish liturgical year, unit by unit.

Our first connector, please recall, comes when we attach the story of Jesus' passion to the Passover celebration of the Jews. That connection is today all but universally acknowledged in New Testament circles. Next we add the Easter narratives in

Matthew that appear to be designed to be read on the Sabbath or Sabbaths of Easter following the Passover.[7] Originally, Matthew's gospel appears to have been designed to start its journey through the Jewish liturgical year on the Sabbath after Easter day or, as we noted earlier, the fourth Sabbath of the liturgical year.

Following the divisions of Codex Alexandrinus, we would thus assign all of Matthew chapter 1 to be read on that fourth Sabbath/Sunday of the liturgical year. That would include the genealogy and the short narrative that chronicled the Annunciation to Joseph. The fifth and sixth Sabbaths/Sundays of the new Jewish year would divide Matthew chapter 2. The birth of Jesus and the visit of the wise men would be assigned to the fifth Sabbath/Sunday; and the flight to Egypt, the slaughter of the innocents, the return from Egypt, and the settlement at Nazareth would be assigned to the sixth Sabbath/Sunday of the Jewish year—or, just to make things confusing, to the third Sabbath of the Christian year, which always ran at least three Sabbaths behind the Jewish year. Recall that in these early Matthean narrations, each detail of the story was related as the literal fulfillment of the scriptural expectations. Matthew even employed the formula, "This was done to fulfill what was written in the prophets."

On the seventh Sabbath/Sunday of the Jewish year or the fourth week after Easter, the story of the baptism and the temptation would be read (Matt. 3:1–4:16). In both 1 Corinthians 10 and Hebrews 5, baptism had been drawn into sermons on temptation. The story was a natural connection, and it appears in Codex Alexandrinus to be a single unit despite its length. Once again, this Matthean narrative was framed by scriptural quotations. John the Baptist was portrayed in the words of Isaiah 40 as "the voice crying in the wilderness," while Jesus was portrayed as the servant figure of Isaiah 42 of whom it was said by the prophet, "I will put my spirit upon him" (Isa. 42:1). The temptation story had Jesus relive the experience of Moses and the Hebrew people in the wilderness. Before Moses received the law, he fasted forty days and forty nights (Exod. 34:28).[8] So

Jesus, before delivering the new law, underwent a similar fast. The story line followed the adventures of Moses in the wilderness. The manna story (Exod. 16) found expression in the temptation to turn stones into bread. The story of Moses striking the rock in the wilderness at Massah/Meribah (Exod. 17) was told as an act in which Moses put God to the test. That found echoes in the temptation story in Jesus' words, "You shall not tempt the Lord your God" (Matt. 4:7). The story of the people of Israel building and worshiping the golden calf (Exod. 32) in the wilderness found its echo in Jesus' words, "You shall worship the Lord your God and him only shall you serve" (Matt. 4:10). In all three temptation episodes, Jesus was portrayed as quoting Deuteronomy (8:3, 5:16, 6:13), and each Deuteronomic quotation reflected the Exodus wilderness journey of Israel. The *midrashic* ability of the scribe who authored the Gospel of Matthew is clearly revealed in this episode. He took a single verse in Mark, "He was in the wilderness forty days, tempted by Satan, and he was with the wild beasts and the angels ministered to him" (Mark 1:13), and he expanded it into a story that portrayed Jesus reliving the stories of Moses and the people of Israel in their wilderness years.

That narrative would bring us to the eighth Sabbath of the Jewish liturgical year and the fifth Sabbath after Easter. Since Passover came after the second Sabbath of the year, it would be at least the sixth Sabbath after Passover.[9] The next unit of Matthew according to the Codex Alexandrinus text would be Matthew 4:17–25, which was the last segment of this gospel prior to the Sermon on the Mount, which was clearly understood by the author to be Jesus' "Sinai" experience. This final preparatory narrative told of the inauguration of Jesus' public ministry, which was keyed to the arrest of John the Baptist, and it was marked by Jesus beginning the task of choosing his disciples. This is noteworthy because Moses, in a narrative just prior to his Sinai experience, was also portrayed as choosing "able men out of all Israel making them heads over the people" (Exod. 18:25). Matthew's Jesus was still reliving the saga of Moses. He was still fulfilling the scriptures. That was the way the mind of the scribe, who was creating this story, worked. That reading would bring us to the seventh week after Nisan 14–15, during which time the fiftieth day after Passover would occur, the time when the celebration of Jewish Pentecost would be observed.

The Jews marked Pentecost with a twenty-four-hour vigil divided into eight segments. It was designed to remember Moses at Sinai and to extol the wonders and virtues of the law. So with the arrival of Pentecost, we discover that Matthew began the first long teaching segment of this gospel, the segment we call the Sermon on the Mount.

To appreciate fully this liturgical order, we need to keep the vigil format in our minds. A vigil was a watch service. The psalm written to be used at Pentecost by the Jews was Psalm 119, a hymn of praise to the Torah, the law. It was the longest psalm by far in the psalter. This psalm was divided into twenty-two stanzas, each marked by one of the twenty-two letters of the Jewish alphabet. That meant that the psalm had an introduction and seven segments made up of three stanzas each. This indicated that the liturgical use of this psalm was to carry the worshiper through the eight segments of the twenty-four-hour watch ceremony that marked the Pentecost celebration. This liturgical purpose was reflected in the internal words of this psalm that reveal its structure. "Seven times a day will I praise you" (Ps. 119:164), the psalm proclaimed. Next, we observe that verses reflecting the various hours of the watch were included in the text with revealing time references. Verse 55 says, "I will remember thy name in the night, O Lord." Verse 62 says, "At midnight I rise to praise thee." Verse 97 says, "Oh, how I love thy law! It is my meditation all the day." Verse 147 says, "I rise before dawn and cry for help." Verse 148 says, "My eyes are awake before the watches of the night."

It goes without saying that a festival designed to give thanks for the Torah would feature in the synagogue worship the portion of the law that recalled Moses on Mt. Sinai and the giving of the Torah to Israel. Most especially it would focus on the Ten Commandments, which opened the Mosaic code.

Can we still think it is a mere coincidence that the first major block of uninterrupted teaching from Jesus in the corpus of Matthew's gospel portrays Jesus on a mountain giving a new version of the Torah? Is it a coincidence that this teaching block occurs in the liturgical calendar some fifty days after Passover, where the Jewish observance of Pentecost would fall? Does anyone believe it is merely a coincidence that the Jewish festival designed to celebrate the giving of the law by Moses at Sinai was marked by this gospel writer with the narrative of Jesus cast as the new Moses? Is it a coincidence that Jesus was said in this segment to be dealing specifically with the content of several of the Ten Commandments?

If one still thinks that this is a coincidence, then that person must be invited to look carefully at the structure of this first teaching segment in Matthew. The Sermon on the Mount also reveals the form of a twenty-four-hour watch vigil, for it divides neatly into eight subgroupings, which would provide a proper Christian reading for each of the three-hour segments of the liturgical watch that marked the Pentecost celebration.

The Sermon on the Mount began with an octave of blessings that we call the beatitudes. The octave was closed by making the first and last reward identical. To both "the poor in spirit" and those who were "persecuted for righteousness sake" was promised the Kingdom of God (Matt. 5:3 and 5:10). That was Matthew's introduction to his Sermon on the Mount. Then the sermon was divided into sections in which each beatitude was the subject of an exposition, one for each of the eight watches of the vigil celebration. This sermon followed a typical Jewish pattern that worked from the eighth blessing backward to the first. The first unit of the sermon (Matt. 5:11–20) is thus an exposition of the eighth beatitude (Matt. 5:10). Matthew 5:21–26 is an exposition of the seventh beatitude on the blessedness of peacemakers (Matt. 5:9). Matthew 5:27–37 is an exposition of the sixth beatitude on the blessedness of the pure in heart (Matt. 5:8). Matthew 5:38–48 is an exposition of the fifth beatitude on the blessedness of being merciful (Matt. 5:7); and so on we go. Matthew's church clearly celebrated Pentecost with a vigil of eight watches with eight lections proclaiming over and over again how the law and the prophets had been fulfilled.

Matthew certainly believed that he was portraying accurately, if not literally, the teachings of Jesus. However, it is very clear that the Sermon on the Mount was a Matthean creation and was patterned by Matthew on Psalm 119, the psalm of Pentecost. Psalm 119 also began with the word "blessed." "Blessed are those whose way is blameless, who walk in the law of the Lord. Blessed are those who keep his testimonies, who seek him with their whole heart, who also do no wrong, but walk in his ways" (Ps. 119:1–3). The whole Sermon on the Mount was a *midrashic* attempt to reveal Jesus as the new Moses presiding at the new Sinai, the giver of the new law of the new covenant. This sermon gathered together what Matthew believed to be the teaching of Jesus and cast it into the appropriate mold of the Jewish liturgical celebration of Pentecost. It came at the exact spot in Matthew's gospel to fit the Pentecost celebration. It included the proper themes of Pentecost. It was modeled on the psalm of Pentecost. What more powerful proof could be provided that this gospel was written against the background of the liturgical calendar of the Jews?

We have now correlated two of Matthew's five blocks of teaching material with Jewish festival celebrations. The passion story and the teaching block in Matthew that came during the last week of Jesus' earthly life have been identified with the celebration of Passover; and the Sermon on the Mount, Matthew's first teaching block, has been identified with the festival of Pentecost. Stretching Matthew's gospel between these two points and following the division of Matthew found in Codex Alexandrinus, we lay out the lections of Matthew on the Sabbaths of the Jewish year and remarkable conclusions follow. Goulder's premise that these five teaching blocks of material were designed to fall on or near the five great celebratory festivals of the Jewish liturgical year becomes all but impossible to doubt. For now each of the five major teaching blocks of Matthew is seen to fall in that calendar on each of the five celebratory festivals of the Jewish year: Pentecost, New Year's, Tabernacles, Dedication, and Passover. Each block of Matthean teaching material is, furthermore, appropriate to the theme of that Jewish festival.

For New Year, John the Baptist, Mark's human *shofar,* who announced the New Year theme of the coming of the Kingdom of God, was reintroduced into the text of Matthew at exactly the spot in Matthew's gospel that would be read on New Year's (Matt. 11:2–15). The old flashback technique was employed since Matthew had used Mark's Baptist story much earlier in his text. John's words are now recalled articulating the New Year's day themes. The second great block of the teaching of Jesus in Matthew introduced the Baptist story, and it was appropriate to the themes of that New Year celebration. It was about judgment, the need for preparation, and the promise of rest in the new Kingdom that was to come (Matt. 10:5–11:1).

We arrive next at Tabernacles in the month of Tishri, and we come to the third Matthean teaching unit. Tabernacles was the festival of the late harvest and focused on the memory of the wilderness wandering years when the Jewish people were living in temporary shelters on their journey to the Promised Land. So this teaching unit, following Mark's guidance, captured the harvest theme with the parable of the sower and its interpretation, both of which concentrate on the harvest. Then the parable of the wheat and tares, another harvest parable, was told. This was followed by the parable of the grain of mustard seed that, when planted, grew from the smallest seed to the greatest of shrubs. Other harvests of hidden treasure, the pearl of great price, and the great catch of fish concluded this segment (Matt. 13:1–53). Once again, it was a perfect liturgical fit.

Continuing this journey through the liturgical year, we walk lection by lection through the Sabbaths from Tabernacles toward the Festival of Dedication. That festival celebrated the light of God coming to the Temple. Again following Mark, the narrative that introduced this festival in Matthew was the account of the Transfiguration when the light of God descended on Jesus. Then the fourth teaching block of Matthew falls precisely after that story. Dedication themes are present again and again in that block of teaching material (Matt. 18:1, 19:1). Finally, to complete the cycle, we observe that the instruction on discipleship that in the chapters in Mark carried Mark's story backward from Passover toward Dedication has also been picked up and reflected in Matthew. He then has Jesus depart from Galilee shortly after the Feast of Dedication to begin his journey to Jerusalem, during which he instructs the disciples in preparation for his departure. The journey preparation of the catechumenate for baptism is thus also reflected in this second gospel to be written.

Matthew is a *midrashic* expansion of Mark. The teaching units of Matthew fall at the five major festivals in the Jewish liturgical calendar. Matthew has front-end loaded Mark because Mark had not covered the first five and a half months of the liturgical calendar. Matthew has provided the exquisite fit of the Sermon on the Mount to cover the one major festival that did not get into Mark's truncated year, which only stretched backward from Passover to Rosh Hashanah, or New Year's.

The organizing principle of Matthew's gospel has been discovered. It was not the life of Jesus or some version of objective history. It was the Jewish liturgical calendar with its festival celebrations. Jesus was preached before the Gospels were written. The Jesus-based preaching was related to the lections read in the synagogue and to the traditional Jewish festivals that came as the Jewish worship year was observed. Mark put these preachments together in a completed form for three reasons: First, to enable the Church to celebrate Jesus as the sacrificial lamb of Passover, Mark related the passion story as a twenty-four-hour vigil. Second, to prepare the newly converted disciples for baptism on Easter eve, Mark placed teaching material into his narrative that suggested Jesus had instructed his disciples on his final journey to Jerusalem. Third, Mark completed his gospel by carrying his readers back to New Year's by adding the Galilean phase to the story of Jesus, and his story was complete.

In time, however, this first gospel became inadequate for many parts of the Church. So Matthew, the scribe, rewrote Mark to make it better serve the needs of his faith community. He covered the months Mark omitted. He dulled Mark's criticism of the Torah, Jewish practices, and the scribes. He expanded the content of the teaching of Jesus so that the five celebratory festivals of the Jewish year could be observed in an appropriate and proper Christian style; and, in the process, he heightened the sense that Jesus was the fulfillment of the law and the prophets. Matthew added greatly to the portrait drawn of Jesus by those who had been touched by his life. But he also interpreted the life of this Jesus in a specifically Jewish way.

By discovering his organizing principle of the Jewish liturgical year, we are enabled to gaze through this Jewish lens at our Lord in a new way and to begin to see him in a new light. Reading the Gospels with Jewish eyes proves once more to be a worthy enterprise for the person of faith who seeks a living God.

8

Luke

Seeking the Jewish Clue That Will Unlock the Third Gospel

Luke's community of Christians was quite different from Matthew's community. Its Jewish members were far more hellenized and therefore less traditionally Jewish. It also included many more gentiles, which meant that those practices that were exclusively Jewish were deemphasized or even neglected. I suggested earlier that Luke himself was, in all probability, one of these gentile members who had first embraced a liberalized Judaism and then had moved into the Christianity that grew from the liberal Judaism.

For Luke's community those Jewish rituals that originally reflected the stages of the Jewish agricultural cycle faded, since the

119

hellenized Jews tended to live in cities and were no longer touched by Palestinian concerns. But all ties with Judaism had not been abandoned. Luke's community originally worshiped on the Sabbath/Sunday of each week.[1] At this service of worship, there was still a regular and ordered reading from the Jewish scriptures, which meant primarily the Torah, but without ignoring either the Former or the Latter Prophets. There was some reason to suggest, however, that synagogue worship services outside Palestine had been shortened considerably. Hellenized Jews, to say nothing of gentiles, allowed themselves to participate in far more activities on the Sabbath than did the strictly orthodox Jews. They were, therefore, not content to spend the whole day in the synagogue. We know, for example, that the readings from the prophets had been shortened dramatically in hellenized synagogues. The ones the Jews call the Latter Prophets (Isaiah, Jeremiah, Ezekiel, and the book of the twelve minor prophets), for example, appear to have been read in Luke's church on a four- to five-year cycle.

There might be reason to think that even the long segment of the Torah assigned to a Sabbath/Sunday to enable the Torah to be completed on a one-year cycle had been subjected to a "technical" shortening in these more liberalized circles. At least it might have been read in three segments, with the first two coming at minor services during the week prior to the Sabbath, with only the final third being read when all the people gathered on the Sabbath/Sunday.

When Mark's gospel made its first appearance in Luke's community, it was enormously popular. It ordered Christian worship as never before, but it also tended to freeze the understanding of Jesus into a set form for the first time. If Luke's fellow worshipers also knew Matthew's gospel, as I think they did, they were grateful that he had expanded Mark to cover the full year, but they were also less inclined to value Matthew, primarily because that gospel emphasized the very ritualistic Jewishness that Luke's community was quietly abandoning. Certainly we cannot help but observe that when comparing Luke with Matthew, every time Matthew changed Mark to make it more traditionally orthodox, and thus more pleasing to his more conservative Jewish audiences, Luke left the text the way Mark originally had written it. But Matthew was, I believe, nonetheless valuable to Luke. For this gospel had opened experiences like the temptation of Jesus to new meaning and it had greatly enhanced the content of Jesus' teaching. Luke appears to have appreciated the teaching, but not the form in which Matthew presented it. Those long teaching segments in Matthew, for example, were far less significant to a community that no longer observed with the same panache the major Jewish festivals for which these Matthean segments had been created. Eight-day festivals, vigils, and midweek observances were not part of the hellenized Jewish experience. Luke's congregation gathered primarily on the Sabbath/Sunday of each week. They were not prone to be there in large numbers at any other time. So, with the exception of the passion story, which in Luke's community was beginning its shift from the observance that occurred on the most holy night in which the paschal lamb was slain into the eight-day span that Christians would someday call Holy Week that culminated in the vigil on Maundy Thursday and Good Friday, Luke tended to relegate the Jewish fasts and festivals into being simply the dominating note in worship on the single Sabbath or Sunday that fell nearest to the time the festival had been traditionally observed. Perhaps these hellenized Jews were the harbingers of that modern American tradition that moves holidays to the nearest Monday to create the convenience of a long weekend.

When we examine the corpus of Luke, we quickly become aware that there is a significant amount of uniquely Lucan material that appears nowhere else in any gospel. New Testament scholars tend to call this the L source. In the past it was asserted that L represented the material available to Luke other than Mark or Q. Lately, the suggestion has been offered that Luke was himself the creative genius who wrote the L material and that his only external primary sources were Mark and Matthew. This latter point of view is convincing to me, as these chapters on Luke will reveal. So, by examining this uniquely Lucan material, insights might be gained into the personhood of this author.

We will derive other insights from the way Luke changed the material from his sources, whether Mark or Matthew, and from those places where Luke quite obviously moved material to a new place in his narrative that was quite different from its location in Mark or Matthew. Strange locations cry out for explanations. Why did Luke move that episode to this position? That is a question we must address. Sometimes Luke would reverse the order of the events described in an earlier gospel. Again, we will try to understand why. These questions lead us into the motive and writing style of the author.

There is a budding universalism in Luke that is either not found, or not found in as total a way, in either Mark or Matthew. Matthew, for example, began his genealogy of Jesus with Abraham, the father of the Jewish nation. Luke, in contradistinction, traced the genealogy of Jesus all the way back to Adam, the presumed father of the entire human enterprise. If gentiles were to be incorporated into the people of God, as Luke intended to do and as the Book of Acts demonstrated, then they needed to have Adam, the father of all, as the common point of origin: for only then could gentiles have some ownership of the heritage that produced the one they increasingly would call Lord and Christ.

This universalism was demonstrated when Luke wrote that the destiny of the Christian gospel was to move from Jerusalem, the center of the Jewish world, to Rome, thought in that era to be the center of the entire world. In Luke's words the disciples were to be "witnesses in Jerusalem, Judea, Samaria, and to the uttermost parts of the earth" (Acts 1:8). Luke told again and again of a Jesus who was the breaker of the barriers that separated the human family. He portrayed Jesus as one who was not bound by the dividing lines that traditional Jews had erected against the poor, the lepers, the Samaritans, the women, or the gentiles. These were the signs of his universal understanding of God.

Luke's gospel certainly accelerated the movement of Christianity into a more cosmopolitan and thus a more gentile world. Yet there is ample reason to believe that Luke still observed certain customs of the Jews, even if he transformed these customs to suit his purposes. Luke seemed well aware of the Jewish festi-val of Pentecost, but he transformed it from being a celebration to remember the time that God gave the Torah to Moses on Mt. Sinai into being a celebration of the time when God gave the Holy Spirit to the church. Law and spirit were frequently con-trasted in the early days of Christianity. However, Luke kept the name "Pentecost" for his celebration, even though that name was created by the number of days separating this festival from the Jewish Passover.

In the Book of Acts, Luke had Paul refer to "the fast," which was clearly a reference to Yom Kippur, the Day of Atonement, which Paul obviously still observed (Acts 27:9). He also por-trayed the disciples as continuing to meet together in the Temple (Acts 2:46) and as going "to the Temple at the time of prayer" (Acts 3:1). So some Jewish worship practices still had power in the circles where Luke lived, until at least as late as the tenth decade of the Christian Era. Luke seemed, therefore, to have continued the basic outline of Jewish worship patterns, albeit in a hellenized and less rigid form.

Among his sources Luke clearly favored Mark over any other, but he did not follow Mark uncritically. Occasionally, he omit-ted episodes or even whole portions of Mark, including the long segment from Mark (6:45–8:26) called by scholars "the great omission." There is also a section of this gospel in which Luke was describing the final journey of Jesus to Jerusalem where Mark seemed to disappear from Luke's view altogether (Luke 9:51–18:14). Luke told the story of John the Baptist's miracu-lous birth, which, as far as we know, was found nowhere else in Christian literature. He introduced into Matthew's birth story such non-Matthean elements as the shepherds, the manger, and the swaddling cloths. He made the annunciation of Jesus' birth be directed to Mary rather than to Joseph, as Matthew had done. He reordered the temptations that Matthew had said oc-curred in the wilderness. Luke broke up Matthew's Sermon on the Mount and distributed its segments throughout his gospel, having Jesus deliver a major portion of it not on a mountain, but on a plain (Luke 6:17–49). Luke took Mark's stories of Jesus' rejection at Nazareth and of the woman who anointed Jesus' feet near the time of the crucifixion and changed them to revealing new positions, in both cases far earlier in Jesus' career.

Luke omitted Mark's story of the feeding of the 4,000. He appears to have changed the parable of two brothers in Matthew (21:28–32) into his parable of the prodigal son. He made a parable out of Mark's story of Jesus cursing the fig tree (Luke 13:6–9). He suppressed Galilee as the scene of the resurrection (Luke 24:6). He probably created the Emmaus road story, about which no other gospel writer seemed to know (Luke 24:13–35).

These are just a few of the more prominent features in Luke's gospel that cry out for some explanation. So, by examining these aspects of his style, we seek to discover both his purpose and his person. This is also the process that will force us, I believe, to see Luke with Jewish eyes, even though we must remember they will be the Jewish eyes of hellenized Jews and gentile proselytes to Judaism.

To begin the process of unraveling the mysteries of Luke, we go first to his own words about why he undertook this gospel writing task in the first place. In the prologue of this gospel, the author stated that he sought to write this account of Jesus "in order." Those words have been badly translated in the standard English texts as "an orderly account." The Greek word used here means "in order or in sequence."[2]

The question is, What is that order? Was it chronological? Did he record the story of Jesus in the order in which Jesus lived or in which it was remembered? Well, that is a possibility. Yet standing in opposition to that suggestion is the fact that an early second-century Christian leader named Papias wrote that Mark had recorded the remembered words of Peter accurately, but "not in order."[3] Perhaps Luke sought to remedy that problem. It is also clear that, as dependent as Matthew was on Mark, Matthew still did not follow Mark's order in every instance. Compare, for example, the order of the miracle stories of Mark 1–5 with the order employed in Matthew 8–9 and 12. Perhaps it could be argued that Luke intended to reorder both Mark and Matthew so that their contradictions would no longer exist. That is certainly another possibility. I do not believe, however, that either alternative explains fully Luke's pledge to write in order, and I part company slightly with my great teacher, Michael Goulder, at this point. I do not find either the order of biography or the attempt to order Mark and Matthew compelling explanations of the order in which Luke said he would write.

Recall that Luke composed his gospel almost sixty years after the earthly life of Jesus had been completed. That would be close to one hundred years after Jesus' birth. This was in a world where records were not written down and biography was based only on memory. Sixty years after the fact would be almost three generations. One hundred years could be as many as five generations later. Would anyone dare to pretend that they could recapture the chronological order of the events of Jesus' birth or of his earthly life and ministry from the vantage point of sixty to one hundred years away? The story of Jesus had existed primarily in oral transmission before Mark wrote in the seventh decade and before Matthew wrote in the ninth decade. Yet neither of these evangelists was following an order other than the liturgical one. During the years when the memory and story of Jesus were transmitted orally, that story had been preached primarily in isolated sermons with no great sense of a connected time frame. Neither Mark nor Matthew claimed the authority of an eyewitness with the ability to recreate the chronological order of Jesus' life. Would Luke then be so foolish as to make this claim? Would he presume that he could compose a new order into which Mark and Matthew would fit properly? Luke was certainly not an eyewitness. He was going to base his story, he told us, on information provided him from those who had previously sought to tell this tale. So the order that Luke intended to follow could hardly have been either the chronological order of the events in Jesus' life, or even some corrected order that would harmonize Mark and Matthew. So our search for what Luke meant by "order" must look beyond these options.

We return therefore to Luke's preamble and begin to search there for additional clues. We discover that Luke in that preamble stated that he intended to make known to Theophilus "the full truth"[4] about which he had "been instructed" (Luke 1:4). The word translated "instructed" can also mean "catechized."[5] So perhaps clues lie waiting if we could understand how that instruction or catechesis took place.

We have already suggested that the Christians, borrowing a Jewish custom, originally prepared their catechetical classes for baptism at Easter. We noted that the journey section, especially in Mark, might well have included something of the substance of the teaching that was given to the converts in catechetical training. Since these lessons from Mark's journey section were also read at Sabbath worship, this would suggest that the catechetical training actually took place on the Sabbath, when the whole community was gathered for worship. Not unlike in contemporary church confirmation or membership classes, the catechumenate received a short instruction course in the ten to twelve weeks prior to Easter. Now, in his prologue, it becomes at least possible that Luke was saying, "I want to tell those of you who have only been catechized the whole Christian story." This gospel would thus lay out the full Christian tradition in which the newly baptized Christians had been instructed but briefly in their catechism training.

The most excellent Theophilus, to whom this gospel was addressed, may have been a specific person. The name Theophilus, however, literally means a "lover of God."[6] So the name of the addressee of this gospel could be generic and deliberately employed to include the whole group of gentile converts in the hellenized church who had recently undergone their catechizing instruction. To call them lovers of God would thus be quite appropriate. In our search to discover what Luke meant by "in order," that becomes our first clue.

The second clue to what Luke meant by his phrase "in order" is found, I believe, in the last words this author placed into the mouth of the risen Jesus. There Luke wrote, "Everything must be fulfilled that is written about me in the law of Moses [that is, the Torah], the prophets and the psalms." Luke went on to say that then "he [Jesus] opened their minds so that they could understand the scriptures" (Luke 24:44-45). Is the order found in Luke's gospel the order that God revealed in the sacred scriptures of the Jews? Is it the order of the Torah? Will these newly instructed "lovers of God" know fully the matters in which they have so recently been catechized when they have discovered Jesus revealed as the fulfillment of their Jewish scriptures of which the Torah was the most treasured and the most revered? As if to remind his readers once more that this might be his organizing principle, Luke closed the Book of Acts with similar words. He said that Paul remained in Rome "trying to convince them about Jesus, both from the law of Moses and the Prophets" (Acts 28:23). Note that once again the Torah, that is, the law of Moses, was mentioned first, suggesting that Luke found Jesus revealed primarily in the Torah. I would like to suggest that the order for the life of Jesus that Luke promised to lay out was not the chronological order of Jesus' life, nor was it the attempt on the part of Luke to harmonize existing gospels, though he would be happy to have insight from both sources, but the order was primarily the liturgical order of seeing Jesus emerge as the "fulfillment of the law of Moses," as that law was read week by week in the synagogue/church of the hellenized Jews of the Mediterranean world. That order was supplemented for sure, as even Luke suggested by references to the prophets and the psalms. It was affected, we also know, by the liturgical year of the Jews. But the order of the Jewish scriptures and primarily the order of the Torah (Genesis, Exodus, Numbers, Leviticus, and Deuteronomy), was the organizing principle by which I now believe Luke wrote his gospel.

Therefore I contend that if we could lay out a yearly calendar of Torah readings supplemented by some relationship to the prophets, and if we could then fit in those festivals and fasts of the Jewish year, as Luke's community observed them, we would see the exact order in which Luke's gospel was written and thus the order against which it must be understood. If we could then stretch Luke's gospel out lection by lection against that background, we would be astonished by how remarkable the fit is. We will also see in this scheme just how it was that Luke used his sources. He rewrote Matthew 1:1 through 4:11 to create his Genesis (Luke 1:5–4:13). He leaned on Mark 1:21 through 3:19 to create his Exodus (Luke 4:14–6:19). He quarried Matthew in rather unique ways to develop his readings for Leviticus (Luke 6:20–8:25). He transcribed Mark 4 through 9 with some rather gaping omissions to provide appropriate readings to correspond with the material found in Numbers (Luke 8:26–9:50).[7] Finally, in his most imaginative piece of writing, Luke created the expanded journey section of his gospel (Luke 9:51–18:14) to correspond to the readings from Deuteronomy. This segment was by far the longest, and that will demand some explanation. It also contained the heart of Luke's teaching material. When Luke completed his use of Deuteronomy (Luke 18:14), he filled out his story with Marcan material for the balance of chapter 18. Then he added the story of Zaccheus (Luke 19:1–10), and a rewritten version of Matthew's parable of the pounds (Luke 19:11–27) to bring his journey up to the edge of Jerusalem, where the events of the final week of Jesus' life were set to unfold (Luke 19:28). That is the scheme I shall seek to demonstrate, but lots of explanation and explication lies ahead.

One further critical decision needs to be made before this Lucan order becomes clear: Where does one start? Again, for the third time, we go back to the critical issue of relationship between the liturgical year of the Jews and the creation of the Christian story. The Jewish readings from the Torah started on the first Sabbath of Nisan in the late winter to early spring of the year (March–April). In the Jewish calendar, there were normally two Sabbaths of Nisan prior to Passover. But since the Passover had come to be thought of as the time of the passion of Jesus, it was for Christians not the beginning but the climax of the Jesus story. It was, however, also not the end of the Jesus story. The end for Christians was not Jesus' passion or suffering, but his resurrection. So the Christian year could not start with Passover. It could not even start when Passover was over. It could not begin until Easter had been celebrated. So if Passover came after two Sabbaths of Nisan, Easter would be on the third Sabbath of that month. Thus the Christian year would begin on the fourth

Sabbath of the Jewish year at the very earliest and would lag the Jewish year by at least three Sabbaths. Later, when the Easter celebration was lengthened to include a second Sabbath, it could lag the Jewish year by even four Sabbaths. It was this discontinuity of starting places that hid for centuries the close relationship between the Christian scriptural story of Jesus in the synoptic Gospels and the Jewish story as recorded in the Torah. When that discontinuity was worked out, however, the connectors all fell into place. So I shall start my study of Luke with the first chapter of that gospel being assigned in the lectionary to the fourth Sunday of the liturgical year of the Jews.

Recall also once more that the Jews used a lunar calendar of twelve months or moons, which gave them only fifty or fifty-one Sabbaths a year. So their lectionary readings had to be flexible enough to accommodate the Jewish custom of adding an extra month called 2 Adar seven times every nineteen years to keep the Jewish calendar from falling behind. Clearly, no calendar explanation will be consistent at all times. It is confusing and perhaps even distorting, but it does not invalidate the connections that are so apparent. Now, having filed those caveats almost by title, let me proceed to the corpus of Luke so that we can read this gospel against the order of the Jewish scriptures and, with Jewish eyes, perhaps see things in the Gospel of Luke we have never seen before.

9

Luke

The Story of Jesus Told
Against the Order of the Torah

GENESIS: THE TORAH READINGS
BEHIND THE BIRTH NARRATIVE

When the story that we call the Gospel of Luke began its journey through the liturgical year of the Jews, it was the fourth Sabbath of that year. The synagogue Torah readings, which started three Sabbaths earlier, were already deep into the Book of Genesis. So if my suggestion is accurate—that the lectionary readings from the Torah ordered Luke's gospel—then I must be able to demonstrate that Luke turned to the Torah readings of

Genesis, and on the basis of those readings he built his birth tradition. Perhaps that process will illumine the mystery as to why Luke's birth story is so different from Matthew's birth story, or why he altered Matthew's birth story so dramatically, as I now believe he did. Since Mark had introduced John the Baptist to inaugurate the adult story of Jesus, so Luke decided to introduce his narrative with the story of the origins of both John and Jesus. Perhaps he was inspired by the fact that the word "genesis" means origins, and it was this Torah book of origins that was going to give order to this first part of Luke's story. So I will seek first the Genesis influences on the birth stories in Luke.

Luke began his gospel by introducing first Zechariah and then Elizabeth, the parents of John the Baptist. He portrayed them, however, quite overtly after the pattern of Abraham and Sarah from the Book of Genesis that was being read in the synagogues. The connections between the two stories are overwhelming.

Both sets of parents were called righteous (Gen. 26:5, Luke 1:6). Both Sarah and Elizabeth were barren (Gen. 11:30, Luke 1:7). Both were advanced in age (Gen. 18:11, Luke 1:7). In both stories the angelic annunciation came to a disbelieving father (Gen. 18:11, Luke 1:11). Both fathers were assured that nothing was impossible with God (Gen. 18:14, Luke 1:37). These connections are far too extensive to be coincidental.[1] The account of the birth of John the Baptist was quite clearly based on the Genesis story.

The readings from Genesis then moved on to new stories of Jewish origins, and Luke moved, not coincidentally, exactly in sync with his Genesis source from Abraham and Sarah to their son, Isaac. Isaac's wife, Rebekah, was expecting twins. The Genesis text informs us that because these unborn children leapt in Rebekah's womb, she went to inquire of the Lord about them. The word of the Lord that Rebekah heard in the Genesis story was that the destiny of these two boys had been set by divine providence while they were still in the womb. Furthermore, it was revealed that the older, who would be named Esau, would serve the younger one, who would be named Jacob (Gen. 25:19–23).

There is only one other story in the entire Bible where a baby leaps in its mother's womb. That is found, again not coincidentally, I would suggest, in Luke's birth story, which he was writing against this background of the Book of Genesis. Under the skill of Luke's pen, John the Baptist and Jesus became the new Esau and Jacob. They were not brothers, but Luke did make them kin in his story so that he could relate them to this Genesis reading. Mary went to visit her kinswoman, Elizabeth, Luke wrote. When she arrived the babe in Elizabeth's womb leapt to acknowledge the Lordship of Jesus, who was still in Mary's womb. The destiny of these two lives, like Jacob and Esau of old, was revealed while they were still in the womb. That destiny was that the older would serve the younger. The Book of Genesis was clearly ordering Luke's story.

The connections that link Luke to Genesis continue at a rate almost too rapid to record. Genesis told of how the barrenness of Rachel, Jacob's favorite wife, was overcome, and Rachel's words are placed by Luke, almost verbatim, into Elizabeth's mouth (Gen. 30:23, Luke 1:25). When Leah, Jacob's other wife, was blessed with children, she proclaimed that God had seen her lowliness and that she would be called "blessed" (Gen. 29:30, 30:13). Luke placed these words, again from Genesis, into Mary's song (Luke 1:48), which we know as the Magnificat. Over and over again, Luke wrote the Genesis stories of the founding fathers and mothers of Israel into his stories of the origins of the one who was to inaugurate the New Israel. Please recognize that Luke knew he was not writing literal history.

Luke next turned his attention to his account of Jesus' birth, and the Genesis lections by this time were well into the story of Jacob. Jacob had parted from his father-in-law, Laban, and had been guarded by a heavenly host of angels (Gen. 32:1 ff.). He had wrestled with an angel at a place called Peniel, which means "I have seen God and lived" (Gen. 32:22 ff.). Jacob had dispatched flocks of sheep and cattle as a peace offering to his brother, Esau (Gen. 32:13 ff.). He was then portrayed as being on the road to his homeland with his expectant wife (Gen. 35). Finally, he reached his home in Bethlehem, where Rachel's child,

Benjamin, was born (Gen. 35:16–21). So, as Luke was creating the story of Jesus' birth, he employed all of these elements from the Genesis narrative. Joseph, like Jacob, was on the road to his homeland with his expectant wife, Mary. His destination was also Bethlehem. The angel with whom Jacob had wrestled and the heavenly host that guarded him announced the birth of Jesus to the shepherds, who then journeyed to welcome the child.

A priest named Simeon next announced that his eyes had seen God's salvation (Luke 2:30). He too, like Jacob, had seen God and lived. Finally, an old prophetess named Anna, who was identified as the daughter of Phanuel, spoke of this child to all who were looking for salvation (Luke 2:36). Phanuel, we note, is simply another way to spell Peniel. The notes from Genesis, in which the origins of Israel are found, appear again and again in Luke's story of the origins of Jesus. Once again, this is not coincidental. It is rather revelatory of the order under which Luke's gospel was composed.

There are other connections on which we cannot dwell, but echoes of Joseph being lost to Jacob can be found in the account of Jesus being lost to his parents for "three days." We are even told that Jacob kept all these things and pondered them, just as Luke suggested that Mary had also done (Gen. 37:11, Luke 2:51) at the conclusion of the birth story.

But with the birth narratives now complete, Luke found the Jewish Festival of Pentecost interrupting the liturgical flow of the Book of Genesis and pushing the Torah readings momentarily into the background. Luke accommodated that in a peculiarly Lucan way. There was no long Sermon on the Mount to celebrate the giving of the law that one can find in Matthew. Luke had a different agenda. Recall, in the Book of Acts, Luke would suggest that the Jewish Pentecost was the appropriate time for Christians to celebrate the gift of the Holy Spirit. Perhaps this image was suggested to Luke by Paul, who contrasted the letter of the law that kills with the spirit that gives life. In any event, the lection in Luke that would be read on the Sabbath/Sunday that marked Pentecost was the story of John the

Baptist, who promised that one mightier than he was coming who would baptize with the Holy Spirit and with fire. It was once again an appropriate lesson for the festival, and it fell at exactly the point in Luke's corpus to coincide with the Pentecost celebration.

Luke next related the story of Jesus' baptism, in which the Spirit descended upon Jesus and the voice proclaimed him God's son. The background lection from Genesis would be the story of the pharaoh naming Joseph as the second person in rank in the entire realm. Pharaoh inquired, "Can we find a man such as this in whom is the Spirit of God?" (Gen. 41:38). Jesus' baptism was for Luke the first Pentecost. The man "in whom is the Spirit of God" had been found. After Jesus' death would come the second Pentecost, when that Spirit would be given to all the people. Again and again, Luke was weaving the themes of the Torah into his developing story of Jesus. He was telling the Jesus story in the order of the Torah!

The Book of Genesis then concluded the Joseph story with the genealogical tables of Jacob's descendants. Once again Luke followed the Torah. He broke his gospel narrative at this point to supply the genealogical table of Jesus' ancestors. That is why Luke's genealogy comes in such a strange place. The order found in the Book of Genesis is determining the order of Luke's gospel. To demonstrate this further, the names of the patriarchs of the Book of Genesis were all over this table. Jesus' first, seventh, and thirty-third ancestors were all named Joseph. The other sons of Jacob were also included: Simeon, twice; Levi, twice; Judah, twice. The patriarchal names of Jacob, Isaac, and Abraham, who dominate the Book of Genesis, also obviously appear.

The final lection from Genesis portrayed the scene of Jacob blessing his children and dying. The world famine predicted in the pharaoh's dream was in full sway. People were crying to the pharaoh for bread, and Joseph reigned in glory as the second in command in Egypt. Against the background of that part of Genesis, Luke has placed his story of Jesus' temptation. By seeing the temptation story against the order found in Genesis, another of the mysteries of Luke's gospel can be solved. Luke has reversed the order of two of the temptations that were found in Matthew. Matthew had Jesus casting himself off the pinnacle of the Temple as the second temptation, with bowing down to worship something other than God as the final temptation. Luke placed the temptation to bow down and worship something other than God second and made testing God by casting himself off the pinnacle of the Temple last. Matthew was referring to the Exodus order following the life of Moses. Luke, however, was following the Genesis order, in which the hungry of the world were clamoring to Joseph in Egypt for bread and needed to recognize that it was not by bread alone that human life lived. Then immediately in that Genesis story, Joseph was portrayed as clothed with human glory by his willingness to serve the pharaoh. Such a temptation Jesus called his disciples to resist, with the words that God only is to be served.

Scholars have been puzzled by this change in the Lucan order for centuries. But when one places Luke's narrative against the background of the Torah readings from Genesis, it becomes clear that Luke has adapted his material to bring it into harmony with that Torah lection. Once more an obvious explanation arises from this lectionary theory of gospel formation.

Before going on to correlate Luke's story with the Exodus readings, there is one other Genesis story that needs to be highlighted. It relates to that unique resurrection episode that only Luke recorded. That was the account of Cleopas and his friend on the road to Emmaus (Luke 24:13–35). Since the Christians had started their gospel tradition on the fourth Sabbath of the liturgical year, while the Jews began reading the Torah on the first Sabbath, there might be something in that earlier part of Genesis that could have provided the basis for the Emmaus road story, and indeed, there was.

The segment of Genesis that would be read when the Emmaus story was the Christian lection for the day would be the account of that moment when Abraham entertained God and two angelic visitors unawares (Gen. 18). These divine visitors made themselves known to Abraham as they ate together. Following that episode, the angelic beings journeyed to Sodom. There Lot invited them to his house (Gen. 19). They were reluctant to come in, but Lot constrained them to do so.

In the Emmaus road story, Jesus was said to have walked with Cleopas and his partner as one unknown. Arriving at their home, Jesus was reluctant to come in, but, like Lot, they constrained him. Thus they too proceeded to entertain a divine presence unawares. Finally, Jesus' divine nature was made known to them in the breaking of the bread, that is, when they ate together. It is an intriguing fit with the Genesis story and does nothing to shake the premise that the order of Luke's gospel was the order of the Torah. Luke was presenting Jesus as one who was in the process of revealing that everything written about him in the law of Moses had been fulfilled.

EXODUS: JESUS FACING THE SAME REJECTION ACCORDED TO MOSES

Before the Torah readings turned to the Book of Exodus, some of the themes of Exodus began to appear in the text of Luke, for they had been employed as Exodus themes in both Mark and Matthew. The baptism of Jesus certainly had echoes of the Exodus Red Sea story. The temptation of Jesus had echoes from the wilderness wanderings of the children of Israel. Nevertheless, Luke stuck fairly closely to his order of the Torah, and, despite the examples of Mark and Matthew, he made Genesis his guide for these narratives.

The first Lucan lection designed to provide Christian insight into the Torah when the Book of Exodus was being read in the worship life of the synagogue was the story of Jesus being rejected by his own at Nazareth (Luke 4:16–30). This story is intriguing because Luke relocated this narrative in his own text from the position in which he found it in the story line of Mark (6:1–6) and Matthew (13:53–58). Both of these gospel traditions had located it much later in their gospels. But Luke moved it so that it followed directly after the story of the temptation. When such a deliberate and overt change is made in the text or texts that are providing an author with his major sources of information, then one must search for some explanation. Changes like this provide entree to the mind of the author and reveal the principles on which the author was operating. That thesis is illustrated rather precisely with the moving of this episode. This dramatic forward shift of the account of Jesus' rejection at Nazareth was dictated, I would suggest, by the fact that in Luke's mind this narrative introduced the major theme from the Book of Exodus as Luke understood that book. It was, in fact, Luke's understanding of Exodus combined with the order of the Torah that suggested this relocation to Luke.

The clue that convinces me of this probability and adds to the credibility of the Torah theory as the underlying order of Luke's gospel is actually found elsewhere in Luke's own writing. In the Book of Acts, Luke created a long speech that was delivered by Stephen (Acts 7:2–53). In this speech Luke rehearsed the history of Israel from Genesis to the moment in which the speech was presumably given. That meant that this speech had to journey through the content of the Book of Exodus and in the process of doing so, it revealed exactly the way Luke understood the second book of the Torah. Indeed, this portion of the Book of Acts actually provides us with a brief Lucan commentary on Exodus. The speech revealed first that Luke clearly found Genesis to be more exciting than the rest of the Torah, for he devoted the first eighteen verses of this speech to recalling events in Jewish history recorded in that book. This attraction to Genesis is also verified in the way Luke wrote the Genesis section of his gospel. Next Stephen was portrayed as racing through Exodus, Leviticus, Numbers, and Deuteronomy, all in the next twenty-five verses. Luke certainly recognized that major portions of Exodus, Leviticus, and Numbers were cultic rather than narrative in nature, making it more difficult to relate the Jesus story to them. Deuteronomy offered something quite different, as this book rehearsed the entire history of the Jews a second time. We shall watch Luke deal with the sparseness of his material until he reaches the rich resources that are to be found in the book of Deuteronomy.

But the significant data, for our purposes, was that the part of Stephen's speech that reflected the Book of Exodus concentrated almost totally on Moses and more specifically on Moses' rejection by the people of Israel after he had served them so well.

Luke's attention in this speech was captured first by the episode in which the forty-year-old Moses slew an Egyptian who was ill-treating an Israelite. Moses assumed, Stephen asserted, in the words Luke placed into his mouth, that God was using him to rescue the people of Israel from their Egyptian affliction (Acts 7:25). The Israelites, however, responded to this Mosaic intervention not by being grateful, but by saying, "Who made you ruler and judge over us?" (Acts 7:28–29). (For the Exodus version of this story, see Exodus 2:11–15.) So, feeling no support and believing that his own life was in danger, Moses fled into the wilderness and lived as a foreigner in the land of Midian (Exod. 2:15 ff.). Forty years later, said Stephen, God appeared to Moses once again, this time in a burning bush. In that experience, God specifically did call Moses to the role of deliverer. Moses was to be the means whereby God would free the children of Israel from their bondage (Exod. 3:1 ff.). In the words of Stephen's speech, God was now, in effect, appointing Moses to be ruler and judge over Israel, so that the question asked by the people in that earlier episode in the life of Moses, namely, "Who made you our ruler and judge?" had now received the answer, "God did!"

Stephen then related all that Moses had done for his people. He recounted the wonders Moses performed in the actual exodus and the leadership he had provided in the wilderness years (Acts 7:36). This Moses, Stephen went on to say, even promised that "God will send you a prophet like me from among your own people" (Acts 7:37).

The point of Stephen's speech was to show that no matter what God had done or what Moses had done for Israel, the response of the people was the same. With consistency, the people rejected God's law and God's chosen agents. The speech of

Stephen concluded with an indictment of those who persecuted the prophets and especially those who have now betrayed and murdered "the righteous one" that Moses had actually anticipated (Acts 7:52).

So Luke, playing on his understanding of the Book of Exodus and Moses, began to show the parallels between Moses and Jesus. The fate of the one whom Moses had promised would one day come was not to be different from the fate of Moses himself. Jesus, at his baptism, like Moses at the burning bush, had been validated by God. Like Moses, Jesus had returned from that sojourn charged by God to deliver his people. Like Moses, Jesus was to be scorned and rejected by his own people.

So it was that in Luke's opening narrative of the Exodus segment of his gospel, Jesus was portrayed as coming to his own town of Nazareth and entering the synagogue. There he took down the scroll of Isaiah, the prophet. He read the words of the appointed text, which, again not coincidentally, portrayed Isaiah as a new Moses leading a new Exodus (Isa. 61:1–2). Jesus identified himself and his life with those words (Luke 4:21); and then, like Stephen had done in the Book of Acts, Jesus began to rehearse the history of the way the people of Israel had treated the prophets. The response of the synagogue congregation was predictable. The new Moses fared no better than had the old Moses. The people rose up in fury and tried to kill him, but he passed through the midst of them, said the Lucan story, and escaped (Luke 4:30). The themes of the Book of Exodus were quite clear in this episode. It was the perfect way for Luke to introduce the Exodus unit of his gospel, and that was why he moved this episode to this location in his gospel.

Luke's next problem was how to build on this theme and provide gospel readings for the whole Exodus segment of the synagogue's liturgical year. He could not use all of the narrative of Exodus at this point. The Passover portions of Exodus he needed to save until his account of Jesus' passion. The baptism counterpart to the Red Sea and the temptation counterpart to the wilderness adventures he had already deployed in his Genesis narrative. He would need portions of Matthew's Sermon on the Mount to tell his Leviticus story, as we shall shortly see. Finally, when one reads beyond the story of the giving of the law at Sinai recorded in Exodus 20, one discovers that the Book of Exodus was consumed with the minutiae of the law in which Luke's hellenist and gentile community had little interest. When Luke wrote the Exodus portion of Stephen's speech in the Book of Acts, these things got not a mention. So how would Luke tell the Jesus story against the Exodus background once he had introduced it with his rejection at Nazareth?

Once again, I believe the clue is found in the Stephen speech and was simply reinforced when Luke made the rejection at Nazareth story the theme song, if you will, to his Exodus lection.

Returning to Stephen's speech, we find these attributes and accomplishments of Moses listed and referred to quite specifically. Moses was "mighty in his words and deeds" (Acts 7:22). He not only led them out of Egypt, but he performed wonders and signs in the process (Acts 7:36). He built the "tent of witness" for them in the wilderness, a place where the holy God was pleased to dwell (Acts 7:44). This tent of witness was the first precursor of the great Temple in Jerusalem that was to come. He could perceive the future, for he anticipated and promised that God would raise up for the Jews, after Moses, another prophet to lead them (Acts 7:37, 52). All of these things the righteous Moses did and was; and despite these accomplishments, his reward was to be rejected.

The next dramatic narrative in the Moses cycle found in the Book of Exodus was the story of the burning bush (Exod. 3:1–22). In that Torah account, Moses perceived God present in a nonmaterial phenomenon, a burning bush that was not consumed. God spoke to Moses out of that flame, directing him to take off his shoes, for he was standing on holy ground. When God made it clear who it was that addressed him, Moses immediately hid his face, for he was afraid to look at God. That was the means through which Moses was called to the vocation of being the deliverer of Israel. It was a memorable episode. But our task is to see if this burning bush story found an echo in that segment of Luke's gospel designed to be read during the Exodus cycle.

When that is the query one makes of the gospel text, then the gospel is read in a new way, a Jewish way. For Luke did place into his text, shortly after the account of Jesus being rejected by his people at Nazareth, a dramatic call story that involved an unnatural and fear-producing phenomenon. The content was different from the story of the burning bush, but the emotional tone was quite similar. In the fifth chapter of Luke, we find the account of the miraculous catch of fish. It was a uniquely Lucan narrative, as it did not appear in his primary sources of either Mark or Matthew. Yet, in the Fourth Gospel, an almost identical story has been included, but there it was placed by John into his resurrection tradition (John 21:4–8). In the two accounts, one found in Luke and the other in John, these similarities are apparent: The disciples have toiled at their fishing trade all night and have taken nothing; Jesus asked the disciples to cast their nets one more time into the sea; the disciples then hauled in a miraculous catch of fish; and finally Peter became in both the focus of the response. Since no one seems to believe that Luke knew the Johannine tradition, the assumption is that John has borrowed here from Luke and that this episode was an original Lucan creation. John, feeling uncomfortable with this story occurring in the early Galilean ministry of Jesus, moved it to Easter, where he could exploit its mysterious and supernatural qualities. However, since Luke designed this story to correspond to the mysterious and supernatural qualities of the burning bush story, those elements in this place suited Luke quite well. Luke was describing a unique awareness of the presence of God. In Luke's account this episode elicited from Peter some very dramatic words. Peter perceived, in this awesome phenomenon, that he was standing on holy ground. His words captured this awe-filled emotion. "Depart from me for I am a sinful man, O Lord" (Luke 5:8). Then Peter received his call to be a fisher of converts, perhaps to lead the mission of the Christian Church:

"From now on you will be catching people" (Luke 5:10, NRSV), the text concluded.[2] Surely this story is reminiscent of the call of Moses. The Exodus motif was obvious, and the oral preacher who lies behind the Lucan narrative had found another text in Exodus for his Sabbath day Jesus sermon.

Luke then turned to a string of Marcan stories to fill out his Exodus readings. In these stories Jesus was portrayed in a fashion strikingly similar to the portrait of Moses as Exodus had revealed him, or perhaps more accurately, as Luke's understanding of the Book of Exodus as disclosed in the Stephen speech had revealed him.

So Luke incorporated this Marcan source. And with just some slight editorial adjustments and an expansion of the story from time to time, he provided gospel lections for the remaining Sabbaths when the Book of Exodus was being read in the synagogues.

When we examine these nine stories, we can see the Moses themes being applied to Jesus again and again. In these narratives Jesus was portrayed as possessing the power to rebuke evil spirits, and he elicited amazement from the crowd who could not believe that he possessed such abilities (Luke 4:35–36). He was portrayed as capable of rebuking fever and banishing illness (Luke 4:39–40). He was portrayed as having the ability to bring wholeness with the touch of his hands and as being proclaimed the Son of God (Luke 4:40–41). He was portrayed as possessing power over nature, and therefore being recognized as holy by Peter (Luke 5:5–8). He was portrayed as one who could cleanse a leper (Luke 5:13), heal paralysis (Luke 5:18), forgive sins (Luke 5:23), transform tax collectors (Luke 5:27), and even create new wine skins into which to pour the new wine of the spirit (Luke 5:37). One would think that a person who could demonstrate all of these signs of divine favor and divine election, and who quite obviously possessed the actual powers of God, would be acclaimed and appreciated by the people he came to save. That, however, had not been the fate or destiny of Moses, and it was not to be Jesus' fate or destiny either.

For before this string of Marcan episodes was concluded in Luke's Exodus section, the signs of Jesus' rejection were already apparent. As we get near the end of this group of stories, hostility appears in the text. "Why are you doing what it is not lawful on the Sabbath to do?" (Luke 6:2). That was the first Lucan sign of this pending rejection. The second sign followed closely on the first. "The scribes and Pharisees watched him . . . so that they might find an accusation against him" (Luke 6:7). Next we read that "they were filled with fury and discussed with one another what they might do to Jesus" (Luke 6:11). Indeed, even the traitor Judas was introduced by Luke in this segment of his gospel (Luke 6:16). The shadow of the cross was already falling across the story of Jesus.

No matter what great things Moses had done, he was still rejected by his people. That was Luke's understanding of Exodus. No matter what great things Jesus had done, he was still destined to be rejected by his people. That was Luke's understanding of Jesus as the new Moses. So Luke used this Marcan material to present and to illustrate his understanding of the history of Israel from the Book of Exodus. He was still telling the story of Jesus based on the order of the reading from the Torah. This lectionary theory is further strengthened when we observe that when Luke's synagogue community completed its reading of Exodus, Luke immediately and abruptly abandoned his following of the Marcan text. He needed to find another source to carry him through Leviticus, and indeed he did.

LEVITICUS: RITUAL PURITY TRANSFORMED BY JESUS

As the Book of Leviticus was being read over the following eight Sabbaths/Sundays, Luke's ingenuity was tested, for in his community, the rules and prohibitions of Leviticus were simply not relevant, and they made little or no contact with the people's lives. So it is quite interesting to see how Leviticus shaped Luke's gospel.

Luke opened this Leviticus phase of his book with three segments of gospel material. The first was the sermon on the plain

(Luke 6:20–49), which included some material from Matthew's Sermon on the Mount. The second was the story of the centurion's slave (Luke 7:1–10), which was also adapted from Matthew (8:5–13). The final segment was a Lucan original, the account of the raising from the dead of the widow's son at Nain (Luke 7:11–17). These three episodes would carry Luke's story into the month of Tishri (October), at which time three major liturgical celebrations occurred in quick succession, all of which had proper readings from Leviticus, as we shall see, but each of which had specific historic themes. That combination would serve to get Luke basically through this difficult Book of Leviticus. Seeking to probe the mind of Luke in this portion of his gospel is absolutely fascinating.

We noted that Luke had followed Mark almost verbatim for his Exodus lessons. At Mark 3:19 this dependency was broken (see Luke 6:19). When Luke returned to pick up Mark once again, he did so with a softened version of the story of Jesus' family coming to take him away, which began at Mark 3:31 (see Luke 8:19–21). This means that Luke had omitted from his text only one Marcan episode (Mark 3:20–30), the Beelzebub story. Into that single omission Luke had placed six lessons, the three episodes previously mentioned plus the three lessons that he would use to cover the major liturgical celebrations of Tishri. These six narratives would fill out most of the Leviticus portion of his Jesus story.

So we return to these narratives, seeking Leviticus clues in them. This section began with Luke having Jesus go into the hills to pray prior to his calling of the twelve. The reference to the hills gave Luke the hook he needed to relay part of the material Matthew has placed into his Sermon on the Mount. In the Lucan narrative, Jesus had returned to the plains with his newly chosen twelve. They were joined by people from Judea, Tyre, and Sidon. The boundaries on the Jesus movement were broadening as this group included both Jews and gentiles. It was to this specifically mixed audience that Luke had Jesus give his version of the Sermon on the Mount. The eight beatitudes that were found in Matthew have been shortened to four in Luke, but four complementary curses have been added. The passage from Matthew's sermon that was selected by Luke as his focus concerned loving one's enemies. It was deliberately designed to counter Leviticus 19:18, where the teaching of the Torah was actually to love your neighbor as your kin, but which had been interpreted as justification for not loving, or even hating, your enemies. The concept of "neighbor" did not stretch in Jesus' day much beyond the boundaries of the clan. Jesus was calling that Leviticus interpretation to a new and higher standard. Luke's climax was "Be ye merciful as your Father is merciful." It was a climax that set him in contradistinction to Matthew, who made the climax of his sermon be the affirmation, "You therefore must be perfect as your heavenly Father is perfect" (Matt. 5:48). Even more important, it set Luke against the tradition of Leviticus, where the ultimate injunction of the Torah was, "Ye shall be holy, for I the Lord your God am holy" (Lev. 19:2). Luke did not believe that either perfection or holiness was the ultimate mark of the Christian life. Those qualities were and are the goals of self-righteous religion that in Luke's time and throughout the centuries has produced enormous amounts of conflict, persecution, and even religious warfare. The attempt to impose a version of either perfection or holiness has resulted only in religious bitterness. Luke was portraying Jesus as calling the Christian to a new level, to a virtue higher than the holiness of Leviticus, higher indeed than the perfection of Matthew. For Luke the virtue of God that he had seen in Jesus was mercy, the mercy of an inclusive and a suffering love. So, be merciful rather than holy was Luke's first message when Leviticus was the text before him. What better way could he have found to introduce his gospel lections that were designed to illumine and to inform the Torah Book of Leviticus?

With his connection with the Torah established, Luke went on to tell the story of the healing of the centurion's slave (Luke 7:1–10). It did not particularly help him with his Leviticus connection, but since Matthew had decided to follow his version of the Sermon on the Mount with this story, Luke did likewise.

Perhaps the only tie-in was that in the Book of Leviticus we find featured the authority of God through Moses to command (Lev. 6:8 ff.) together with a series of ritual commands that follow. The story of the healing of the centurion's servant turned on the acknowledgment by the centurion that Jesus did not have to be physically present. He only had to say the word, to command, and it would be accomplished (Luke 7:6–10). This story also served one other item of Luke's agenda. Before he completed his Luke/Acts corpus, he would show how Jesus broke the barrier separating Jew from gentile. This story pointed in that direction.

One Sabbath lection remained before the advent of the fall festivals began to occupy Luke's attention. For that slot in Luke's lectionary, he crafted the story of the raising of the widow's son at Nain (Luke 7:11–17). In some ways this story anticipated the Jewish New Year, Rosh Hashanah, that first of the Jewish fall festivals. That festival called the people of Israel into the Kingdom of God, where the scriptures suggested that the deaf would hear, the blind would see, the dead would be raised, the poor would hear the gospel. Luke had accounted for some of those signs in the stories of Jesus' power that marked his Exodus section, but nowhere had he yet suggested that Jesus had possessed the power to raise the dead. Such a wonder could hardly be a minor theme that he could just drop in passing. It would not be credible to say, "Oh, by the way, he also raised the dead." That experience was too startling not to be enshrined in a narrative. So on this Sabbath/Sunday before the new year dawned, Luke told the story of a young man, the only son of a widow, who was raised from the dead. The story appears to be patterned on 1 Kings 17, where Elijah raised a widow's son to life. Portraying Jesus as a new and greater Elijah was a prominent subtheme for Luke.[3] This was not an easy comparison, however, for Elijah's miracle occurred in the widow's home. Luke's miracle occurred as the funeral procession was literally carrying the body to its burial. So we seek other sources. Following the lectionary outline, we note that the Torah lesson for that Sabbath would come from near the middle of Leviticus.

Searching there, we find the text that may well have shaped Luke's story. In Leviticus 10:1–14 two young men, Nadab and Abihu, the sons of Aaron, have died and are being carried out of the camp to their burials. So Luke appears to have amended his Elijah story to catch this Leviticus note. If so, we can observe once again that it was the Torah that gave order to Luke's narrative about Jesus.

Luke's worshiping community had long ago downsized the major Jewish feasts and fasts to a single theme for the worship on a single Sabbath/Sunday. So it was that when the month of Tishri arrived, three major observances came in such rapid succession that they dominated synagogue worship for three straight Sabbaths.

The first day of Tishri was the traditional Jewish New Year. The Torah justification for this day was found in Leviticus (23:23–25). New Year, or Rosh Hashanah, was followed quickly by Yom Kippur, the penitential Day of Atonement, which also normally did not fall on the Sabbath. The Torah justification for this holy day was also found in Leviticus (23:26–32). Then came the feast of Tabernacles, the major harvest festival of the Jewish people, which was originally an eight-day celebration. This was proscribed by Leviticus also (23:33–36). So Luke could turn to these High Holy Days without abandoning his task of showing how Jesus fulfilled all things written about him in the law of Moses, the Torah, for these observances still grounded him in Leviticus. To celebrate these great occasions on the nearest Sabbath in hellenized Jewish circles was refreshing to Luke because they each gave him a specific focus. Almost any contemporary liturgical leader welcomes the return of Advent, for example, after the long and somewhat less well defined Sundays of the Pentecost season have finally been concluded. At least for Luke, these festivals meant that for three weeks the themes for his gospel would be provided by the emphasis of these three celebrations, while the Book of Leviticus was still present in the background.

Mark, we noted earlier, had made John the Baptist, with his call for repentance and his warning that his task was to prepare the way for the coming of the Lord, the major thrust of his new year message. John's voice was portrayed as the warning *shofar,* and his message embodied the primary theme of this new year celebration; namely, that the Kingdom of God was drawing near. Like Matthew, however, Luke had already used this Marcan material by having the baptism of Jesus come in the opening part of his text to inaugurate the beginning of Jesus' public ministry. So, following Matthew's example, Luke also resorted now to the time-honored technique of the flashback.

John's disciples, Luke began, had reported to John in prison the things they had heard about Jesus. John then sent these disciples to inquire as to whether or not he was the expected one who would inaugurate the Kingdom of God, or were they to wait for another. Luke, having already told the story of the raising of the widow's son, now felt free simply to say that at that very moment, he healed many of their sicknesses and infirmities. Then, turning to John's disciples, Jesus began to quote from Isaiah 35, the traditional lesson appointed for the festival of Rosh Hashanah, where the signs of the inbreaking of the kingdom were recorded. "Go tell John what you see and hear: The blind see, the lame walk, the lepers are cleansed, the deaf hear, the dead are raised up and the poor are evangelized" (Luke 7:18–35). No more appropriate new year's lesson could have been written, for those were the marks of the coming kingdom, said the Jewish scriptures (Isa. 26:19, 29:18–19, 35:5–6, 61:1–5).[4]

Luke, who had subordinated John to Jesus at his birth, now went on in this episode to continue that mild negativity. Many others in the early Church had identified John with the nameless messenger Malachi, and especially with the figure of Elijah, who was to come before the Lord. Luke suggested rather that John only came in "the spirit of Elijah." He went on to divide Jesus from John with an enormous chasm. John was the greatest of all in the first dispensation, but, Luke continued, the least in the Kingdom of God was greater than John (Luke 7:28). In the Book of Acts, this Lucan denigration of John would appear again as he would write that those who have received only the baptism of John did not possess the Holy Spirit (Acts 18:25). But throughout this episode, the new year themes were in fact the first call of the dawning kingdom, the call to repentance. This episode was at exactly the right place in Luke's gospel to fit the liturgical needs of Luke's community to celebrate Rosh Hashanah.

If that was a proper New Year's text, Luke's next episode was an exquisite choice for the observance of the Day of the Atonement. When one sees this narrative in this place, which was unique to Luke, one once again gets a deeper insight into how Luke used his resources and how the liturgical practices of the Jews shaped his gospel.

Yom Kippur, or the Day of the Atonement, was a somber time of repentance and confession for the Jews. It was described in Leviticus 16, and these readings continued into the holiness code of Leviticus 19. At this ceremony the sacrificial lamb that came to be called the Lamb of God was slain. Next the people symbolically and ceremoniously placed their sins on the back of the scapegoat. Laden with those sins, the goat was driven into the wilderness (Lev. 16:20–22). In this manner atonement was accomplished and the people were purged. The people were then admonished to avoid all types of sexual defilement as they were outlined in Leviticus. So lectionary readings from Leviticus continued to provide the background for Luke even as the holy days of the liturgical calendar dominated his story momentarily.

But how was he going to interpret atonement from a Christian perspective? The way he chose to do this was both unique to Luke and deeply insightful to his Torah order. There was a story in the tradition that Luke decided would be the perfect atonement lesson after some Lucan editorial revisions had been added. That story, found first in Mark but repeated in Matthew, was the account of the woman who came to Jesus while he was sitting at a meal, in the home of Simon the Leper. This woman anointed Jesus' feet with a costly ointment. In both Matthew and Mark, this story took place shortly before the crucifixion, and there was in neither narrative a hint of scandal or impropriety connected with the story. The only indignation expressed was over the cost of the ointment and the sense of waste found in this extravagant act. But to that complaint Jesus replied, "Let her alone ... She has done a beautiful thing to me ... She has anointed my body beforehand for burial ... Wherever the gospel is preached in the whole world, what she has done will be told in memory of her" (Mark 14:6, 8, 9). Matthew's version of this story was not significantly different (Matt. 26:6–13).

But for Luke to transform this episode into the lesson for atonement required some changes. So he went to work. First, Simon the Leper in Mark and Matthew became Simon the Pharisee in Luke. For his atonement story, Luke wanted to contrast forgiveness with righteousness. Second, the woman became a prostitute. Luke called her euphemistically "a woman of the city who was a sinner" (Luke 7:37). The context reveals that there was no question that this meant that she was a prostitute. Third, Luke heightened the sensual quality of the act. Only in Luke's version of this story did the woman "wet his feet with her tears and [wipe] them with the hair of her head." She then kissed his feet and anointed them with the ointment (Luke 7:38). It was a powerfully sensual scene in which Jesus was himself assumed to have been sexually defiled by his having allowed this woman to touch him in this way. The host immediately made this judgment. "If this man were a prophet, he would have known who and what sort of woman this is who is touching him, for she is a sinner" (Luke 7:39). To this Jesus responded with a parable that related forgiveness to love, not to righteousness (Luke 7:40–47). Then Jesus pronounced the woman forgiven and was thus portrayed as claiming the God power of being the source of forgiveness and absolution. So it was that in Luke's hands this episode became a powerful atonement day story. Forgiveness was God's free gift in the Christ who removed the necessity for sacrificial lambs and scapegoats, since he had himself taken away the sins of the world. The themes of Yom Kippur were clear, and this transferred and transformed story came in Luke's gospel at exactly the right place in the liturgical calendar to reveal Jesus as the fulfillment of the expectations of that book of the Torah known as Leviticus.

The next celebration in Luke's community would be the occasion when the shrunken observance of Tabernacles, the great harvest festival of the Jews, would be observed. Sometimes a Sabbath would separate the Yom Kippur observance from Tabernacles. Luke seemed to provide for that with a transition piece that we find in the opening verses of chapter 8 (Luke 8:1–3). It related the cleansing of certain women, including Magdalene, Joanna, and Suzanna, as well as others, of certain evil spirits and infirmities. The Book of Leviticus had many prescriptions for the purification of women (see Lev. 12, 18, 19, 20). So the major organizing theme of Luke's gospel was still operative.

When the Feast of Tabernacles arrived, Luke needed a harvest message for his next lection that would reveal that this Jewish celebration had also been brought to fulfillment in Luke's Christ. So what do we find at this point in Luke's story? Well, there was first of all the parable of the sower, which focused on the results of sowing that are revealed at the harvest (Luke 8:4–8). Second, to make sure we got the point, there was the long and elaborate explanation of that parable (Luke 8:9–15), once again focusing on the harvest. Third, there was a teaching bit on the meaning of light. Since light just happened to be one of the minor themes of Tabernacles, that also served Luke's purpose. Finally, Luke softened the story of Jesus' mother that he had taken from Mark (3:31–35) and concluded it with a word of blessing to those who both "hear the word of God and do it." This narrative allowed Luke to draw the nice contrast to those in the parable of the sower who merely heard the word of God and held it fast (Luke 8:15). The harvest Luke was interested in was the harvest of conversion, not the harvest of crops.

Once again we observe that these Lucan lections form a stunning fit with the liturgical year of the Jews, which consisted of Torah readings into which the festivals and fasts of the Jews were inserted. It was this liturgical year that we see time after time giving order to Luke's placement of his episodes and even to the content of Luke's episodes.

Luke then added another transition story. This one described how Jesus calmed the sea (Luke 8:22–26). It was a story taken from Mark and appeared not to be related to Leviticus at all. Clearly, Luke was ready to move on; and perhaps he felt he had gotten from Leviticus for "his order" all that it had to give. So with this story, he concluded his Leviticus cycle of readings.

NUMBERS: PRELUDE TO LUKE'S GRAND FINALE

The Book of Numbers would also be a challenge for Luke, but at least now he had Mark to guide him, for Mark also had had to cover the Sabbaths between Tabernacles and that point shortly after the Feast of Dedication when the journey to Jerusalem began. So Luke was content to lean on Mark, but he worked those Marcan themes into his text so that his order might be preserved and to enable him to arrive at his grand climax, where the Book of Deuteronomy would offer richer possibilities. The first four chapters of Numbers were involved with a census and with counting the people of Israel. Then, in Numbers 5:1, the text stated that those with menstrual irregularities were to be put outside the camp, as well as those who had had contact with the dead. The uncleanness of contact with the dead was expanded in Numbers 9:6 ff. So in the first lection in Luke's gospel that fell under the sway of the Book of Numbers (Luke 8:26–40), the author has set the stage for dealing with the Numbers theme of things that were unclean.

Jesus and his disciples, having crossed the lake, arrived at the country of the Gerasenes, who were unclean gentiles. There they confronted a demon-possessed man who lived among the tombs of the dead, a place believed by the Jews to be a source of uncleanness. Nearby these gentile farmers had herds of unclean swine. So Jesus came into an area where uncleanness was everywhere. First, said Luke, Jesus freed the man of the demons. In the process of achieving that, however, he caused the drowning of a herd of swine. This forced the Gerasenes to ask him to leave, and so he did. But, for Luke's purpose, Jesus had not only entered the world of the ritually unclean, but he had also prevailed over it. The laws of the Torah had found a new fulfillment in him. Luke had thus introduced the Book of Numbers, and he had set the stage to enable him to deal redemptively with the other prescriptions that would be found in that book.

In the next two episodes that fell under the sway of the Numbers cycle, Luke dealt with the specific sources of uncleanness mentioned in Numbers 5. The first was the story of the woman with a menstrual discharge (Luke 8:40–48). Luke's text said that she had had "a flow of blood for twelve years." In this unclean state, Luke noted, she touched Jesus. The result was not that Jesus became unclean, as Numbers would have led you to believe, but that the woman was herself healed. This narrative concluded with the words, "Daughter, your faith has made you well. Go in peace." It was a striking commentary on, and a transformation of, the content of the Book of Numbers.

The next Lucan lection continued this theme. This was the story of the raising of Jairus' daughter (Luke 8:49–56). In this narrative Jesus was portrayed as actually taking the hand of the dead child. This meant that he was in defiling physical contact with a dead body. Once again, however, as Luke told his story of the Christ, the defilement was transformed and overcome. Jesus did not become unclean. Rather death itself was defeated, and life was restored to the deceased person. The Torah was meeting its fulfillment in Jesus and was being transformed in the process by the gospel.

Numbers then moved on in chapters 13 through 15 to portray Moses as sending out twelve men to spy out the land of Canaan. One of the twelve, a man named Hoshea and called the son of Nun, was from the tribe of Ephraim (one of the two Joseph tribes). This man Moses renamed Joshua. When these spies returned, only Joshua and a man named Caleb were faithful to the conviction that God was with them and would lead them to victory. All of the others cowered in fear before the Canaanites.

So, once more not coincidentally, my lectionary theory would suggest, in Luke's next episode (9:19) Jesus was portrayed as sending out twelve men, not to spy out the land, but to preach and heal. We need to be reminded once again that the names Joshua and Jesus were identical in Hebrew. So the faithful

Joshua/Jesus, who was a minority voice in the Numbers story, was transformed into the new Joshua/Jesus, who now did the sending; and the twelve returned, not cowering in fear, but victorious. They had seen the signs of the Kingdom.

Luke next moved into the story of the feeding of the 5,000. It appears not to be correlated, at least not directly, with a Numbers story, but rather with the Exodus manna story and with an Elijah story (1 Kings 17:8–18) in which the food supply was not exhausted. This was followed by Jesus teaching on his identity and offering predictions of his suffering and death. Here again these passages appear not to be related to Numbers in any discernible way, though threats against the life of Moses were commonplace in this book. It was simply another transition piece for Luke. There was another festival on the horizon, and there are times when the assigned passages in the lectionary do not sing for the preacher. Perhaps that was Luke's experience here.

Into the liturgical calendar there now came the minor Jewish festival called Dedication, or Hanukkah. It was not mentioned in the Torah, but received a major emphasis only in the second century B.C.E. during the victories of the Maccabees over the Syrian overlords. Hanukkah celebrated the time when the light of God was believed to have returned to the Temple. So Luke provided, as Mark and Matthew both had done before him, a story that we call the transfiguration, in which the light of God that once came to the Temple was now portrayed as descending on Jesus (Luke 9:28–36). Unlike Mark and Matthew, however, Luke related that story to the Book of Numbers. In Numbers (16:42 ff.) we are told that the cloud of God covered the tent of meeting and the glory of the Lord appeared upon that meeting place. It was the first experience of the light of God coming to the worship center of Israel.[5] In his story of the transfiguration, Luke simply brought these themes into his gospel. Then Luke followed the transfiguration with the story of Jesus healing the epileptic boy (Luke 9:37–43), some teaching about discipleship (Luke 9:43–45), the argument about who was greatest (Luke

9:46–48), and finally the account of the man who cast out demons in Jesus' name (Luke 9:49–50).

The Lucan story then culminated with Jesus "setting his face" toward his destiny. Balaam had "set his face" in Numbers 24:1, but that connection might be too weak to press.[6] The latter part of Numbers was concerned only with how the land of Canaan was to be divided. It offered little material for Luke to work with, so he followed Mark until he was ready to start his journey section. Numbers closed with Moses in the plains of Moab by the Jordan. Jericho and the Promised Land lay in front of him. He was leaving the wilderness behind forever. Luke closed his Numbers section with Jesus setting his face toward Jerusalem and preparing to leave Galilee forever. It was not a perfect fit, but Luke has done the best he could do with the scanty material provided in Leviticus and Numbers. In retrospect it was rather impressive.

Luke has thus reached the turning point of his story at 9:51, and the Book of Deuteronomy was the reading from the Torah that he would confront. If the order that Luke was following was the order of the Torah, then we must be able to identify the Book of Deuteronomy with this final segment. For when this journey ended, Jesus was in Jerusalem and the story of the passion, told in terms of the Passover, would have to commence.

DEUTERONOMY AND THE JOURNEY NARRATIVE

The journey section in Luke is quite unusual. It was clearly written against the background of Deuteronomy, yet it was three times longer than those segments of Luke's gospel that he had written against the backgrounds of Genesis, Exodus, Leviticus, and Numbers. Its unusual quality did not stop there. If we follow the divisions found in Codex Alexandrinus that have been a faithful guide up to this point, we discover that there were almost three Lucan lections available for every Sabbath remaining during which Deuteronomy was to be read in the liturgical calendar of the Jews. The journey section of Luke was unusual in still a third way. The material contained in this section was in large measure unique to Luke; that is, the vast majority of this material appeared in no other gospel tradition of which we are aware.

Much of the special source speculation in regard to Luke arose as an attempt to answer questions raised by this segment of this gospel. I now think that it is far more probable that Luke himself was the creative genius behind this material. That will not be a comfortable thought for some, for it would mean that such familiar and treasured parts of the gospel tradition as the parables of the good Samaritan, the prodigal son, the lost sheep, the Pharisee and the publican, and Lazarus and Dives, as well as that charming story about Mary and Martha squabbling over who was helping in the kitchen, all of which are in this section, must therefore be seen as not original with Jesus. They rather originated, I now suggest, with Luke. Luke surely believed that he was being faithful to the tradition that Jesus inspired, but nonetheless Luke was the creator of this material. It does not go back to Jesus. That is my conclusion, and the lectionary theory of the way Luke organized his gospel gives great weight to this conclusion. For these uniquely Lucan pieces can be related rather dramatically to the Book of Deuteronomy. Indeed, when the journey section of Luke is laid out against the Book of Deuteronomy, it becomes quite evident that Luke's journey section is a commentary on Deuteronomy, or an attempt to retell the story of Deuteronomy in the light of the teaching of Jesus.

The very way in which Luke introduced this section of his gospel reveals the Deuteronomic connection. "When the days were near for him to be received up, he set his face to go to Jerusalem. And he sent messengers ahead of him" (Luke 9: 51–52). The Greek forms of the verbs used in this opening sentence were unique even to the rest of Luke. They were characteristic, Professor C. F. Evans has argued, "of the narrative style of the Septuagint."[7] This opening sentence suggested, according to Professor Evans, "a situation analogous to that of Moses" at the edge of the Promised Land. It was indeed reminiscent of the opening lines of the Book of Deuteronomy. There Moses was pictured as just beyond the Jordan in the wilderness. Israel would journey from Horeb to the borders of the Promised Land. It would be, said the text, an eleven-day journey. The Book of Deuteronomy, we pause to note, was read in the synagogues over eleven Sabbaths. It was the similarity of the introduction to both Deuteronomy and the journey section of Luke's gospel that caused Evans to propose that this section of Luke was modeled quite specifically on Deuteronomy. This contribution was made before anyone had suggested that Luke's whole gospel might have been organized on the basis of the Torah or that the order Luke set out to demonstrate in his story of Jesus was in fact the order of the Torah. So suddenly, from an independent source, one aspect of the lectionary theory is confirmed. Dr. Evans outlined the parallels in great detail. I shall but sample his genius.[8]

In Deuteronomy Moses chose twelve men and sent them out to search the land. They returned with fruit and pronounced the land good (Deut. 1). In the corresponding segment of Luke's journey segment, Jesus appointed seventy disciples in addition to the twelve and sent them out into the land. They returned with joy. They did not bring fruit, but Jesus was made to observe "the harvest is plentiful, but the laborers are few." (Luke 10:2).

In Deuteronomy Moses sent messengers to an alien nation, bearing words of peace and asking them to sell his emissaries both food and water. The king of this nation, however, refused, and so the alien nation was destroyed (Deut. 2:26–30). In the corresponding segment of Luke's journey section, Jesus sent the seventy out with a message of peace. They were told to eat and drink what was set before them. If rejected, they were to wipe the dust of that town off their feet, and a destruction like that of Sodom and Gomorrah was promised to the rejecters (Luke 10:4–16).

In Deuteronomy, despite Moses' fervent prayer to the Lord, he was refused entry into the Promised Land. Only those born in the wilderness would be allowed to enter the Promised Land, and that would be with Joshua, not Moses (Deut. 3:28). In the corresponding segment of Luke, Jesus gave thanks to the Father, who it was said concealed things from the wise and understanding and revealed them only to the babes who would accompany Jesus into the Kingdom of God (Luke 10:21), they being the ones to whom the Son would reveal these things.

In Deuteronomy the Decalogue was rehearsed by Moses (Deut. 5,6). In the corresponding section of Luke's journey section, Jesus responded to the question of the lawyer by asking him, "What is written in the law?" The lawyer answered with a summary of the Ten Commandments. First, he recited the Shema: "The Lord is one," and is to be loved with all your heart, soul, and strength. To this was added the Levitical requirement that you should also "love your neighbor as yourself" (Lev. 19:18). The leaders of the Jews had long summed up the Ten Commandments in this way (Luke 10:25–28). The parallels thus continued.

In Deuteronomy Moses told the people that they were to destroy the foreigners with no mercy (Deut. 7:1:2). If you do this, Moses promised, God will keep you from evil and will even lay this evil on those who hate you (Deut. 7:15). In Luke, in the corresponding segment, Jesus was portrayed as giving the parable of the good Samaritan in which the foreigner, whose worship was judged to be corrupt, was portrayed as showing mercy on the Jew who had fallen upon evil fortune (Luke 10:29–37).

In Deuteronomy Moses asserted that human beings did not live by bread alone, but by everything that proceeded out of the mouth of God (Deut. 8:1–3). In the corresponding segment of Luke, we are told of Jesus' visit to the home of Mary and Martha. Martha was busy preparing food, under the assumption that food was the most important aspect of life. Yet Mary was said to have chosen "the good portion." She sat at the feet of the Lord "to listen to his teaching" (Luke 10:38–42), to be fed by "everything that proceeded out of the mouth of the Lord." What a marvelous correlation with the Deuteronomic text.

In Deuteronomy God has dealt with Israel on the way to the Promised Land as a father was said to deal with a son. He has cared for Israel, fed Israel, disciplined Israel, and brought these people through the various tests of the wilderness. God has been the source of their power and their glory (Deut. 8:4 ff.). In the corresponding section of Luke, Jesus was teaching his disciples to pray to the God who was called "Our Father," whose name was to be hallowed, who fed them their daily bread, who led them through temptations, and who alone possessed the power and the glory they sought. This was followed by the parable of the friend in need who came at midnight. It concluded with the line: "If you who are evil know how to give good gifts to your children, how much more will the heavenly father give the Holy Spirit to those who ask him" (Luke 11:1–13).

In Deuteronomy, in a discussion on what was clean and unclean, Moses exhorted Israel to destroy every place of worship dedicated to idols and to come to the Lord's true sanctuary in Jerusalem, with tithes and offerings. You may eat meat, however, Moses said, in any place, but not until its blood has been drained lest it be unclean (Deut. 12:1–16). In Luke Jesus dined with a Pharisee who did not understand the difference between inner cleanness and outer cleanness. Jesus also pronounced woe on those who tithed insignificant things but neglected justice and the love of God (Luke 11:37–44).

In Deuteronomy Moses taught that every seventh year the debts of the Jewish people were to be forgiven by their fellow Hebrews. A Jewish servant or slave, for example, who had served for six years must be freed in the seventh year (Deut. 15:1–18). In the corresponding section of Luke, Jesus on the Sabbath released a woman from a peculiar type of bondage, the bondage of infirmity. To this gift of freedom, the leader of the synagogue registered a protest, since Jesus' gift of healing of this woman was not done during one of the six working days of the week. Jesus responded that the Sabbath was exactly the proper day to free one bound in servitude to an illness for eighteen years. That was triple the amount of time a Jew could be enslaved according to Deuteronomy. Luke's text noted that at this rebuttal, the people rejoiced (Luke 13:10–21).

In Deuteronomy we are told that the scribes could grant immunity from the Lord's battle to those who had built a house but not yet dedicated it, to those who had planted a vineyard or those who were betrothed to a wife (Deut. 20:1–7). In the corresponding section of Luke, Jesus gave the parable of the great feast from which invited guests had asked to be excused because, said the parable, they had bought a field, or purchased five yolk of oxen, or married a wife. This action enabled the banquet to be thrown open to the poor, the maimed, the blind, and the lame (Luke 14:15–35), who would inherit the Kingdom of God that Jesus proclaimed.

In Deuteronomy, if a man had a rebellious and stubborn son who talked back and would not obey his parents, a riotous liver and a drunkard, the father must bring that son to the elders of the city to be put to death (Deut. 21:18–21). In the corresponding section of Luke, Jesus told the parable of a man who had a rebellious, demanding, and disrespectful son. This son had wasted his father's substance in riotous and drunken living, but the father of this son did not execute him. Instead, he welcomed him home with open arms and great honor when "he came to himself"(Luke 15:11–32). Once more Luke called the people to the inner meaning of the Torah. It was not righteousness but rather a new kind of holiness, marked by love and forgiveness.

In Deuteronomy Moses gave injunctions against the oppressive treatment of the poor in Israel, whether the poor were brethren or aliens in their midst. Each person, said Moses, must pay for his own sins and when one comes before the judge, the innocent person would be rewarded and the wicked person would be punished (Deut. 24:10–25:3). In the corresponding section of Luke, Jesus told the parable of Lazarus and Dives, in which the poor man was oppressed by the rich man, which resulted in each being sentenced. Lazarus the poor man went to eternal reward and Dives the oppressor went to eternal punishment. The rich man in torment tried to get a message to his brothers, but was told that one person cannot be responsible for another person's sin or another person's blessing (Luke 16:19–31).

In Deuteronomy Moses said when you come to the Promised Land, you shall go to the Lord's sanctuary and say, "I have given the tithe to the Levite, the fatherless and the widow. I have obeyed the commandments. I have not been unclean. I have done all that the Lord commanded of me, so God should look down and bless God's people Israel" (Deut. 26:1-15). In the corresponding section of Luke, Jesus was portrayed as telling the parable of the Pharisee and the publican. In this parable the Pharisee said, "I have kept the commandments, I fast twice a week, I give tithes of all that I get." But it was the publican, said Jesus, who was blessed because he approached God in humility (Luke 18:9-14).

At this point the teaching of Deuteronomy ended and the book concluded with a series of blessings and curses. So, not surprisingly, at this point Luke's journey section ceased its independent commentary and returned to Mark for material. For our purposes we need to note that these were not all of the connections between Deuteronomy and the journey section of Luke, but they represent a sufficient sample to suggest that Luke had modeled his journey section directly on Deuteronomy. Perhaps even more significantly, it suggests that Luke had quite deliberately created most of these traditions and the teachings, even the parables of Jesus found in this journey section of his gospel, in order to cast Jesus into the mold of Deuteronomy. Jesus, for Luke, was not only the new and greater Moses, but he was also the fulfillment of all that Deuteronomy anticipated. Certainly, Luke has succeeded in providing teaching lections for the Christian community that corresponded to the teaching lections that Deuteronomy provided for Israel in this seminal book of the Torah.

One problem, however, remains to be solved for this lectionary thesis. Luke had provided in his journey section sufficient lections for thirty-three Sabbaths. Yet the reading of Deuteronomy in the synagogue was normally completed in approximately eleven Sabbaths. Does the suggestion that Luke was developing his gospel on the order of the Torah break down at this point? I think not, but it does require an explanation.

Recall that in the chapter on Mark, we suggested that the Book of Deuteronomy had been used by the Jews as the material to prepare proselytes for circumcision, the ceremonial bath, and incorporation into Judaism at the time of the Passover. We also suggested that the Christians took over this pattern for their converts, with baptism taking place on Easter eve, the Eucharist replacing the Passover meal, and the teaching of Jesus found in the journey section of each gospel replacing the words of Moses in Deuteronomy as their preparation. Evidence from ancient second-century Christian sources, such as the Didache, or third-century sources, such as the writings of Hippolytus, bear witness to the fact that such catechetical instruction was customary. The Didache was in fact catechetical material based in large measure on the Book of Deuteronomy. A work by Cyril of Jerusalem in the fourth century C.E. suggested that these instructions were given at the rate of three a week or eighteen over a six-week period of time.[9] To give an earlier hint to that pattern, we have also discovered that pious Jews went to synagogue thrice weekly—Saturday evening, Monday, and Thursday—to hear the Torah of the coming Sabbath,[10] and that pattern was thus also used for the converts who, then as now, appeared to be among the most pious. The journey section suggests that in Luke's Church this thrice-weekly pattern of instruction was also in practice. The Lucan journey section was Jesus instructing his disciples for the time when he would not be with them. That was the situation for disciples in Luke's Church. Furthermore, this catechetical material in Luke's journey section was roughly organized into groups of three lections each, rotating around a central theme. So with Deuteronomy as his guide, but with the practice of providing three preparation sessions per week for converts as his model, Luke wrote this catechetical material for his Church to use three times a week as the candidates were prepared for baptism. In the process he portrayed Jesus as the one who not only replaced Moses but called the teaching of Moses found in Deuteronomy to a new and higher level. He also had used the text of Deuteronomy again and again as the basis on which to demonstrate that everything written about this Jesus in the law of Moses had been fulfilled. Deuteronomy also gave wings to Luke's understanding of Jesus, and it helped Luke to create some of his gospel's most enduring images. Deuteronomy held before its readers what it called "the two ways"—one was the way of blessing and the other was the way of a curse (Deut. 11:26 ff., 30:15–19). Luke was clearly affected by that understanding of Christianity as "a way of blessing," for in the Book of Acts he described the Christians as those "belonging to the Way" (Acts 9:2). He also referred to himself as one who "persecuted this Way" (Acts 22:4). The way that led to life in the Book of Deuteronomy had now been deeply invested by Luke with Christian content so that "the way" in Deuteronomy became a synonym for Christianity itself.

When Deuteronomy was about to close, Moses was pictured as commissioning Joshua to lead the children of Israel into the Promised Land (Deut. 31:23). In Luke the new Joshua would soon go over the Jordan to complete his journey and to prepare for the climactic moments of the crucifixion and resurrection (Luke 18:35 ff.). When Jesus approached the city of Jerusalem, he wept over it, and the content of his teaching shifted. He began to say, in such parables as the wicked husbandman (Luke 20:9–18), that the history of the Israel that rejected and killed the ones whom God had sent was about to be enacted yet again. The way of life and death, the way of blessing and curse, had been delineated, but Israel was still destined to choose death. The new Moses would not escape the fate of the first Moses.

The passion story was now in sight. The Book of Deuteronomy was complete. The liturgical year for the Jews had begun anew with the beginning of the month of Nisan. Luke completed his journey section by continuing his threefold practice. He included three Marcan episodes in his text for the first Sabbath of Nisan. He next employed his long apocalyptic chapter (Luke 21) to be the Christian version of the end of the world to continue the Genesis story of Noah and the final destruction of that ancient world, which was the Torah reading for Nisan 2. Then the events of the passion unfolded in eight sections.

The Gospel of Luke was written to illumine the Torah with occasional references to the prophets and the psalms, with a bow to the liturgical year of the Jews and with an attempt to harmonize the texts of Mark and Matthew. But above all, it was to illumine the Torah, to show Jesus as the fulfillment of all that Moses wrote. This was the work of a convert to Judaism. He did his work well, so well indeed that only eyes trained to see things from a Jewish perspective will be able to see the meaning of the gospel that bears the name of Luke.

THE OUTLINE OF LUKE'S GOSPEL PLACED AGAINST
THE TORAH IN THE JEWISH LITURGICAL YEAR

Month	Sabbaths	Holy Days	Torah	Luke
Nisan	1		Genesis 1	Luke 20:19
	2			
14th–15th Nisan		Passover (eight days)		
	3			Luke 24: end
	4			Luke 1
Iyyar	1			
	2			
	3			
	4			
Sivan	1			
		Jewish Pentecost (Vigil)—Shavuot		
	2			
	3			
	4		Genesis 50	Luke 4:13
	5		Exodus 1	Luke 4:14
Tammuz	1			
	2			
	3			
	4			
Ab	1			
		Ninth of Ab		
	2			
	3			
	4			
Elul	1			
	2		Exodus 40	Luke 6:19
	3		Leviticus 1	Luke 6:20
	4			
	5			
Tishri	(First Day)	Jewish New Year—Rosh Hashanah		
	1			
	2			
		Atonement—Yom Kippur		

Month	Sabbaths	Holy Days	Torah	Luke
	3	Tabernacles (eight days)— Sukkot	↓	↓
Cheshvan	4			
	1		Leviticus 27	Luke 8:25
	2		Numbers 1	Luke 8:26
	3			
	4			
	5			
Kislev	1			
	2			
	3	Dedication— Hanukkah		
	4			
	5			
Tebeth	1		Numbers 36	Luke 9:50
	2		Deuteronomy 1	Luke 9:51
	3			
	4			
Shebat	1			
	2			
	3			
	4			
Adar	1			
	2			
	3	Purim		
	4			
Nisan			Deuteronomy 34	Luke 20:18

Acts and John

A Very Brief Glimpse

This analysis of how the synoptic Gospels of Mark, Matthew, and Luke might have come into being certainly does not exhaust the content of the New Testament. It does, however, suggest a perspective through which the entire New Testament can be read. Above all, it confronts us with the Jewish dimensions of the New Testament that were not just present in, but dramatically shaped, the Christian story. It has enabled us to discover Jewish content present in almost every verse. The same insight would have become obvious if our focus had been on that part of the New Testament that we call the Epistles, whether they be the Pauline Epistles, the pseudo

Pauline Epistles, the General Epistles, or the Book of Hebrews.[1] To set the epistles into their historic setting and to see the Jewishness of these parts of the Christian tradition is, however, beyond the scope of this book.

So is a treatment of the Book of Revelation, that premier late-first-century piece of Christian apocalyptic literature. I suspect this book will get a great deal of attention as Western civilization navigates its way through the transition into the third millennium of the Christian Era. It will be quoted quite frequently and with a strange literalness by those who traffic in predicting the end of the world in order to produce sufficient fear among people, for it is religiously tinged fear that enables religious charlatans to manipulate their audiences for their own benefit. I am always amazed at the ability of the doomsday preachers to create a response from those who think that arbitrary dates like 1000 C.E. and 2000 C.E., created by arbitrary human counting systems, are somehow significant to God and the divine plan for the world. This is especially so since the best guess we can put together from the most highly regarded resources now suggests that Jesus was born somewhere between 8 B.C.E. and 4 B.C.E. This means, of course, that we have some time ago entered the third millennium and no one noticed! But despite the fact that the Book of Revelation will get millennium attention, I will resist the temptation to be one of its attention givers in this volume.

There are, however, two remaining books in the canonical Christian writings that I cannot ignore, even if I also cannot treat them with the attention they are deemed to require. These are, of course, the Book of Acts and the Gospel of John. These books impinge directly on the content of this volume, yet they still remain only tangential to my primary task. Both Acts and John, I am certain, had liturgical uses at their inception. Both books were in all probability tenth-decade pieces of work. Both reflect the tensions that divided the increasingly rigid orthodox Jews from the Christian worshiping community, which was made up of a combination of both Jews and gentiles. Both would be deserving of treatment far beyond what they shall receive here; and yet not to give them at least some brief attention would leave my task feeling incomplete. So, out of my need to present a context that is whole, even though the content will not be exhaustive, let me incorporate Acts and John into this study with at least a few appropriate brush strokes.

The Book of Acts was written by the same author who created the Gospel of Luke. It serves as a companion piece, a kind of volume 2 in the Lucan corpus. For these reasons I shall bring it first into my focus.

I see no reason to doubt that the Book of Acts was originally created and constructed on the very same models that we have discovered present in the Gospels. That is, it too was born as a lectionary book that was designed for reading in Sabbath/Sunday worship settings. If we are accurate in assessing its date (ca. 90 C.E.–95 C.E.), it would have been written in that period of time when the Church and the synagogue were separating. It would thus fill a growing liturgical need in the newly independent Christian Church.

In the traditional synagogue liturgy, we have noted, as many as three lessons per Sabbath might be read. The essential one was from the Torah, but there was also a reading from that part of the sacred text known as the Former Prophets, and generally a third reading from what the Jews called the Latter Prophets. However, as the synagogue moved farther and farther away from Jerusalem and Judea and thus from the traditional practices of the Jewish homeland, these latter two readings began to decline in their appeal. For that reason they began to suffer the liturgical fate of being shortened dramatically. The Latter Prophets (Isaiah–Malachi) began to be read on at least a four-year cycle; and even within that framework, the Book of Ezekiel seems to have been ignored in some circles.

The Former Prophets (Joshua–Kings), on the other hand, just seemed to grow less and less relevant to the hellenized Jews and gentiles who now made up the separating Christian Church. This biblical material basically traced the history of the Jewish people after the death of Moses. It recounted the conquest of Canaan under Joshua and the period of loose confederation reflected in the Book of Judges. This material culminated in Israel's rising demand for a king, which emerged in the twilight years of the revered judge named Samuel. It then chronicled the history of the Jewish kingdom. It recounted the story of the first king, Saul. Then it dwelt in great detail on what was regarded as the golden age of Jewish history, the successful reigns of David and Solomon. It told the story of the division of the nation into two warring principalities, called Israel and Judah after the death of Solomon. Finally, it recounted the destruction of Israel at the hands of the Assyrians in 721 B.C.E., and later the fall of Judah to the Babylonians in 598 B.C.E. to 586 B.C.E. It is easy to understand that while an aura of importance continued to surround the Torah for more than a century into Christian history, this reading from the history of the Jewish nation that constituted the second reading in the synagogue worship tradition began to lose its appeal in Christian circles. "Since Jesus, not Moses, was the founder of this new faith tradition," someone was bound to have asked, "why do we not substitute for our second reading, which traditionally described the adventures of the Jews after the death of their founder, a description of the adventures of the Christian people and their movement following the death of our founder, Jesus?" Since necessity is always the mother of invention, the need for such a book created the necessity for its being written.

Luke was clearly the candidate for authorship, since he, more than any other gospel writer, lived on that cusp between the Jewish past that produced Jesus and the gentile future to which Luke clearly believed that Jesus belonged. Whether Luke and Acts were originally written together as two parts of a single work, or whether some time (no more than five years at the most I would guess) elapsed between the two, no one can say with certainty. What can be said with certainty, however, is that Acts was written to parallel the Gospel of Luke at points so numerous that doubt is simply not an option. Furthermore, since the Gospel of Luke was written to be a lectionary book to be read in order at the liturgy on the Sabbaths/Sundays throughout the year, there is little reason to doubt that this was also the purpose of the Book of Acts. Indeed, the Book of Acts provides us with some internal evidence that it was designed to fit a liturgical year.

To build this case, it is important first to cite the obvious. The Book of Acts is approximately the same length as Luke and Matthew. Since both of those books were designed to provide a lection per week, as well as to provide for readings to mark the festivals and fasts of the Jewish liturgical year, we can begin with the assumption that the length of the Book of Acts does not disqualify it for consideration as a proper lectionary book. The fact that it is divided into fifty-two lections in the early manuscripts further strengthens that claim. Fifty-two lections would provide a lection per Sabbath of the Jewish year, with enough flexibility to accommodate those added days when the Jewish calendar would be brought into harmony with the Julian calendar, and this enabled the Jewish calendar to remain relatively constant with the annual cycle of darkness and light.[2]

Second, there was one obvious reference early in Acts to a major Jewish festival. Acts built its story of the coming of the Holy Spirit into the life of the Church as the dominant theme of its observance of Pentecost. We met this understanding of Pentecost earlier in our examination of Luke's gospel. To the Jewish people, Pentecost celebrated the giving of the law by God to Moses at Mt. Sinai, and it was observed fifty days after Passover. Matthew, writing out of his Jewish context, followed this Jewish lead and provided his Sermon on the Mount as his Pentecost reading. Luke, on the other hand, believed that what the law had been to the Jews, the Holy Spirit was to the Christians. So he used the Sermon on the Mount material at another place in his drama and made his Pentecost story in his gospel the account of John the Baptist announcing that one would come after him who would baptize with the Holy Spirit and with fire (Luke 3:16). Luke was clearly anticipating in his gospel the Pentecost story in the Book of Acts. It is easy to imagine this portion of Luke being read alongside the Pentecost story in Acts in the worship life of that late-first-century Christian community. Indeed, the baptism of Jesus by the Spirit was also paralleled with the baptism of the Church by the Spirit. If that liturgical connection can be so easily made, then armed with this insight, we begin to look for others. They are not difficult to locate.

The Gospel of Luke began with the account of Jesus' conception. That was the moment of his entry into a new realm in which he would accomplish his purpose as the bringer of salvation. Mary, Jesus' mother, was for Luke the point of entry. In the Book of Acts, the story of Jesus' ascension paralleled his conception and inaugurated the drama. The ascension was also the moment of his entry into a new realm in which he would bring his purpose to a new fulfillment, breaking its limitations and thus making salvation universally available. It is interesting to note that only Luke has suggested that Jesus' mother was present at this second entry story in his corpus (Acts 1:14).

In the gospel, after the story of Jesus' baptism and temptation, Luke began his Exodus segment with the account of Jesus' rejection in Nazareth. In the gospel account, we are told that when Jesus came to his home in Nazareth, the initial response of his fellow Nazareth citizens was quite positive (Luke 4:20–22). Jesus proclaimed that he spoke as one on whom the Spirit of God rested. He justified this claim by an appeal to the prophet Isaiah (Isa. 61:1–2). In the corresponding segment of Acts, we discover that when the Christian Church came to its home in Jerusalem, the initial response was likewise quite positive (Acts 2:37). Peter in Jerusalem had preached just as Jesus had done in Nazareth (Acts 2:17–36). Like Jesus, Peter claimed that he spoke as one on whom the Spirit of God rested. Like Jesus, he justified this claim by an appeal to one of the prophets (Acts 2:17–21, Joel 2:28–32). In both instances rejection came quickly (Acts 3–5, Luke 4:29–30). Jesus was cast out of the city with the intent of destroying him by hurling him from the brow of the hill on which the city was built (Luke 4:29). Peter was arrested and put in custody (Acts 4:3–4).

In both instances the escape provided for each was murky. Jesus simply "passing through the midst of them" (Luke 4:30) went away. Peter was found guilty but released nonetheless since this sign was "manifest to all the inhabitants of Jerusalem"

(Acts 4:16). In both episodes the sticking issue was that no boundary could be placed on the love of God and thus the message was clear that gentiles must be welcomed to God's salvation (Luke 4:25–27, Acts 2:1–13).

Later parallels continue to be noted between Jesus in the gospel and Peter in the Book of Acts. In the gospel Jesus stopped the potential negativity of the crowd of people by feeding the multitude (Luke 9:10–17). In Acts Peter stopped the potential negativity of "the hellenists" by making provisions to feed the widows (Acts 6:1–6). Jesus appointed seventy to assist him (Luke 10:1–12). Peter appointed seven to assist him (Acts 6:5–6). In the gospel Herod drove Jesus out of Galilee (Luke 10:31–35). In the Book of Acts, Herod tried to kill Peter (Acts 12:1–3). The failure of Israel to fulfill its vocation was a major theme in Luke 10–12. The Church arriving at the realization of despair about Israel was a major theme of Acts 8–13. In the gospel Jesus made reference to Jonah, the prophet who went to preach to the gentiles of Nineveh (Luke 11:30). In Acts Peter, who represented the risen Christ, ventured forth from Joppa, the point of departure for Jonah (Jon. 1:3), to baptize Cornelius the gentile and thus to launch the gentile mission of the Church. One can hardly conclude that these points of contact are coincidental. Acts was written to be read in worship alongside the gospel. The gospel described the Jesus who was the fulfillment of the Jewish scriptures. The Book of Acts described the way in which the Christ experience was shared throughout the world.

In the climactic chapters of Acts, which were dominated not by Peter, but by Paul (Acts 20–28), we discover that Paul has also been portrayed as reliving the climactic events in the life of Jesus. Once again, this happened with such regularity that it simply could not be coincidental. And once again, we get the very broad hint that the Book of Acts was written to be read in tandem with the Gospel of Luke.

Both Jesus and Paul made a long journey to Jerusalem to meet a destiny that involved suffering (Luke 9:51–18:43, Acts 19:21–21:16). Both delivered farewell discourses, Jesus in the upper room (Luke 22), Paul at Miletus (Acts 20:17 ff.). Both recorded prophecies of their deaths (Luke 18:32, Acts 21:10 ff.). Both were portrayed as obedient to God's will (Luke 22:42, Acts 21:14). Both had the crowd call for their deaths (Luke 23:18; Acts 21:36, 22:22). Both endured false accusations (Luke 23:2, Acts 21:28). Both were deemed innocent by representatives of the State (Luke 23:4, Acts 26:31). Both endured the same number of trials. For Jesus it was first before the Sanhedrin (Luke 22:66) and then before Pilate (Luke 23:1), Herod (Luke 23:8), and Pilate again (Luke 23:13). For Paul it was first before the Sanhedrin (Acts 23), and then before Felix (Acts 24), Festus (Acts 25), and Herod (Acts 26). Both had a final supper (Luke 22:14–27, Acts 27:35). Both experienced death, though for Jesus it was crucifixion (Luke 23) and for Paul it was the symbolic death of shipwreck in the deep (Acts 27:39–44). Both were raised after three days, Jesus from the grave (Luke 24:1 ff.) and Paul, who, when lifted from the sea, was given three days to recover (Acts 28:7). Both finally arrived at the Promised Land, Jesus by ascending into heaven (Luke 24:50–53), Paul by reaching his destination in Rome (Acts 28:16).

There is also data to support the thesis that Luke wrote many of the episodes in Acts, not from memory or even from word of mouth, but *midrashically* from texts in the Hebrew scriptures, just as we have discovered he did in the gospel. The story of Ananias and Sapphira (Acts 5:1–11), for example, appears to be related to the account of Hananiah in Jeremiah (28:15–17). The story of the Ethiopian eunuch who was evangelized by Philip (Acts 8:26–40) was certainly influenced by the account of the only other Ethiopian mentioned in the Bible (Jer. 38:7–13). His name was Ehed-melech and, not coincidentally, he was also a eunuch. Even the Damascus road story and the heroic role played by Annanias in that drama are cast into significant historic doubt when one recognizes that nowhere in the Pauline corpus is such an experience or such a man ever mentioned. On and on we could go, but that is sufficient to challenge the literalism that surrounds the Book of Acts and to suggest that it too will be understood only when it is read through Jewish eyes as a lectionary book written *midrashically* and designed to complement and parallel the reading from the gospel.

When we look at Acts as a lectionary book and as a companion volume to Luke's gospel, designed to provide an alternative in the liturgy to the reading from the story of Israel's history, other interesting insights develop. Through the centuries people have had questions about some of the things that appeared to be so strange in this volume when they were read as history. The Book of Acts ends in an unusual way. It was written perhaps as much as thirty years after the death of Paul, but it included no mention of that death. It has been referred to as incomplete, with its final chapter somehow missing. It concluded with Paul arriving in Rome, settling in, teaching as he could about the Lord Jesus for two years unhindered. At this point it stopped abruptly. But if Paul's arrival in his promised land of Rome was designed to parallel the final events of Jesus' life, including his arrival via the ascension into his promised land of heaven, then the closing of the Book of Acts at that point is both logical and consistent. Besides that, a lectionary book had to come to an end when the liturgical year was complete.

To the complaint that far too much time in Acts was dedicated to storms and shipwrecks, the lectionary theory would suggest that since this section of Acts, which described the passion of Paul, paralleled the passion of Jesus, then its length is quite understandable. It had to provide sufficient material to parallel the Holy Week gospel readings.

It has also been suggested that in Acts Paul's trials are painfully repetitive. However, if the four trials of Paul are designed to provide parallels to the four trials of Jesus, it becomes quite understandable.

When it is suggested that when Acts leaves both Philip and Peter, they never again reappear in this story unless they cross Paul's path, it needs to be noted that when the Gospel of Luke has Jesus leave Galilee, he also never returned. Please note that only Luke, of all the gospel writers, refused to allow the story of resurrection or the Resurrected One to be cast in Galilee. Luke has written his story to take the message of Christ first to Jerusalem from Galilee and then to the uttermost parts of the world from Jerusalem. Luke never returned to any site or person unless the forward progress of his narrative required it. Thus the lectionary theory solves many of the mysteries that commentators of the past confronted when they looked at Acts as if it were a volume in Church history. That assumption, which was a product of the Western gentile mind, had the effect of hiding for centuries the essential Jewishness of the Book of Acts and the liturgical role in synagogue worship for which the book was in fact composed.

The Gospel of John offers an even greater challenge. This book alternately thrills me and exasperates me. I think that, better than any other piece of Christian writing, this gospel captures the profundity of the experience of Jesus as the Christ. I also believe that in a number of debates over facts in the gospel tradition, wherever John and the synoptic Gospels clash on details, truth normally has resided with John. Yet I do not think that there is one word in the Johannine text that Jesus actually came close to saying. To literalize the text of John's gospel, more than any of the other gospel traditions, brings a far greater distortion to the Johannine message. I grieve when I see how literalized Johannine words played so major a role in the great theological debates of the third, fourth, and fifth centuries and how they led to such rigid doctrinal positions in the Church as the Incarnation and the Trinity. It is not that I consider the reality these doctrines seek to articulate to be wrong, for certainly I do not. However, in history the literalized words of the Johannine text joined forces with the Greek thinking fathers of the Western Church to produce a theological system that is as foreign to our day as anything I can imagine. Yet that system is still called Christian orthodoxy. There is a vast difference between the truth of one's experience of God and the literalness of the truth of the words that one uses to articulate that experience.

My experience, for example, as a Christian, is that Jesus is for me the bread of life, the living water, the door, the vine, the way, and the resurrection, but I am confident that the Jesus of history never literally claimed to be any of these things. So that the Johannine "I am" sayings were never literally spoken by this Jesus. Indeed for him they would have been all but unthinkable. I find the literal Jesus of history to be only dimly present in the Fourth Gospel, yet having said that, I still need to register that this gospel continues to feed my faith more deeply than any other.

I can find in the Fourth Gospel that the name of God revealed at the burning bush to be "I am" was applied to Jesus by the early Christian community. We see this, not just in the "I am" sayings, but in those two unique and dramatic Johannine claims attributed to Jesus: "When you have lifted up the Son of Man, then you will know *I am!*" (John 8:28), and "before Abraham was, *I am*" (John 8:58).

I am intrigued by the hints that perhaps there is some connection between the seven-day creation story of Genesis and the constructed order of John's gospel. At least John's gospel appears to be written between "In the beginning" (John 1:1, Gen. 1:1) and "It is finished" (John 19:30, Gen. 1:21). I note the similarity between the God who completed his work on the sixth day and rested on the seventh with the Jesus who completed his work on the sixth day, rested in his tomb on the seventh day, and then emerged on the first day of the second week to inaugurate the new creation.

John's development of Lazarus into a figure of history who symbolizes the Christ also amazes me. I think John's Lazarus existed first, not in history, but in Luke's parable of Lazarus and Dives. Both stories, the parable in Luke and the raising of Lazarus from the dead in John, turn on the phrase "if they do not hear Moses and the prophets, neither will they be convinced if someone should rise from the dead" (Luke 16:31). That which was a warning in Luke's parable became the reality on which the Fourth Gospel turned in John's episode of the raising of Lazarus. Indeed this raising not only failed to convince the authorities of Jesus' relationship with God, but it became the very reason the authorities sought to kill Jesus. Both Lazarus and Jesus in John's gospel were buried in a tomb (John 11:17, 19:41). Both tombs were sealed with a stone (John 11:38, 20:1).

Both had a woman named Mary outside the tomb weeping (John 11:21–37, 20:1). One was raised back to this earthly life on the fourth day by Jesus' intervention (John 11:29). The other was raised into God's presence on the third day (John 20:17–18) by Jesus' own power. "I am ascending," he said. John also portrayed Lazarus as the brother of Mary and Martha of Bethany, though no other gospel writer seemed to know of this brother. John was a sophisticated symbolizer and Lazarus was clearly one of his primary symbols. So was water being turned into wine (John 2:1–11), the concept of being born again (John 3:1–15), and many, many others.

I am also fascinated, but not yet convinced, by the possibility that John's whole gospel with its signs and long theological discourses was originally written to be part of a seven-week liturgical observance designed to instruct and prepare, with fasting and prayer, converts to Christianity in anticipation of their baptism. This was thought to be the practice of the Asian Church in Ephesus, where John's gospel supposedly was written, and this proposal leans heavily on the Johannine identification of the day of the crucifixion with the day the paschal lamb was slain, as well as trying to make sense out of references both to days and to weeks found in the Johannine text. This theory would suggest that John 1–11 was designed to lead one through four weeks of preparation. John 12–19 was the text for Holy Week, with John 20–21 leading the worshiper through the joys of Easter day and two Sabbaths afterward. Such an idea has much to commend it, but not enough yet to make me want to defend the theory.[3]

My knowledge of John, if by that one means having read almost every major English-language commentary on this gospel published this century and many in the nineteenth, is not insignificant.[4] However, my sense that anyone has yet found the key to unlock the original intention of this author is still uncertain. I also believe that the definitive work on John has not yet been written. It will not be, in my opinion, until someone can place this book into its original Jewish setting, discern the motive and the agenda of its original Jewish author, and in this manner open the mysteries hidden away there for so long. The great contribution of the Fourth Gospel is that it continues to feed Christians in every generation on many levels, whether they know its well-kept secrets or not.

But having spent most of my time seeking to open primarily the synoptic Gospels, and employing only brush strokes to include in this analysis both the Book of Acts and the Gospel of John, I now want to turn back to the specific issues in the life of this Jesus that my analysis has raised and to seek to find a way to understand these events as something other than objective events of remembered history. I want to propose that, rather than trying to discern whether the things said and done in the Gospels actually happened, we need to begin to explore these episodes as attempts by Jewish authors working against the background of a Jewish liturgical year and Jewish lectionary readings to process and write about the Church's experience of Jesus in a specifically Jewish way. Such an approach will destabilize again and again the claims of the literalists, but it will also open a door into the realm of the spirit in our postmodern world for those of us who seek a new way into the wonder of God.

◇◇◇

Part Three

Looking with Jewish Eyes at Critical Moments in the Christian Faith Story

11

Jewish Stars in the Story of Jesus' Birth

I trust that I have demonstrated thus far that it is more difficult than most imagine to read the Christian scriptures with little or no knowledge of their Jewish past. It is impossible, in my opinion, to understand those Christian scriptures without a profound knowledge of that Jewish past. I intend to illustrate that reality with very specific examples in this section of the book. To make this case, I will focus on the most familiar parts of the gospel material, the parts Christians think they know best: the birth stories of Jesus, the stories of the crucifixion, the resurrection, the ascension, and the outpouring of the Holy Spirit. In this process, quite inevitably, questions will be raised about that fine line between the reality to which the stories point and the *midrashic* style in which the stories are told. In the Western

Christian world, the two have been so intermingled as to be thought almost identical

Have you ever wondered what Isaiah, Solomon, the queen of Sheba, David, Micah, Abraham, Sarah, Isaac, Elijah, Zechariah, Balaam, Balak, Malachi, Aaron, Elisheba, Miriam, and Moses had in common? At least one answer would be that these stars in the Jewish firmament, who populate the pages of the Hebrew scriptures, made cameo appearances in the stories of Jesus' birth in the New Testament. Does that surprise you? You have read those stories, you say, countless times, and you have never met Solomon, the queen of Sheba, Elijah, and the others there before. That fact should awaken you to the possibility that there might be more to these narratives than you have imagined. The appearances of these heroes of the Jewish past actually form a rich tapestry of interpretive background without which the lovely and familiar birth stories have little or no meaning. Those birth stories are not and were never intended to be historic descriptions of events that actually happened, and the presence of these Jewish stars, once our eyes are opened to see them, makes that abundantly clear. Each Jewish star, for example, illumines, not a fact about Jesus' birth, but an element of the Church's memory and faith in regard to the impact of the adult Jesus of Nazareth. Yet, I think it is fair to say that few Christians would know this Jewish background well enough to identify either these stars or their meaning. These stories are read with little or no awareness of the interpretive power present in the references and allusions that point us toward Hebrew history. So my task now is to lift this Hebrew background out of the shadows and into full consciousness, and in the process to call people into a deeper appreciation of the power, depth, and nonliteral significance of the birth narratives in Matthew and Luke. It is also my intention to show how those birth stories reveal adult themes and adult insights that illumine dramatically the person and the work of Jesus of Nazareth.

Identifying the Jewish roots present in the stories of Jesus' birth, however, will not complete the interpretive task for which these narratives almost scream. For onto the Jewish background of these stories has been laid first of all 2,000 years of Christian tradition that developed slowly, generation by generation, as these stories were told and retold and as they were acted out in pageants while being viewed by countless millions. Next we Christians have piled onto this combination fantasies, myths, legends, and the creative imagination of the ages. These facts make it incredibly difficult for most people to separate out these various levels found in the stories of Christmas even in their own minds.

If any group of church people, for example, were asked to identify the mode of transportation used by the wise men as they journeyed from afar to bring their gifts to the Christ child, almost without exception or hesitation they would answer, "They came on camels. Everybody knows that!" They would be absolutely secure in the truth of that answer. But the fact is that no camels are ever mentioned in the biblical story of the wise men. Those camels are simply not present in the biblical text, as a quick reading of Matthew 2 will reveal. Where then did the camels come from? How did they get so firmly planted in our imagination and on our Christmas cards? The camels were in fact the product of the Jewish *midrashic* tradition developed by the creativity of the author of Matthew's gospel. The camels that our imaginations have assigned, in the tradition, to the wise men actually came out of Isaiah 60, on which I suspect Matthew built major portions of his birth narrative. In Isaiah 60 kings were said to have come to the light, to the brightness of God's dawn (v. 4). They came on camels (v. 6) and, not coincidentally, they brought gold and frankincense (v. 6). No myrrh was mentioned in this Isaiah chapter, but that text did say that kings also came from Sheba (v. 6). It was the Sheba reference that immediately sent the scribe who created Matthew's story back to a search of his biblical sources to read an earlier account in which another royal visitor came to pay homage to another king of the Jews. The queen of Sheba's visit to King Solomon (recorded in 1 Kings 10:1–13), revealed that she too traveled with camels and that she came bearing spices. "Never again did spices come in such quantity as that which the queen of Sheba gave to King

Solomon," said the text (1 Kings 10:10). The most popular spice in the Middle East was myrrh, a fragrant resin found in various shrubs and trees in south Arabia that was used in perfumes, in beauty treatment, in the scenting of clothes, and in embalming. So it was that among the first stars from the infinitely rich cast of Jewish characters to make guest appearances in the birth narrative of Jesus were Isaiah, Solomon, and the queen of Sheba. They are in the background of the story of the magi, and apart from them, the magi become nonsensical.

Also in that account of the magi we meet Balaam and Balak (Num. 22–24). Their narrative was another ancient Jewish story of yet another figure who came to do the bidding of a king. From that narrative Matthew lifted the Star of David that he had rise in the east.

So Jewish eyes reveal that the star, the magi, the gifts were not original with Matthew. They all arose out of the Jewish scriptures on which Matthew depended when he wrote his gospel in the tradition of *midrash.*

A second appearance of Isaiah is found in the word "virgin." Both Matthew and Luke use this word, although only Matthew identified its Jewish source. The word came originally from an Isaiah text, "Behold a virgin shall conceive and bear a son, and his name shall be called Emmanuel" (Matt. 1:23, based roughly on Isa. 7:14). In Matthew's narrative, this text was actually revealed by God to Joseph in a dream (Matt. 1:20–24). The unique thing about this text is that the word "virgin" does not appear in the original Hebrew passage in Isaiah. It is simply not there! Matthew has developed an idea based on a concept that was not present in the original source Matthew was quoting. The word "virgin" did not enter the Book of Isaiah until it was translated into Greek some 500 years after Isaiah had written these words and some 200 years before the birth of Jesus. The translators chose the Greek word *parthenos* to translate the Hebrew word *almah. Almah* means a young woman in Hebrew. It never means virgin; the Hebrew word *betulah* was used for that. However, in the Greek word *parthenos* the concepts of young woman and virgin were merged. So it was only in the word *parthenos* that the connotation of virgin entered the reading of Isaiah. That, however, did not deter Matthew, who built his whole narrative around this mistranslation. He probably never checked the original Hebrew. Though Luke borrowed the virgin idea from Matthew, he made no reference to the determining text. Perhaps Luke was aware of its destroying weakness. Early Jewish leaders also called this anomaly to the attention of the Christians, but to no avail. The Christians were ecstatic with their discovery and heady about their power. They were like the person who exclaimed, "My mind is made up. I do not want to be confused by the facts." But in the word "virgin," Isaiah (albeit a translated Isaiah) made yet another appearance in the birth narratives.

Solomon appeared a second time, at least in echo, in Luke's reference to the baby Jesus being wrapped in "swaddling clothes." Swaddling clothes (or cloths, to be more accurate to the Greek text), along with the manger, were the key identifying marks the angels gave to the shepherds. "Ye shall find the babe wrapped in swaddling clothes and lying in a manger" (Luke 2.12 KJV). I use the King James Version here because the Revised Standard Version loses the power of the symbol by translating "swaddling" as "bands of." However, the Greek word found in this text is the clue to locating its biblical antecedent. So, once again, armed only with that word, we search the rich heritage of the Jewish sacred story in order to find and understand its significance. This search leads us to the apocryphal book known as the Wisdom of Solomon, in which Israel's wealthiest and in some ways most powerful king had observed, "I was nursed with care in swaddling clothes, for no king has had a different beginning of existence" (Wis. 7:4, 5). So Jesus, who was believed by the author of Luke to be the ultimate king of the universe, was portrayed as coming to this world in a way reminiscent of Israel's most resplendent king. He came at his birth in the garb of swaddling cloths.

Luke's reference to a manger brought the prophet Isaiah once more into the birth narrative. This would be Isaiah's third appearance in the Christmas stories. This manger proved to be a

rich addition to the later Christian imagination. The word translated as "manger" literally meant crib or feeding trough. From
this single word, over the centuries the story of the stable populated by various animals has entered our imaginations and our
tradition. Pictures have been painted and songs have been sung
that include the animals in the stable in the rich tapestry of nativity celebrations. But those stable animals are like the camels.
They are the products of our human creativity. There were no
animals in the stable in Luke's gospel, primarily because there
was no stable. This is hard for people to believe until they are
forced to read the gospel text in search of either the nonexistent
stable or its nonexistent animals. Despite the inevitability that
every schoolchild will tell you that Jesus was born in a stable
surrounded by animals, the fact remains that these familiar elements of the story are the products of our fantasy. There was
rather but one word in the text—the word "manger"—and
around this single word the idea of a stable filled with animals
has been built. For our purposes, however, we need to recognize
that the concept of the manger was another *midrashic* gift from
Isaiah to the developing Christmas tradition.

In the first chapter of Isaiah, the prophet bemoaned the fact
that "the ox knows its owner and the donkey its master's crib
[or manger], but Israel does not know, my people do not understand" (Isa. 1:3). The people of Israel, said Isaiah, simply did
not know the God who was their master. They did not even recognize that they were fed each day from the crib of God's
bounty. So Luke, leaning on this text from Isaiah, decided that
the Christ who was, for this writer, the embodiment of the true
and faithful servant of God, and who was, even more, to be
identified ultimately as God's son, God's complete revelation,
must be placed into the master's crib or manger at his birth so
that at least the ideal and representative Jew could be said to
know the God to whom this manger/crib belonged. So Isaiah is
yet again present in this *midrashic* drama of Jesus' birth as
Matthew and Luke were creating it.

King David came next across this Jewish stage, accompanied
by another prophet, whose name was Micah. "For to you is

born this day in the City of David" was the message of the angels (Luke 2:11). The manger from the Book of Isaiah had been
placed in David's city, and into that manger the new king was to
be found, wrapped in the swaddling cloths that were said to
have surrounded King Solomon. David, recall, was a shepherd
boy called from his pasture land in Bethlehem to be the King of
Israel. In the developing life of the Christian Church, David
would prefigure the one who would become the Good Shepherd
unto whom all those who travail and are heavy laden would be
said to come. Since David had been a child of Bethlehem, so the
folklore of the Jews had proclaimed that the messiah who would
arise from the line of David, who would be a branch from Jesse,
David's father, also had to be born in Bethlehem. It was the
prophet Micah who had put this Jewish expectation into writing. "But you, O Bethlehem Ephrathah, who are little to be
among the clans of Judah, from you shall come forth for me one
who is to be ruler in Israel, whose origin is from old from ancient days" (Mic. 5:2). Bethlehem was also the place where
something called the Migdal Eder, the tower of the flocks, was
located. This tower, which was said to have helped in the guarding of the sheep, was mentioned twice in the Hebrew scriptures
(Mic. 4:8 and Gen. 35:21). Those two references, together with
the memory of David as the shepherd boy, helped to create the
familiar nativity scene that portrayed shepherds keeping watch
over their flocks by night, near the city of David, in the narrative
written by Luke. So David and Micah have now joined Isaiah,
Solomon, the queen of Sheba, Balaam, and Balak as heroes from
the Jewish past who practically dance across the stage in the
midrashic birth stories of Jesus of Nazareth.[1]

With this Jewish lens through which we have begun to view
the stories of Jesus' birth, we now turn and look backward to the
narrative of the birth of John the Baptist, with which Luke
opened his gospel. There we discover cameo appearances in the
text by other Jewish heroes like Abraham, Sarah, and Isaac.
John's birth, like the birth of Jesus, was also a wonder, Luke asserted. No, it was not the wonder of the supernatural birth resulting from the operation of the Holy Spirit on the Virgin Mary

that was said to have produced Jesus as God's son in some physical, biological way. It was, however, a supernatural birth that required divine intervention to reverse the processes of nature. That is to say that John's birth was miraculous, but it was not of the same magnitude of miracle as was the birth of Jesus. The parents of John the Baptist were old. They were beyond the childbearing age. Conception would therefore require an act of God.

That kind of conception had happened before at another critical point in Jewish history, and we have already noted it in the chapter that revealed Luke's dependency on Genesis. In that story of Abraham, it appeared that God might not make good on the divine promise to create of Abraham and Sarah a nation of people more numerous than the stars of the heavens or the sands of the sea. Abraham had reached the ripe old age of 100, said the biblical text, and his wife, Sarah, was ninety. "It had ceased to be with Sarah after the manner of women" (Gen. 18:11), said the author of Genesis in his rather delicate description of the postmenopausal reality. But God intervened by sending an angelic messenger who spoke to Abraham to assure him that God would act to give him not just a child, but a son. "Is anything too wonderful for the Lord?" this story concluded (Gen. 18:14). So Sarah conceived and in her old age "bore Abraham a son," as God had spoken. The child, Isaac, was the fruit of this divine action. The incredible manner of Isaac's birth signified that a new chapter was about to begin in the history of the people of the covenant.

This Abraham/Sarah/Isaac story was picked up and retold by the author of the Gospel of Luke, and it formed the background to the story of Zechariah and Elizabeth, the parents of John the Baptist. Their child, like Isaac, was to be a sign that a new chapter was about to begin in the history of the people of God.[2] So in the story of Zechariah and Elizabeth, the ultimate parents of the Jewish nation, Abraham and Sarah, were recreated. They emerge with their son, Isaac, out of the Hebrew past to join the list of Jewish stars who are allowed to play their *midrashic* roles in the drama of salvation that Luke was describing in the story of Jesus' birth.

The angelic messenger who brought to Abraham the annunciation of Isaac's birth was nameless. Luke, however, has leaned upon the post-Exilic development of angels in Jewish thought to make his story more angel specific. So Luke named the angelic messenger that he had appear to Zechariah in the Temple. His name was Gabriel. That name enabled Luke once more to journey back into the Hebrew tradition to find details with which to embellish his story of the angelic visitor. In this manner the prophet Daniel entered the Christmas story.

In the eighth, ninth, and tenth chapters of Daniel, the angel Gabriel appeared by name for the first time in biblical literature. This heavenly being came to Daniel at a time of prayer, just as Luke had him do to Zechariah (Dan. 9:21, Luke 1:10). Indeed, Luke had developed his narrative in such a way as to suggest that Zechariah was in the most sacred place possible. Zechariah had been chosen by divine lot to offer the incense in that portion of the Temple known as the Holy of Holies. It was while he was about this duty that his prayers were interrupted by Gabriel. Both Daniel and Zechariah were petrified in their respective stories (Dan. 10:8, Luke 1:12). Both received the angelic message in their fear. Both were reassured by the angel (Dan. 12:10, 11 and Luke 1:13). Both were left without the ability to speak (Dan. 10:15, Luke 1:20). Both narratives ended with a song that pointed to a fulfillment yet to come when "a king of bold countenance shall arise. . . . who will grow strong in power" (Dan. 8:23, 24) or "when he has raised up a mighty savior for us" (Luke 1:69). This segment of Luke's story closed with it being said of John the Baptist that he "grew and became strong in spirit" (Luke 1:80). Surely this narrative from Daniel has also shaped Luke's story of the visit of the angel Gabriel to Zechariah. So Daniel is now joined to the growing cast of Jewish stars who play across the stage on which the birth tradition of Jesus was being developed.

One might think that this would be a sufficient collection of ancient Jewish heroes with which to populate the birth story, but the surface of the *midrashic* tradition has only just begun to be scratched. We are to meet still others before this drama is complete. Those who deny the *midrashic* influence on the writing of the gospel narratives must find some new way to explain this overpowering reality once awareness of it is born. Those who are not knowledgeable about the heritage of Judaism, out of which the gospels flow, will never understand, so they will read these birth accounts without the key that unlocks their meaning. For the birth stories of Jesus are not remembered biographical details related by either Mary or Joseph as the unlearned tradition of the past once asserted. They are rather the rich *midrashic* weaving and reweaving of the sacred moments of the Jewish past around the life of Jesus of Nazareth in whom the original Christian community, which was composed predominantly of Jewish people, had come to believe that God was at work anew. This process revealed the growing connection among these original Jewish Christians that the divine presence was once more in human form. In time their experience would lead them to assert that this divine presence in Jesus was both unique and complete. So watch as other Jewish heroes emerge in the drama.

John the Baptist, said the Gospel of Luke, came "with the spirit and power of Elijah" (Luke 1:17), and suddenly this figure from the Jewish past is before us. John the Baptist came to be identified with the messenger of the Lord "who will prepare your way" (Mark 1:2) and as one who was the voice "crying in the wilderness" (Mark 1:3, Luke 1:4). The first reference was from Malachi (3:1) and the second was from Isaiah (40:3). Malachi went on to identify his messenger with the prophet Elijah, whose task it was to prepare the world for the coming of that "great and terrible day of the Lord" (Mal. 4:5). The word "Malachi," by which this last book of the Old Testament has come to be known, was not the name of the author of this book as was the case in the other prophetic works. The title of this book, Malachi, is rather a Hebrew word which meant "my messenger" (see Mal. 1:1). So Malachi, "my messenger," was identified as the nameless one, who came in the spirit and power of Elijah to prepare for the advent of the Kingdom of God. All of this went into the task of shaping the account of John the Baptist in the Christian story. Just to make sure that this point was not missed, John the Baptist's appearance was described in the gospels to coincide with the appearance of Elijah. John was "clothed with camel's hair," wearing "a leather belt around his waist." He emerged like Elijah from the desert, and he ate a desert diet of "locust and wild honey" (Mark 1:6, Matt. 3:4). In the Hebrew scriptures that shaped this story of John the Baptist, it was said of the prophet Elijah that "he was a hairy man with a leather belt around his waist" (2 Kings 1:8), who lived in the wilderness (1 Kings 17:1–4). The locusts that accompanied the wild honey as the diet of the desert were also kosher, declared the Book of Leviticus (11:22). John was thus created or, perhaps more accurately, shaped to be the Elijah type messenger and forerunner. John became the life that the Christians believed was foretold in the story of the nameless messenger who wrote the book we call Malachi. So Elijah and Malachi join the cast of Jewish characters that parade across these gospel narratives of Jesus' birth.

John's parents were said to be named Zechariah and Elizabeth. Are those names real? Or are they chosen deliberately to send a *midrashic* message about who this John was and what his role in salvation history, as the Christians understood it, was to be? Names were vitally important in the *midrashic* tradition of the Jewish people. Names sent messages. Names embodied proclamations. So now we raise the question and possibility that the names Zechariah and Elizabeth were deliberately chosen for their *midrashic* capability. If that is so, then what would those meanings be? So we turn once more to the scriptures of the Hebrew people to explore those sacred stories with our imagination freed to embrace new ideas.

There were a number of Zechariahs in the Hebrew sacred texts, but one of these was clearly powerful and influential in the development of the Christian story beyond all others. This was the author of the prophetic book that bears the name Zechariah. Texts from the Book of Zechariah appear again and again in the gospel tradition. This book, as was the book we call Isaiah, was written by more than one author. Chapters 1 through 8 of the prophet Zechariah reflect a period of history perhaps 100 years earlier than chapters 9 through 14. In chapters 1 through 8, a priest named Joshua, who was described as "anointed by God," was the religious leader of the nation (Zech. 4:14). Not only were Joshua and Jesus the same Hebrew name, as we have noted on many occasions, but the words translated "anointed one" and "messiah" came from the same Hebrew roots. So early Christians who were also Jewish expositors of the scriptures might look at these texts as overwhelming proof of a place in which the scriptures were fulfilled in Jesus of Nazareth. Joshua the anointed one would be read as Jesus the Messiah. Of this Joshua/Jesus, for example, it was said that God set before him a single stone with this inscription upon it: "I will remove the guilt of this land in a single day" (Zech. 3:9). Echoes of the developing Christian idea of Jesus as God's atoning sacrifice were seen by Christians in this text. Other references to this portion of Zechariah were seen in the account of the transfiguration which we have already noted.[3]

The latter portion of the Book of Zechariah (9–14) closed with the anticipated return of the Lord of Hosts to the Temple in Jerusalem to inaugurate the Kingdom of God (Zech. 14). An Elijah-like figure, it was said, would prepare the way. This note was then picked up in the next book of the Bible, the aforementioned Malachi. Again, the messenger who prepared the way for the Lord was called Elijah (Mal. 4:5). When the Lord comes he will, said Malachi, "purge the worship of Israel. He will purify the sons of Levi [the order of priests] till they present right offerings to the Lord" (Mal. 3:3). Only then, asserted Malachi, will my name be "great among the nations," from "the rising of the sun to its setting" (Mal. 1:11). This newly emphasized note in Malachi simply reaffirmed an earlier note from Isaiah, who wrote of the Temple, "My house shall be called a house of prayer for all people" (Isa. 56:7).

Please keep in mind that Malachi, the nameless messenger, as just noted, had been identified early in Christian history with

John the Baptist. The immediate predecessor in the Bible to the Book of Malachi was Zechariah, which pointed toward the message of Malachi. Why not capture this truth by using the name Zechariah for the father or the immediate predecessor of John the Baptist? Since the Messiah to whom the Elijah/John the Baptist figure was to point was destined to claim the Temple for all people, why not also place the father of John in the Temple for the moment in which he received the angelic message? It was too tempting a possibility to be ignored, and it fit the *midrashic* tendency to use names to convey messages.

But what about John the Baptist's mother, Elizabeth? What could that name reflect that would cause it to be chosen? It was a rare name among the Hebrew people. There was only one Elizabeth in the Jewish sacred story other than this mother of John the Baptist. And even that one was spelled differently in Hebrew, making the connection a bit more difficult to make. The other biblical Elizabeth was called Elisheba. She was the wife of Aaron, Moses' brother and the first high priest of the Jewish nation. Aaron occupied that position from Israel's days in Egyptian slavery to its birth in the Promised Land as the Jewish state. Aaron thus was revered as the one who established the priestly tradition in Israel. The Levites, who gave order to the liturgical life of the nation and of the Temple, were the spiritual children of Aaron.

Aaron, his brother Moses, and his sister Miriam were important figures both for good and ill in the wilderness years. Aaron crafted the golden calf for the people when Moses was delayed on his mountain rendezvous with God in search of the Torah (Exod. 32). Miriam was portrayed as the one who stood watch over the baby Moses as he was nestled in a basket amid the bulrushes on the Nile River to escape the purge led by the pharaoh (Exod. 2:1–10). She was the author of the Song of Triumph sung on the eastern side of the Red Sea (Exod. 15:20 ff.). She also led a rebellion against her brother Moses and was supported in this rebellion by her brother Aaron (Num. 12). She was a far more significant figure than her sister-in-law, Elisheba. It must be noted that the Hebrew name Miriam would be written Mary in

Greek. In Luke's story Mary was a far more significant figure than Elizabeth, who Luke called Mary's "kinswoman" (Luke 1:36). Indeed, the suggestion that John the Baptist and Jesus were kin, perhaps even "cousins," as John Wycliffe first suggested in the fourteenth century, rests totally on this one word, "kinswomen," in Luke's birth story. Was that word a Lucan hint that he was crafting his story on a theme from the Moses family history? He started with the name Mary, the name by which Mark had identified Jesus' mother in the second Marcan scriptural reference to her (Mark 6:1–6). Relating that name to other Marys/Miriams in the Hebrew sacred story, he happened upon the account of Miriam, Moses' sister, who had a kinswoman named Elizabeth/Elisheba. Then he fleshed out his narrative by making the new Elizabeth a member of a priestly family, a tradition that descended from Aaron, who was married to the first Elizabeth/Elisheba. He then topped this off by portraying the relationship of Mary and Elizabeth after the analogy of the relationship between Miriam and Elisheba. If they were sisters-in-law, then their offspring would be first cousins. There is certainly enough data here to provide a meaningful fit in the *midrashic* tradition. So the galaxy of Jewish stars continued its parade through the birth stories of Jesus and was now joined by Zechariah, Moses, Aaron, Miriam, and Elisheba.

The birth narratives of Jesus were not even yet finished with this task of providing material that would reveal Jewish heroes making guest appearances, but we will pause here, before continuing in the next chapter, just to reflect on what I hope is an eye-opening new view of a tiny portion of the material we call Gospels.

Can you not see how rich reading the gospel with Jewish eyes can become? Perhaps on an even more poignant note, can you not see how the anti-Jewish bias of the ages has impoverished the Christian Gospels even for the Christians? Can you not grasp the excitement that comes when eyes are opened to see these birth stories as they were intended to be seen by the Jewish authors who crafted them so carefully? Can you not imagine that if all these dimensions lie hidden in this small segment of gospel material, how much more there will be when we can read the entire New Testament through the lens of Jewish eyes? But for now, just gaze at these birth stories whose Jewish content we have just begun to understand, and embrace the fact that there is available to us a significantly different way to read the Gospels, as soon as we have accepted the fact that they are Jewish books.

12

Joseph

The Shadowy Figure

Have you ever wondered about Joseph? He was that strong, silent male who stood guard over the manger and is portrayed in the traditional crèche scene at Christmas. He has been the subject of such Christmas hymns as "Joseph dearest, Joseph mine, help me cradle this child divine." He starred in the medieval song called "The Cherry Tree Carol," in which he expressed his doubt about Mary's virtue. In this case, when Mary requested Joseph to gather her some cherries, he replied with some feeling, "Let the father of the baby gather cherries for thee!" The cherry tree, however, responded to this attack on Mary's virtue by bowing low to make its cherries available to her without Joseph's assistance, and Joseph was filled with remorse. W. H. Auden's Christmas oratorio, "For the Time Being," also plays on the theme of Joseph's doubt and his internal debate about what it means to be a cuckolded husband.[1] Through the ages, many images have circulated around this figure.

When I ask a group of adults in a church setting to tell me whatever they know about Joseph, the answers are predictable. Typically, they include such data as he was a carpenter, he lived in Nazareth, and he was kind and just. There is also a sense abroad that Joseph was an older man, and perhaps that he died before Jesus was grown. Sometimes other bits of tradition are present in their memories, such as the story of his flight to Egypt with Jesus and that Joseph seemed to have had lots of dreams. Some add further that perhaps he was previously married so that Jesus might have had some half brothers and sisters. Separating truth from fantasy, legend, and developing tradition is not always easy.

In order to set the stage, let me first go to the texts of the Bible and lay out the data about Joseph that is sometimes hidden in that book. First, Joseph was not mentioned in any of the writings of Paul. That proves very little, but it is a fact. It is also a fact that Mary, the mother of Jesus, was not mentioned in the Pauline corpus either. The only Mary that Paul mentioned appears to be a member of the congregation at Rome. Of her, Paul wrote that she "has worked hard among you" (Rom. 16:6). But there is no hint that this Mary was the mother of Jesus, and there is not even a legendary tradition that located Jesus' mother in Rome. At the very least, we can state that to the degree that Paul represented Christianity in the fifth, sixth, and seventh decades of this common era, there was no interest in Jesus' origins or his parentage at that stage in the development of the Christian story.

Second, Paul's writing gives us no indication that he had ever heard of or had any interest in the miraculous birth traditions. As we have already observed, Paul stated in a very matter-of-fact way that Jesus, like everyone else who enters this world, was "born of a woman" (Gal. 4:4). He also said that Jesus "was descended from David according to the flesh" (Rom. 1:3). Further-more, Paul referred to James as "the Lord's brother" in his epistle to the Galatians (1:19). There is no reason to think that the use of the word "brother" *(adelphos)* here meant anything other than a literal blood brother. Yet, despite these obvious and human refer-ences, Paul clearly believed that God was in this Christ "reconcil-ing the world to himself" (2 Cor. 5:19). Reading Paul makes it quite apparent that this early Christian had no trouble affirming the lordship and the divine nature of this Jesus and that he did so without any reference either to Jesus' family of origin or to the possibility that he had a sibling. The clear assumption that these data suggest is that the legends that came to surround Jesus' birth had simply not been born by the time Paul did his writing. With-out these legends, please recognize that there was no need to pro-vide Jesus with an earthly father or to explain any unusual circumstances that hovered around his origins.

The mystery thickens when we come to the next biblical fact, namely that the first gospel to be written, Mark, also makes no mention of Joseph in any verse of its text. Yet it is in this gospel that, for the first time in Christian written history, we are given some slight biographical data about the family of Jesus.

In the first Marcan reference to Jesus' family, we learn that on one occasion "the mother and brothers" of Jesus came to him when he returned to Nazareth (Mark 3:31–35). It was not a friendly visit, for this gospel writer had said earlier that when his family heard some things about him, they went to seize him, for people were saying, "He is beside himself" (Mark 3:21). This phrase, "beside himself," was a colloquial Semitism that meant literally "outside himself" or "out of his mind," and it described a severe mental disturbance. His harsher critics, said Mark, were suggesting that Jesus was demon-possessed (Mark 3:22). In this story Mark said that Jesus rebuked his family; for when he was told that his mother and brothers were outside asking for him, he said, "'Who are my mother and my brothers?' and looking around on those who sat about him, he said, 'Here are my mother and my brothers! Whoever does the will of God is my brother and sister and mother'" (Mark 3:33–35). The tone of this passage was negative, even disinheriting. Surely, a woman who had undergone a virgin birth would not have had doubts about the mental health and mental balance of that offspring! The virgin tradition was clearly one of which Mark did not know. But for the purpose of the Joseph inquiry, it needs only to be noted that in this first gospel reference in the New Testament to the family of Jesus, there was only a mother, who was nameless, and brothers, who were also nameless. No earthly father had yet been mentioned anywhere.

A bit later in Mark's narrative, the second reference to the family of Jesus was chronicled (Mark 6:1–6). In this passage, for the first time in the Bible, we learn that his mother's name was Mary, and that the names of his four brothers were James, Joses, Judas, and Simon. We also learn that he had "sisters." It was a plural word in the text, which implied that there were at least two. The sisters, however, being female, were not deemed important enough in this patriarchal society to be given names. But still there was no reference to a father, much less a father named Joseph. Indeed, that name at this moment had not yet been heard anywhere in the Christian story that we can today identify. Mark, for one, displayed no evidence that he even knew of the existence of such a person.

Even more fascinating in this segment of Mark's gospel are two additional pieces of data that later Christian legendary development seemed simply to ignore.

First, in this second Marcan reference to Jesus' family, Mark referred to Jesus as "the carpenter." "Is not this the carpenter?" the crowd asked. That biblical fact is simply not present in the conscious mind of the popular Christian tradition, so please note it and let it register: in the first gospel to be written, not only was there no mention of Joseph, but also it was Jesus who was identified as the carpenter! The portrait that most of us have in our minds of the boy Jesus assisting his father in Joseph's carpentry shop is simply not supported by the first gospel to be written.

Second, in this same passage, Jesus was called "the son of Mary." This was the way in which the name of Jesus' mother entered the Christian tradition. Furthermore, only in these two passages of Mark's gospel was the mother of Jesus mentioned at all. We need to have it register that neither of these original gospel references to Jesus' mother was flattering. Both place her into a relationship of tension with her son. So it is fair to say that Mark, the first gospel writer, accorded the mother of Jesus no status. He did not place Mary at the scene of the crucifixion, nor did he locate her at the tomb of Jesus on Easter day. He certainly did not honor her as a special receptacle of God's divine favor. There was also a hint of scandal in the phrase that this second Marcan passage used when it referred to Jesus as "the son of Mary." To call a Jewish man, in this era, the son of a woman was to suggest that his paternity was in question or at least unknown. That scandalous note would be heard again in the later gospels, the most noteworthy reference being found in a verse in John where an angry crowd hurled an enigmatic charge at Jesus in the words, "We were not born of fornication" (John 8:41). The assumption present in the tone of this comment was that in the minds of the crowd perhaps Jesus was born of fornication. Please note that in neither Mark nor John, where these scandal-tinged words are heard, was there a narrative of a miraculous birth that might temper, at least for the readers of these gospels, the hints of illegitimacy that echo in these two texts. These verses remain in the New Testament as unsuppressed clues to an early battle that clearly centered on the legitimacy of Jesus' origins. At some point after Christians fought off charges based on the scandal of the cross, they clearly had to fight off charges based on the scandal of the birth.

When we put together the earliest data available to us in Christian written history, we discover that Paul seemed to think Jesus' birth was normal, that he was "born of a woman" and that "according to the flesh" he was descended from David. Mark, who appeared to know of no birth tradition, miraculous or otherwise, had only two references to Jesus' family, both uncomplimentary. If Mark was our only source for knowledge of Jesus' family of origin, we would know only that he had a mother named Mary, four brothers, and at least two sisters and that not one of them was portrayed as being particularly supportive of Jesus. We also have to observe that there was no father anywhere in this gospel and the only Joseph ever mentioned in Mark's corpus was Joseph of Arimathea, who appeared in the burial narrative. This is the only material available to us from Christian written history until we come to the ninth decade of this common era. For most people, so sure that the legends and traditions that they have recited and heard so often were the original notes in the biblical story, these elementary biblical facts alone constitute a remarkable realization. It is fascinating when people actually begin to read the text of the Gospels and to see how many of the blanks in the story have been filled in, not by scripture, but by imagination.

To continue compiling biblical facts, we turn our attention next to the later gospels of Matthew and Luke. Here we become aware that Joseph never appeared in either of these gospels outside the stories of Jesus' birth. No narrative about the adult Jesus ever included Joseph. Take away from Matthew and Luke the birth stories, including the story of the boy Jesus being taken up to Jerusalem at age twelve, and Joseph disappears from those gospels. So Joseph appeared to play a role on the stage of these gospels only as a character solely identified with the late-developing miraculous birth tradition. Outside those birth stories, Joseph was not even referred to by name in either gospel. On the single occasion in Matthew where a reference was made to the father of Jesus, it was not by name, but rather by inference. That came in a text where Matthew edited a Marcan passage to change the original meaning and to make the Marcan text compatible with Matthew's birth story.

We mentioned that Mark had two stories about Jesus' family in the corpus of his gospel. We also know that Matthew had Mark in front of him as he wrote and that he used Mark extensively. So it becomes of great interest to see how Matthew would relate to the two rather negative Marcan references to the family of Jesus, since Matthew had begun his story with a picture of Jesus' family experiencing his supernatural birth and receiving the gifts of adoring magi. After such experiences, a hostile family would be all but impossible to imagine.

The first Marcan family reference Matthew simply omitted. Since he actually omitted as few as sixty verses of the entire Gospel of Mark, that omission itself becomes significant.

The second family reference in Mark Matthew changed deliberately and provocatively. In Mark's gospel the crowd, seeking to understand the power they had experienced in this Jesus, said incredulously, "Is not this the carpenter, the son of Mary?" As we noted, there was a tinge of scandal in these words. They certainly would not do in a gospel that had already explained Jesus' divine origins and where a father had already been installed in the family circle. So Matthew changed these words: Where Mark had written, "Is not this the carpenter?" Matthew changed it to read, "Is not this the carpenter's son?" Mark's designation of Jesus as "the son of Mary" was changed by Matthew to read, "Is not his mother called Mary?" It was a bit of editorial genius. With just a few slight changes, Matthew had placed a father who was a carpenter into the narrative. (We already know from the birth narrative in Matthew that this father was named Joseph.) He had removed the hint of scandal. He had transformed the negativity between Jesus' family and himself. But because we have the original Marcan text, we can see Matthew's changes as a skillful redaction that enabled his earlier account of Jesus' birth to be in harmony with this family episode. From this single Matthean editorial addition has come the image of the earthly father of Jesus being a carpenter, and pictures of Jesus helping his father in Joseph's carpentry shop entered the world of medieval art. Joseph was not as major a figure in Luke's birth narrative as he was in Matthew, and some of his adventures in this account, we have noted previously, were patterned after Jacob's adventures in the Book of Genesis.[2]

When we turn to John, we discover once again that Joseph, the father of Jesus, never appeared as an actual character in the narrative of this gospel either. He was, however, referred to twice in the corpus of this tenth-decade book. Both of these Johannine references simply called Joseph the father of Jesus, with neither embarrassment nor explanation. The first Johannine reference to Joseph is found in the conversation between Philip and Nathaniel, in which Philip said, "We have found him of whom Moses in the law and also the prophets wrote, Jesus of Nazareth, the son of Joseph" (John 1:45). The second reference was placed into the mouths of critical Jews who were murmuring against Jesus because in their minds he was claiming a divine origin. So John quoted them as saying, "Is not this Jesus, the son of Joseph, whose father and mother we know?" (John 6:42). For the Fourth Gospel, which has no birth story in its pages to suggest otherwise, Joseph was assumed to be the father of Jesus. Yet the fact remains that Joseph never appeared in this gospel except by these two oblique references to his name.

So, building on our growing base of biblical facts, we need to embrace the reality that not one appearance, other than a reference to his name, was made by Joseph in any episode in any gospel from the adult life of Jesus. Almost everything we know about Joseph comes out of the birth traditions of Matthew and Luke.

For now, file in your mind the fact that the birth stories, which did not come into being until the ninth decade of the Christian Era, are the entire source of our knowledge of the shadowy figure of Joseph. This means that since Joseph appeared nowhere in Christian writings before the ninth decade, he was clearly neither an original nor an early part of the Christian story. So a new, and for some disturbing, question begins to invade our consciousness. Was Joseph a legendary character developed by the tradition to fill in an enormous blank in the story that existed as the virgin birth tradition was developed? Was he a fictitious character created first by Matthew and then incorporated by Luke? That possibility becomes larger and more focused as these data accumulate.

We turn now to the earlier of the two birth stories in Matthew with a question of new intensity. If the author of Matthew's gospel created the character of Joseph, did he do it out of the thin air of his fertile imagination? That may appear to us to be a possibility, but that was not the Jewish style. It was rather the tradition of a Jewish scribe like Matthew to search the sacred texts of his faith tradition for material on which he could draw when he wrote a new chapter in the sacred story. If he had come to believe that Jesus was a new revelation of the ancient God of the Jews, he would seek to relate Jesus to his Jewish roots. Matthew also wanted to expand the boundaries of his Judaism so that this faith tradition might acknowledge as its own the life of this Jesus in whom, to him, God was so clearly present. So Matthew introduced Joseph in the birth stories by pulling together many of the symbols of the rich Jewish past.

Who was Joseph for Matthew? He was "the husband of Mary of whom Jesus was born who is called Christ" (Matt. 1:16). He had a father named Jacob (Matt. 1:16). He was "a just man and unwilling to put her to shame" when he discovered her to be "with child." So he resolved to "divorce her quietly" (Matt. 1:19). He was the recipient of divine messages through his dreams (Matt. 1:20, 2:13, 2:19, and 2:22) and in one dream he was addressed by the angel as "son of David" (Matt. 1:20). The divine origin of Mary's baby was revealed to him in his dream. Even the exact biblical text for which this virgin birth was a fulfillment was revealed to him in his dream (Matt. 1:22, 23)! The name by which this baby was to be known was also revealed in a dream (Matt. 1:21). He was warned in a dream to flee to Egypt in order to save the child's life (Matt. 2:13). He was ordered to return from Egypt in a dream (Matt. 2:20). Finally, he was warned in a dream not to remain in Judea, but to withdraw to Galilee (Matt. 2:22). Each action, the virgin birth of Jesus, the flight into Egypt, the return, and the choice of Nazareth as a home, was done in order "to fulfill what the Lord had spoken by the prophet," and the scriptural allusion was implied, driving readers into the Hebrew texts (Isa. 7:14, Hos. 11:1, Isa. 11:1 or 4:3, Judges 16:17).

The only other detail worth noting from this portrait drawn by Matthew was that Joseph was portrayed as always obedient to the divine instructions. "He took his wife" (Matt. 1:24), "he rose and took the child and his mother by night and departed to Egypt" (Matt. 2:14), "he rose and took the child and his mother to the land of Israel" (Matt. 2:21), and "he went and dwelt in a city called Nazareth" (Matt. 2:23). Finally, the Matthean text asserted that Joseph did not "know" his wife "until" she had borne a son (Matt. 1:25). It was a verse that clearly did not anticipate the future doctrinal development of Mary's perpetual virginity. The Hebrew and Greek word translated "know" carried the connotation of sexual intimacy. The Hebrew scriptures said, "Adam knew his wife, Eve, and she conceived" (Gen. 4:1).

With the birth narrative complete, Joseph disappeared from Matthew's gospel save for that single reference that was a redactional insert into Mark to which I previously referred.

Before Matthew wrote his gospel, the name of Joseph had never been mentioned in connection with the story of Jesus' origin. The Joseph that we meet in Matthew is always responsive to the direction of a text from the Hebrew scriptures. So we are forced once again by our data to ask some increasingly obvious questions. Is it possible not only that Matthew invented Joseph, but also that we can discern the Jewish *midrashic* methods that he employed to accomplish this literary task? If we can admit that possibility for just a moment, two additional major concerns need to be addressed. First, what scriptural basis was there for his choosing the name Joseph? Second, what features in the life and character of Matthew's Joseph can be identified in the story of other Josephs in Hebrew history that might have colored his portrait? In order to enter this Jewish exercise in the creation of a sacred story, we need first to imagine Matthew the scribe poring over the Hebrew scriptures in search of clues that this Jesus was in fact the promised Messiah of Israel, foretold and spoken of in the scriptures and in the prophets.

There were, first of all, still present among the Jews—after all these centuries of life and death, war, conquest and defeat—the ancient divisions between north and south, between Galilee and Judea, between the sons of Joseph and the sons of Judah. Judah, according to the New Testament, was of the tribe of Israel through whom the promise of God was to be fulfilled (Matt.

1:3, Luke 3:33). That was more a reflection of history than it was the law of primogeniture, since Judah was not the first born of Jacob/Israel but was rather his fourth-born son (Gen. 29:31–35). But the tribe of Judah became the most powerful tribe, and it was this tribe that produced King David and the whole Davidic royal line. It was in large measure the loss of the Davidic line in the sixth century B.C.E. during the Babylonian defeat and Exile of Jewish history that caused the birth of the ideal messiah king to enter first the folklore and then the mythology of this people. A king "like unto King David" had to be of the royal line, and therefore this messianic figure would be from David's tribe of Judah. He had to be born in the city of David's birth, Bethlehem, a tradition that undoubtedly shaped the birth narratives that Matthew in large measure created. So it was that Joseph, the earthly father of Jesus, had to be a son of David. But Jesus also clearly hailed from Galilee; he was known as a Galilean, as a Nazarene, and as Jesus of Nazareth. Since Galilee was the vestigial remains of the Northern Kingdom, and the Northern Kingdom had been predominantly the tribe of Ephraim, who was the son of Joseph, this part of Jesus' background needed also to be recognized. So Jesus was of the royal line of David through the tribe of Judah, said Matthew, but he was also a son of Joseph and emerged out of the people of the Northern Kingdom. So first of all we need to note that Jewish history was well served in the choice of this name for Jesus' earthly father.

Second, in the writing of the book of Chronicles, which at least one New Testament scholar in the United Kingdom regards as a *midrashic* rewriting of the books of Kings,[3] the teachers and scribes had wrestled with the issue of primogeniture. So they addressed the question of why the royal line had not come through Reuben, the first born of Jacob/Israel, and secondarily what was the relationship between Judah and Joseph and their respective tribes in this matter of royal succession. In that passage (1 Chron. 5:1–2), the Chronicler argued that Reuben was denied the birthright because "he polluted his father's couch" and "his birthright was given to the sons of Joseph." The Chronicler went on to say that "though Judah became strong among his brothers and a prince [David] was from him, yet the birthright belonged to Joseph." So Matthew may have begun his creation of the person called Joseph in the certainty that the scriptures had given the birthright of the messiah to Joseph, and he symbolized this by choosing this name for Jesus' earthly father. By making this Joseph a son of David and thus of the house and tribe of Judah, he wove together all his themes.

A second, and in my opinion even more convincing, argument may have been developed in Matthew's further searching of the scriptures, this time in regard to the name Jesus. Names in the Jewish tradition reflected both one's character and one's role or destiny in the drama of salvation. He was named Jesus by the angel, said Matthew, for "he will save his people from their sins" (Matt. 1:21). The name Jesus, which is a Greek spelling, lent itself to that interpretation. This name, when written in Hebrew or Aramaic however, became Yeshuah or Joshua and meant "God is salvation." Joshua/Jesus was not an uncommon name in Jewish circles, but there were only two Joshuas who played important roles in Hebrew history; so we now turn to examine these two figures of history for clues as to the interplay between the names Joseph and Joshua/Jesus in the birth narratives.

The best-known Joshua in the Hebrew scriptures was the successor to Moses, who fought the battle of Jericho and who led the Israelite conquest of Canaan. Since the early Greek-speaking Jews would have read the book of Joshua in the Greek Septuagint version of the Hebrew scriptures, we need to be aware that in that version, Joshua would be spelled Jesus. So ancient references to one named "Jesus" were scanned with particular interest by early Greek-speaking Jewish Christians. Connections between the Joshua who succeeded Moses and Jesus are easy to identify. Joshua fulfilled the promise of that for which Moses had prepared the way, just as Jesus fulfilled the promise of that for which John the Baptist had prepared the way. Joshua created extended daylight in order to accomplish his purposes (Josh. 10:12–14). Jesus, having accomplished his purpose, caused darkness to reign over all the earth as he died (Matt. 27:45,

Mark 15:33, Luke 23:44) and then became the source of eternal light and was called "the light of the world."[4]

But of even greater significance for our purpose, it must be noted that this first Joshua/Jesus was a descendant of the tribe of Joseph, who was given an inheritance in Ephraim (the son of Joseph) and who was buried in Ephraim (Josh. 19:49–50, 24:30). So if the ancient Joshua/Jesus of Jewish history was a son of Joseph, why not tell the story in such a way that the latter-day Joshua/Jesus might also reflect this heritage and, without compromising the claim that Jesus was of the royal line of Judah, make certain that he was also known as a son of Joseph?

The second Joshua/Jesus of significance in the Hebrew scriptures was less well known. He was a priestly leader of the post-exilic period of Jewish history and was mentioned in Zechariah (1–8) and in Haggai (1:2). This Joshua and his co-ruler, the political leader named Zerubbabel, were called in Zechariah God's "anointed ones" (Zech. 4:14). The words "anointed one" carried with them the connotation of messiah or Christ, for the Hebrew word *mashiach* from which both the words "messiah" and "Christ" were derived literally means "the anointed one." So a biblical reference to "Joshua, the anointed one" in the book of Zechariah, when read in the Greek translation, would be very close to "Jesus the Messiah or Christ." There is much that could be said about the influence of the book of Zechariah on the early developing shape of the Christian story,[5] but for my purposes now, I simply want to note that the second major Joshua/Jesus who appeared in the Old Testament had a father whose name was variously spelled Jozadak, Jehozadak, Jose-dech, and Josedek. I submit that this is too close to Joseph to be ignored. So the two primary biblical figures in Jewish history who bear the name Joshua/Jesus were both related to a paternal figure named Joseph or to a variation on that name. When these facts are added to the suggestion in 1 Chronicles that the "birthright" belonged to Joseph, the case becomes firmer. These Hebrew sacred traditions could have constituted sufficient justification for the author of Matthew's gospel to add his bit to the fulfillment of the scriptures by suggesting that the earthly father of Jesus, who was called Christ, would be named Joseph.

Once the name was chosen, then the character of the man had to be created. Matthew did that in chapters 1 and 2. Joseph was, said Matthew, a just man who was planning to abide by the directions of the Torah, and, rather than submit his betrothed either to shame or to execution, he sought a more compassionate alternative. A text in Deuteronomy (22:23–25) suggested that a betrothed virgin who was violated in the city should be executed, but a betrothed virgin violated in the country should be spared. The difference in proscriptions was related to the fact that in the city one could cry for help and be heard, but cries for help in the countryside would be in vain, for no hearers were likely to be near. In this latter case, the betrothed would be returned to her father's house as "damaged goods" and the marriage canceled. It was that understanding of the Torah that Joseph appeared to be following in Matthew's story, and this was what presumably made him a "just" or "upright" man and fed his reputation for kindness. Joseph was a wronged man who did not seek justice or revenge.

That was also true of the major Joseph in Hebrew history, whose story was told in Genesis 37–50. He did not seek revenge on his brothers who had wronged him. Recall that this was the Joseph of the "coat of many colors," the Joseph who was handed over to gentiles by his brothers. Joseph, after some hazardous experiences that resulted in his incarceration, then rose to power in Egypt and ultimately saved both his brothers and his father, Jacob, from death by bringing them down to Egypt to live in the land of Goshen. The method this Joseph used in his rise to power was his ability and reputation as an interpreter of dreams. He interpreted the dreams of the pharaoh's butler and his baker, and indeed of the pharaoh himself. This was not a new Egyptian-developed gift in Joseph's makeup, for the original hostility that his brothers felt for him was a direct result of Joseph's ability with dreams. In his boyhood dreams, we are told, Joseph portrayed his brothers as bowing before him under a variety of symbols (Gen. 37:19). When his brothers conspired to kill him, they said of him, "Here comes the dreamer" (Gen. 37:19). So dreams were deeply associated with Joseph the patriarch.

I would suggest that it was in these various elements of this ancient biblical portrait of Joseph the patriarch that Matthew found the inspiration on which he built the character of Joseph that he placed into his birth narrative. Embrace the similarities! Both the Joseph who was the earthly father of Jesus, as Matthew created him, and the Joseph who was the patriarch of ancient Israel had fathers named Jacob. Both Josephs had lives and careers marked by dreams, and both Josephs played dramatic roles in salvation history. Joseph the patriarch had saved the People of the Covenant from death by taking them down into Egypt to live. Matthew's Joseph saved from death the child of promise who came to establish the second covenant by taking him down into Egypt to live. Surely that was not coincidental, but was rather the result of the Jewish *midrashic* technique of opening the scriptures so that Jesus could be seen as the fulfillment of the law and the prophets.

When the time came in Matthew's narrative for Jesus to be brought home from Egypt, the angel said to Joseph in a dream, "Those who sought the child's life are dead" (Matt. 2:20). When God spoke to Moses in Midian to send him back to Egypt to deliver his people from bondage, the text used these words: "For all the men who were seeking your life are dead" (Exod. 4:19). This textual similarity served Matthew's later task of identifying Jesus with Moses in a *midrashic* manner.

Before closing the Joseph story, let me state that Luke disagreed with some of Matthew's details about Joseph. It is not my intention to trace those disagreements in great detail,[6] but I will lift into a concentrated glance the disagreement over the name of Joseph's father, for it illustrates beautifully the principle that I am seeking to develop.

Matthew had stated, as we have noted, that the father of Joseph was named Jacob (Matt. 1:16), but Luke maintained that the father of Joseph was named Heli (Luke 3:23). It is only with Jewish eyes that sense can be made of this disagreement.

Luke patterned his story of Jesus' birth out of different *midrashic* sources from within the Hebrew scriptures. In Luke's account of the Annunciation to Mary, in his recording of Mary's song that we call the Magnificat, and in the description of the boy Jesus going up to the Temple in Jerusalem, we have three unique narratives that are peculiar to this author alone. Luke's sources for these traditions, however, appear to be largely drawn from the Jewish story of Hannah and Samuel (1 Sam. 1–3). God, through a priest, announced to Hannah that she would have a child (1 Sam. 1:17). To that annunciation Hannah had replied, "Let your maid servant find favor in your sight" (1 Sam. 1:18). God, through an angel, had announced to Mary that she would have a child. Mary responded, "Be it unto me according to your will" (Luke 1:38). Hannah's song, which begins, "My soul exults in the Lord and my strength is exalted in the Lord" (1 Sam. 2:1–10), is dramatically akin to the song that Mary sang, which began, "My soul magnifies the Lord and my spirit rejoices [exults] in God my savior" (Luke 1:46–55). Hannah and her husband took Samuel to the Temple in Jerusalem when he was of age (1 Sam. 1:22), just as Mary and Joseph took Jesus to the Temple when he was twelve (Luke 2:41–50). Recall that in the Samuel story, the old priest who promised the birth of the child Samuel to Hannah was the same priest whom Samuel served in the Temple. His name was Eli. He was of an age to have been Samuel's grandfather. So Luke, continuing to lean for his details on the Samuel material, made the father of Joseph, or Jesus' grandfather, bear the name Eli; but since he did it under the Greek spelling, Heli, few people grasp that connection quickly. It was another clear *midrashic* use of ancient sources by the gospel writers and signals rather loudly that we are not dealing with history in these gospel narratives. We are, in fact, dealing with *midrashic* interpretations by Jewish people seeking to process their experience of God in Jesus of Nazareth in a traditional Jewish way.

I suspect that Joseph, the husband of Mary, never existed. That to me is a better explanation than his early death to account for the fact that Joseph never appeared in any adult story of Jesus. Joseph, I believe, was a product of a *midrashic* Jewish use of their sacred scriptures that created a narrative out of the Jewish past to interpret biblically the meaning of the presence of God that had been met and experienced in Jesus of Nazareth. The concern of Jewish writers was not to relate biographical facts, but to interpret within the framework of their faith tradition the meaning of the experience that they had with the living God. So Joseph as Jesus' earthly father, patterned after the Joseph of the book of Genesis and symbolized by the fathers of the two major Joshua/Jesus figures of Hebrew history, entered the Christian story in the ninth decade from the pen of the Jewish/Christian scribe who wrote the book we call Matthew. Had there been no gentile captivity of the Bible, it would not have been the dawn of the twenty-first century before these obvious *midrashic* details were brought to the consciousness of the average Christian. Nor would these details, once enunciated, seem so radical and so new to either the biblically illiterate or to the biblical literalists of our day.

The question still remains: Who was Jesus' father? The only honest answer is that we do not know, and we cannot find out short of an inquiry in the Kingdom of God.

What is important is to discover the experience that caused people to assert, that in some way that was beyond their ability to doubt, they believed that they had met the holy God in and through the life of Jesus of Nazareth. They were convinced that this "God presence" was quite frankly beyond the capacity of human beings to create. So it was that through a myriad of different images, they sought to explain just how this "God presence" got into Jesus of Nazareth. It happened at the resurrection, said Paul (Rom. 1:3, 4). It happened at the baptism, said Mark (1:9–11). It happened at his conception, said Matthew (1:23) and Luke (1:31–32). Jesus was the eternal Logos, or Word of God, enfleshed, so the "God presence" was always his, said John (1:14). It is the experience of the God presence that is important, not the explanation of the God presence. So the Jewish people who had met this presence in Jesus searched the Hebrew scriptures seeking to make sense out of this reality. But we Western, non-Jewish, gentile Christians literalized the explanations because we did not know how to appreciate Jewish books written in a Jewish style and employing Jewish methods. When we develop Jewish eyes with which to read the Gospels, much of that difficulty will fade away.

13

How the Virgin
Birth Tradition Began

We have now examined from several angles the birth tradition of the New Testament. We have seen how these stories were constructed. We have identified both the contradictions and the *midrashic* elements found in these narratives. We have stated the conclusion of the vast majority of New Testament scholars that these lovely and provocative narratives cannot be literalized and that, indeed, that was never their purpose.

But these conclusions raise some brand-new and rather fascinating questions. If the virgin tradition was not placed into the Christian story because it was literally true, then why was it placed there at all? What did it mean? How did it manage to get attached to the life of Jesus? What was its journey? Where did it originate?

It is not enough just to point to the number of virgin births that floated in the religious legends of the Mediterranean world. Nor is it an adequate explanation to suggest that the Christians simply adapted one of those accounts to heighten the Jesus story and to explain what they perceived as his divine origins. That explanation might be partially true, but we still must face the fact that many other traditions can be found in the religious legends of the Mediterranean world that were not incorporated into the Christian story. So why this one in particular? Such an inquiry sets us off once again to explore the Jewish story that lies hidden underneath the texts of the Gospels.

Blocking our way into what lies beyond the words of scripture are first the great superstructures of piety and theology that Christians have constructed over the centuries on top of the virgin birth tradition. These superstructures have been identified in the common mind for so long with the essence of Christianity that tampering with them or the foundation stone on which they stand is an emotional and frightening task to some. In Roman Catholic circles, both the devotion that has been focused on the Virgin and the development of the various Marian doctrines, such as the immaculate conception, the perpetual virginity, and the bodily assumption of the Virgin, seem to imply a literalism about the virgin birth that we now know the biblical texts will not support.

In Protestant circles it came to be believed that the very claim of divinity for Jesus and his status as the Son of God required the literal historicity of the virgin birth stories. This claim has been defended vigorously through the centuries, despite the fact that the most divine portraits of Christ to be drawn in the New Testament came from the pens of Paul and John, neither of whom appear to have acknowledged the supernatural aspect of Jesus' birth or to have believed in this tradition of a literal biological divine origin. In the case of Paul, he appears not to have heard of it. In the case of John, he appears to have denied it.

So our first task is to recognize that an analysis of the texts from the stories of Jesus' birth will not support the later doctrinal development. Mary did not, as ancient piety has suggested, confide the secrets of Jesus' birth to her physician, Luke. Nor was Joseph the source of the unique details of the Matthean narrative.

But once again, this simply begs the question of the original need, the original intention that caused some person or persons in the early Christian tradition to decide that the narrative of a virgin birth could be adapted to the story of Jesus of Nazareth. So into the dark recesses of that pre-gospel tradition of the Christian Church we now venture.

The virgin tradition, I would argue, came out of the natural development within the Christian story and arose for two primary reasons. First, there was the *midrashic* attempt to read the Hebrew scriptures in terms of the Jesus experience. Second, there was a need to create an apologetic protective wall behind which to defend the origins of Jesus as attacks from the traditional circles of conservative Judaism began to increase in negativity and intensity following the destruction of the Temple in that fateful year of 70 C.E. Let me trace each of these elements in a bit more detail.

Explaining the power of the Jesus experience, putting the reality that came to be called the resurrection into rational words, was the critical task of the first generation of Christian people. They believed that, in some dramatic and profoundly real way, they had met the Holy God in the life of this Jesus and that the death of this Jesus did not put an end to that experience. How does one put that into words? How does one explain just how it was that God had come to dwell in Jesus?

Turning first to Paul, we observe that his task was far more to proclaim than it was to explain. He was content to state that God was in Christ. He did not seek to explain how it was that this divine presence got there. He wrote his deepest faith convictions: "I am sure that neither death nor life . . . will be able to separate me from the love of God in Christ Jesus, our Lord" (Rom. 8:38). Despite the fact that Paul did not seem to know of a birth tradition, in his later epistles, Paul did ascribe to Jesus some preexistent status. In Philippians we get the sense of Jesus as God's divine emptying (Phil. 2:5–11). In Colossians and Ephesians, neither of which is universally ascribed to the authorship of Paul, we get a sense of the cosmic Christ on a divine mission from God to redeem and restore the creation, but never was there a hint that these affirmations compromised the humanity of Jesus or created the necessity for a supernatural point of entry into the human arena (Col. 1:15–20; Eph. 1:9, 10, 2:14, 15). Indeed a much stronger case could be made that the writings of Paul took what later came to be called "adoptionism" as his explanation. That is, because Jesus did the reconciling work of God's agent, God adopted him into heaven, gave him a name above every name, and made bowing in reverence at the name of Jesus an appropriate stance for worshipers (Phil. 2:5–11). In Paul's mind Jesus came to be identified with God's first creation, whose task it was to put all things in subjection under his feet, and then the reconciling son would himself be subject to God the Father (1 Cor. 15:27–28). Any suggestion that the Jewish Paul was a trinitarian thinker is to write a massively revisionist bit of theological history. Particularly is this so since the classical doctrine of the Holy Trinity did not get fully formulated until the fifth century C.E.[1]

In the most overt reference to these convictions, Paul placed together some words that became, I believe, determinative in the development of a later miraculous birth tradition. Paul wrote to the Romans (1:4 ff.), God "designated" Jesus as the *"son of God* in power according to *the spirit of holiness* by his *resurrection from the dead"* [emphasis mine].

So, in the mind of Paul, Jesus was declared or designated to be *God's son,* a title used first in Jewish history to refer to the King of Judah or Israel (see Ps. 2:7, 72:1). The declaration was made by the *spirit of holiness,* a vague Pauline concept that would later evolve into the third person of the Trinity and be called "the Holy Spirit." But for Paul it was the spirit of God that animated life and that was seen in the analogy of the wind *(ruach)* and thought to be similar to the breath *(nephesh)* that God breathed into Adam at the dawn of creation. Again, it is terribly important that later trinitarian language not be read back into Paul. Finally, we note that this declaration of the sonship of God as the meaning of Jesus came at the time of "his resurrection from the dead." It was the Easter experience that forced on Paul and the early Christians the necessity of answering the questions, "Who is this Jesus?" and "Whence comes his power?" Those were the same questions we are told later in Mark that the crowd was asking when echoes of the debate about his origins began to be heard in the later gospel tradition (Mark 6:1–6). That, however, is to get a bit ahead of my story. For now, let me simply note that, for Paul, God designated Jesus "his son," that God did it by "the spirit of holiness," and that the time of this designation was the resurrection. Paul wrote his epistle to the Romans no earlier than 53 C.E. and no later than 58 C.E., so this was the stage of the debate, as reflected in Paul in the sixth decade of the common era, or some twenty-three to twenty-eight years after the crucifixion.

We move now to Mark, which was written a little more than a decade after Paul's letter to the Romans, and perhaps as long as five years after Paul's death. Mark opened his work with the claim that his story was the gospel of "Jesus Christ the Son of God" (Mark 1:1). One could hardly write of Jesus as the Son of God in the first verse of one's book and then postpone the announcement of how he became the Son of God until the end of the story. So Mark dealt with this inconsistency by moving the proclamation of that divine origin to the beginning of his story. If Jesus was designated Son of God at the resurrection for Paul, then surely he was also the Son of God during his earthly life, even if no one recognized it. So Mark covered his problem in two ways. He wrote his story, accounting for the lack of understanding in both the disciples and the world by saying that Jesus wanted to keep his real identity a secret until the final dramatic Easter revelation. Therefore those who glimpsed Jesus' true identity were to tell no one, for his time had not yet come (Mark 7:36, 8:30, 9:9). In this way Mark could account for the behavior of the disciples, whom he was to picture as betraying, denying, and forsaking the Son of God. It was because his identity was a secret, Mark was arguing, so that even his disciples did not understand.

The second way that Mark dealt with this issue was to move the divine designation of Jesus as God's son from the resurrection, where Paul had located it, to the inauguration of Jesus' public ministry. For Mark, that inauguration was not the birth of Jesus, but the baptism of Jesus. So this first gospel opened with the story of Jesus coming to John the Baptist at the waters of the Jordan River. But please observe how each of the Pauline elements was incorporated into Mark's baptism story. At the baptism, God designated Jesus to be God's son. In that Marcan episode, the heavens were split so that the divine voice could be heard. Paul only asserted that God was the designator of the divine nature of this Jesus. Mark, however, expanded this narrative by including the actual words God used when that divine designation was proclaimed, "You are my son, the Beloved; with you I am well pleased" (Mark 1:11). This content, in typical *midrashic* form, was actually lifted out of the ancient Jewish scriptures. The words were taken from Isaiah (42:1) and from the Psalms (2:7). The tradition, enriched and augmented by the *midrashic* principle, was growing.

Furthermore, we can find the meaning of Mark's words by searching out the context in the Hebrew scriptures from which they were taken. Isaiah 42 was the first time the figure who came to be called "the Servant" or "the suffering Servant" emerged on the stage in Jewish history. This figure was clearly used again and again in the developing Christian story, as we shall see in subsequent chapters.[2] So Mark has begun this part of the christological interpretive process.

Psalm 2:7 was reflective of the development that took place in Jewish thought between the time when titles like "the Son of God," "the anointed one," and "the messiah" were given to the earthly King of the Jews and the time when the King of the Jews did not exist except in either memory or fantasy. The Davidic royal line began with the coronation of King David (ca. 1000 B.C.E.), and it ended in the destruction of Jerusalem at the time of the Babylonian exile (ca. 598–586 B.C.E.). After this time, when no human occupant was sitting on the Jewish throne, the Jewish people began to dream of that ideal king who would someday restore the throne of David and who would inaugurate anew the Kingdom of God. In time this messianic figure was transformed in Jewish fantasy and in Jewish prayers to a divine and even a preexistent figure. From the writing of Daniel (ca. 165 B.C.E.) on, the messiah was identified as the Son of Man, who sat at God's right hand and who rode on the clouds of heavens (Dan. 7:13, 14). This apparently supernatural figure would, at the end of time, be God's agent in establishing the new heaven and the new earth. So these words from the Psalms, along with these references from Daniel, were added to the developing interpretation of the Jesus experience. One can see that Mark was in fact expanding the original Pauline declaration dramatically.

In Paul the divine designation was made "by the spirit of holiness." So Mark, not content just to give narrative content to the declaration in Paul, now proceeded to develop Paul's "spirit of holiness" into a much more specific entity or being, called the Holy Spirit. When the heavens opened at Jesus' baptism, the spirit descended like a dove and rested on Jesus. It was then that the heavenly declaration was made (Mark 1:9–11).

Please note what happened as the tradition developed. First, the divine designation by God was given content. Second, the defining power of the *midrashic* use of ancient texts had been applied to Jesus. Next, the spirit of holiness had become the Holy Spirit, a presence of God and from God who could now act as a distinct entity. Finally, the moment that this divine declaration was made had migrated from the climactic end of Jesus' life, where it rested for Paul, to the inauguration of his public ministry, where it appeared in Mark. Even so dramatic an expansion as this would not be the place where the development came to rest.

When Matthew and Luke came to be written in the ninth decades, they introduced the birth tradition. Both of them seemed to say that Jesus' life, his divine sonship, and therefore his ministry began not with the resurrection, as Paul had suggested, and not with his baptism and the inauguration of his public career, as Mark had suggested, but rather with his actual human beginning, at the moment of his conception. Thus Matthew and Luke, in rather different ways, continued the development of the essential elements of the Pauline proclamation that God designated Jesus to be God's son by the spirit of holiness.

In Matthew the proclamation was delivered to Joseph by God in words spoken by an angel through a dream. The child is "of the holy spirit," the angel declared in this dream (Matt. 1:20). He was to be called Emmanuel, which means "God with us" (Matt. 1:23). In Luke the proclamation was delivered outside a dream by Gabriel, God's messenger, to Mary. The child "will be great and will be called the son of the most high, and the Lord God will give to him the throne of his father David and he will reign over the house of Jacob forever and of his kingdom there will be no end" (Luke 1:32, 33). In both stories "spirit of holiness" had been further developed into the Holy Spirit. This spiritual power or spiritual being was receiving firmer definition. The spirit had become somehow the source of life in conception, perhaps even the male agent, if you will. So all of the elements of Paul's announcement were present. The designation that Jesus was the divine Son was in these birth accounts, though once more the tradition has developed into a narrative form with content that filled in the blanks that were present in the earlier proclamations. The "spirit of holiness" was present in these narratives, though now not only in a much more concrete form but also on the pathway that would lead to its transformation into the Holy Spirit as a separate "persona" in a triune God. The major difference was the continued backward journey of this ultimate revelatory moment. What had occurred for Paul at the resurrection had migrated in Mark to the baptism, but now it had come to rest in the moment of conception for both Matthew and Luke. One would think it could go no further, but that would be not to understand the power of developing theology.

John, the last gospel to achieve written form, was dated at least five to six years at the shortest point, and fifteen years at the longest point, later than the gospels of Matthew and Luke. The author of this final gospel to be written began with the assertion that Jesus both came from God and had returned to God. His divine nature did not begin at resurrection or at baptism or even at conception. He was the Logos of God, present with God and in God at the dawn of creation (John 1:1–14). He was the word spoken by God in creation that caused the world to come into being (John 1:3). This word was "made flesh" and dwelt among us "and we beheld his glory; the glory of the only begotten of the father, full of grace and truth" (John 1:14).

The migration of this divine declaration about the source of Jesus' holiness was now finally complete. To trace that migration, however, does not end our search to understand how this virgin tradition came to be born as a part of the Christian explanation. So, to follow that story, I return now to the first biblical references to Jesus' family of origin[3] found in Mark in order to call to remembrance two details. In the first Marcan reference to Jesus' family of origin, we noted that only a mother, unnamed, and some brothers, also unnamed, were mentioned. In this narrative (Mark 3:19b–35), both the family and the scribes from Jerusalem were suggesting that he was "beside himself" or was actually possessed of the devil. This was the biblical context in which Jesus was pictured as beginning to talk about blasphemy against the Holy Spirit. He declared blasphemy against the Holy Spirit to be an unforgivable sin, an eternal sin. This, the text suggested, was because his critics were beginning to ascribe both the power of Jesus and his origins to the devil (Mark 3:23–35). This context makes it at least probable that, by the time Mark wrote, a requirement for membership in the life of the Christian Church had been established, which was the acknowledgment of the divine origins of Jesus. Membership in the body of Christ required that the origins of Jesus be recognized as holy, indeed as having been rooted in the power of the spirit. This community of faith had also begun to call itself the body of Christ.

Luke, writing in the Book of Acts some twenty-five years later, had suggested in his Pentecost story that the Church had been known since its birth as the community of the Holy Spirit (Acts 2:1–13). Entry into the Church was to be accomplished by being born of the Spirit, a phrase that is still used in evangelical and charismatic circles today. For one, therefore, to deny that Jesus, the Lord of this Church, was not born of the Spirit would be blasphemous.

Yet it is clear that these blasphemous attacks were already abroad by the time of Mark and that they had been launched by those whom Mark called "scribes from Jerusalem." The aim of these attacks was clearly to defame Jesus by pointing to his ill-defined origins.

We need to be aware that the Jewish tradition did suggest that base-born people frequently became religious agitators. "No bastard shall enter the assembly of the Lord" (Deut. 23:2), said the Torah. So perhaps what was really going on in this Marcan passage was an early expression of the charge of illegitimacy being leveled at Jesus. For this early Marcan gospel record to suggest that Jesus was "beside himself," to portray the mother and brothers of Jesus as trying "to take him away," was startling to the developing tradition. For Mark's gospel also to contain no mention of a father, earthly or otherwise, in its only references to Jesus' family laid the Christians open to the hint of scandal. When that same gospel referred to Jesus as "the son of Mary," it certainly added fuel to this fire for, as we noted earlier, that designation implied that there was no known father.

Other biblical sources, like the epistle to the Galatians, suggested that Christianity very early divided into two camps, one of which was headed by James, the Lord's brother, and was very orthodox and conservative. The other was headed by Paul, and it was open to such things as setting aside the absolute requirements of the Torah and allowing gentiles into the faith community (Gal. 1:2). This epistle revealed that Jesus was clearly a source of division and agitation even among the early Christians, to say nothing of his being a source of controversy among the Jews. Note that in these passages James, the Lord's brother, who according to Josephus was martyred before Mark's gospel was written, was portrayed in a very negative light and the Jerusalem Jews were viewed even more negatively. They were indeed blasphemous. So from a very early time, it seems likely that the Christian Church had to defend Jesus from attacks from traditionally observant Jewish circles, and these attacks centered on the sources of his power and thus on his origins. Was he of the devil, Beelzebub, or of God? Was he base-born or was he the child of the Spirit? Undoubtedly, such attacks raised questions of Jesus' paternity. But up to this moment, the question had not yet been addressed by a story that purported to demonstrate that Jesus' birth was at the instigation and by the power of the Holy Spirit. Such an idea was, however, clearly developing.

It is difficult to date with absolute certainty the writing of the epistle to the Hebrews, but there are those who argue persuasively for a date at least earlier than the Gospel of Matthew (80 C.E.–85 C.E.). In any event, this book appears to come out of an early and fairly Jewish period of Church history, or at least it was developed inside a deeply Jewish part of the Christian Church. Some have suggested that the epistle to the Hebrews was originally a homily based on Psalm 110.[4] It clearly portrayed Jesus as the sacrificial lamb of the Day of the Atonement. It had no specific concept of a resurrection, but focused strongly on what came to be called the exaltation, or the ascension. It suggested that Jesus had entered the heavenly realm in much the same way that the sacrificial animal went up to God on the smoke of the burnt offering (Heb. 4:14 ff., 9:12, 9:24). Jesus, in the Book of the Hebrews, would have been carried on the clouds into the heavenly realm as both the great high priest and the perfect offering.

Jesus was not, however, part of the regular priesthood of the Jews. So this epistle wrestled with how it was that Jesus could offer the perfect sacrifice. This query was answered with the help of a text in Psalm 110 (v. 4) that referred to the priesthood of one called Melchizedek. He too was not of the regular Jewish priesthood. Yet Abraham had, according to the Book of Genesis, acknowledged his priesthood by presenting to him tithes and offerings (Gen. 14:18). Levi, the father of the Jewish priesthood, had yet to be born, so he was carried, the tradition suggested, in the loins of Abraham. Levi, it was said, present in Abraham's seed, thus recognized the priesthood of Melchizedek. So a priest after the order of Melchizedek was the image that the author of Hebrews used to validate his claim for Jesus, who had entered the heavenly place to make intercessions on behalf of the people (Heb. 7:1-10, 15-19).

Melchizedek came out of nothing, said the tradition. He appeared in the Hebrew story and disappeared just as quickly. It was also said of him that he had no father or mother or genealogy (Heb. 7:3). The debate that centered on Jesus' origins and the Christian claim that he was holy and of the Spirit, was thus now joined with this suggestion in the epistle to the Hebrews that the ideal high priest, Melchizedek, after whom Jesus was modeled, had no human origins. The stage was thus set for the story of Jesus' miraculous birth to enter the tradition, and enter it did.

It came first in the work of Matthew, the most Jewish of the gospel writers. This author would use a miraculous birth story to counter the charges of Jesus' base birth that were abroad in conservative Jewish circles. He would demonstrate that those who called Jesus "the son of Mary," as if he were one whose paternity was in question, simply did not understand his origins. He would reject their charge that he was of Beelzebub by asserting that he was born at the initiation of the Holy Spirit. He would place that truth into a literal narrative that would support the words of Jesus that anyone who thought that his origins were base was in fact guilty of the unforgivable sin of blaspheming against the Holy Spirit.

So the story of the virgin birth, with its affirmation of paternity by the Holy Spirit, took shape in Matthew's mind, and "the carpenter, the son of Mary" in Mark (6:3) became "the carpenter's son whose mother is called Mary" in Matthew (13:55). But, as a Jewish scribe, Matthew had to be true to his scribal training. He needed to ground that assertion in the scriptures of his people. So Matthew, searching the sacred story of the Hebrew people to find a text on which he could develop his story of Jesus' holy origins, fastened on to a verse in the Greek translation of the Book of Isaiah (7:14). "Behold a virgin shall con-

ceive and shall bring forth a son and you shall call his name Emmanuel, which means 'God is with us.'" And so it was that the
virgin entered the Christian story. It did not matter to Matthew
that the word "virgin" was not in the original Hebrew text. It
did not matter that the historic context in which the words of
Isaiah were written was the siege of Jerusalem by the Syrians
and the army of the Northern Kingdom in the eighth century
B.C.E. It did not matter that the child in Isaiah who was to be
born to this woman was to be a divine sign that Jerusalem
would survive that particular siege and the life of the nation
would go on, as indeed it did. Matthew's task was to demonstrate to the critics of this Jesus who were attacking his origins
that they were so deeply in error that they were in danger of
placing themselves into a status beyond the possibility of forgiveness. They were guilty of calling that which was of the Holy
Spirit evil. They had actually confused God with Satan. It was a
powerful assertion and a provocative story. But few people
through the centuries were to recognize that the origin of what
came to be known as the Christmas story was born as a polemic
against those most conservative factions of Jerusalem Jewry
who sought to diminish Jesus' influence among the more open
Jews by asserting that he was base-born, illegitimate, of the devil
himself.

Luke developed the story without once referring to Matthew's
exceedingly problematic virgin text. Luke's added witness served
to solidify this tradition of a divine origin for Jesus, and so this
tradition began its journey through history. On that journey the
story of Jesus' birth, as we have noted, picked up other legends,
fantasies, mythologies, and folklore of the centuries and carried
them along with it.

Before closing this chronicle, it is important to recognize that
the virgin birth tradition suffered a momentary eclipse when the
Fourth Gospel appeared in the tenth decade. Perhaps this author
saw that the birth story had already been literalized, and he did
not want its essential truth lost in such nonsensical literal images. As we noted earlier, this gospel portrayed Jesus quite simply as the child of Joseph and Mary, but the theme of being born

in and of the Spirit was not lost by this writer. For John, Jesus had been born on two levels. He was born not just of the will of the flesh, but also of the Spirit (John 1:13). Indeed, his flesh became the vehicle through which his spirit was made known. So must everyone be, John argued, who comes into the Christian faith. The believer must be "born again." No, that did not mean to return to one's mother's womb to be born a second time, as Nicodemus, literalist that he was, seemed to believe (John 3:1–15). It meant that having been born as Jesus was, according to the flesh, one must also be, as Jesus was, born of the Spirit, born to the wonder and reality of God. Life in the Spirit was life that was whole, real, transcendent, and open. It was life through which God could be seen calling, healing, loving, and making all things new and whole. It was this life that Jesus came to bring.

The virgin birth story had a fascinating history of development. When the story was finally written, like all similar stories, it met its fate among the literalizers, and so its power was lost among those who do not understand myths as vehicles through which wordless truth can be conveyed. The meaning of this symbol, however, was and continues to be profound. In Jesus we have met a presence of God that human life alone could not have created. God has come among us offering life, love, and being to this world. Those who respond and accept the divine invitation to let this power be born in them as believers are to be introduced to the meaning of the Holy Spirit. In that Spirit we too are carried beyond all of our human limits into the wonder and transcendence of God. When we live in the realm of the Spirit, we know that the ultimate purpose of God was met in this Jesus, whom John quoted as having said, "I came that they may have life and have it abundantly" (John 10:10). For abundant life is always life in the Spirit that carries us into the timelessness of God.

14

He Died According
to the Scriptures I

We have already suggested that the story of Jesus' passion appears to be the first part of the gospel tradition to achieve written form. It was created to tell the story of the last days of Jesus against the background of the Jewish festival of Passover. It was this festival of Passover, I will now try to demonstrate, that shaped the narrative more than did the memory of objective eyewitnesses.

The Passover was one of three Jewish festivals that had to be celebrated in Jerusalem. The other two were Pentecost (Shavuot) and Tabernacles (Sukkot). The Jews were thus quite familiar with the tradition of going up to Jerusalem to celebrate a major festival. So the drama of Jesus' passion had to begin with his journey to Jerusalem, for that was the way all major Jewish festivals began. This parade was followed in Mark, Matthew, and

Luke by the story of the cleansing of the Temple. That story pictured Jesus in an unforgettable way. He had twisted a rope into a whip. He overturned the tables of the money changers. He loosed from their pens the sacrificial animals. Finally, we are told, he uttered the plaintive cry, "My house shall be called a house of prayer for all people, but you have made it a den of thieves."

Most people are not aware that the prophet Zechariah, the author of the next to last book in the Old Testament, after describing the festival of Tabernacles in his fourteenth chapter, closed his prophetic work by stating that when the Lord returned to inaugurate the Kingdom of God and to reclaim his Temple, "there shall no longer be traders in the house of the Lord of hosts on that day" (Zech. 14:21). Are we then dealing in this gospel story with the remembered history of a literal cleansing of the Temple? Or is this another example where a story from the Jewish past has been used to shape the presentation of the life of Jesus? This case is buttressed when we recognize that the words attributed to Jesus in this Temple episode are lifted directly out of the books of Isaiah and Malachi. Jesus does not appear to be terribly original. He simply quotes the prophets of old. Following this episode, there is in each of the gospels of Mark, Matthew, and Luke a strange chapter that described the end of the world, which we have already identified as reflecting the themes of the synagogue readings on the Sabbath before Passover. With the apocalyptic chapter complete, the real drama of the cross began with narratives of the act of betrayal, the last supper, the arrest, the trial, and finally the crucifixion. Surely, we think, in these traditions we are dealing with remembered history. The narratives are so graphic that they are riveted to our memories. Judas Iscariot is a name still used in our speech today whenever betrayal is experienced, whether it be in the world of religion, politics, or economics. The account of Peter's denial, the trial before Pontius Pilate, the mocking crown of thorns, and the various details of the crucifixion are all part of our remembered history. But have you ever stopped to realize that they are remembered primarily because they have been relived in the liturgy year after year? Is it possible that that is also where they started? Even the last words of Jesus from the cross have been preached on in three-hour services from so many pulpits that phrases like "My God, my God, why have you forsaken me?" "I thirst," and "Father, forgive them for they know not what they do" are etched into our memories. We also know, though perhaps in a more vague way, the story of Jesus' burial that featured Joseph of Arimathea, primarily because that burial story was closely linked to the familiar Easter tale of the visit of the women to the tomb of this Joseph on the "first day of the week."

So vivid are these details, so clear are the pictures they paint, that there remains a general consensus in both church and society that these stories surely were literally created from vivid eyewitness recollections. The assumption is made, without much internal debate, that what we read here are literal and historic facts. Indeed, to think otherwise for most church people is almost inconceivable. Yet that easy leap from familiar data to historic accuracy has been challenged increasingly in the last century, not by critics of the Christian faith who have abandoned organized religion in droves, but rather by the world of New Testament scholarship. Between the academy in which our clergy are trained and the pews in which our church members sit is a gap in knowledge of enormous proportions. Indeed, that gap might better be described as a void. To listen to the sermons of many clergy, one would have to conclude either that they did not learn what is readily available in the centers of theological study or that they have decided not to share it. Perhaps a better explanation might be that this generation of clergy, unable themselves to process what they have learned or unable to correlate it with what they themselves believe, decided simply to ignore or suppress this biblical scholarship for as long as they could. If that is a more accurate explanation, then maybe what we are facing today is that the time limit on that process of ignoring or suppressing biblical scholarship has now finally run its course. For many claims can be made about the passion story of the gospels, but claims of historical accuracy of literal facts are not among those that will stand.

I do not mean to suggest for a moment that Jesus of Nazareth was not in fact crucified by the Roman authorities. That indeed remains a fact of history. Nor do I even wish to suggest that some experience of incredible power did not occur after that crucifixion that had the effect of reconstituting the band of disciples and convincing them that this Jesus, the crucified one, was alive, was available to them, and perhaps most profoundly, was a part of who God is and who God has always been. That experience indeed broke into history with erupting, transforming, ecstatic power and gave birth to a movement that was destined to grow into the Christian Church and to wield enormous power in Western civilization. Whatever that transforming power we now call Easter or the resurrection was, it changed the course of human history in dramatic, measurable, objective ways. There is no doubt both that he was crucified and that after his death he was believed to have been restored to life.

But I do intend to say as powerfully as I can that the biblical descriptions of those originating moments in Christian history grew out of the liturgical practices of the early Christian Church far more than they did out of remembered history. Furthermore, I do intend to suggest that to a degree unimagined by the vast majority of contemporary Christians, most of the details of the story of the cross were shaped by Jewish worship patterns and by the Jewish sacred story of antiquity. Beyond that, I want it to be clear that what the Gospels give us in the passion story is far more a theological interpretation than it is a literal narration of the climactic moments in the life of Jesus. Finally, I intend to confront this massive misunderstanding of the Bible that permeates the religious establishment with an alternative view that will deliver the modern believer from the tyranny of literalism. Biblical literalism arises, in my opinion, out of a blindness that has been created both by an ignorance of and a prejudice against the Jewish origins of our Christian faith. Our biblical ignorance, I will suggest, is a direct result of the gentile attitude toward the Bible.

We are told in Mark, the first gospel to be written, that when Jesus was arrested, "all" of the disciples "forsook him and fled"

(14:50). A noticeable moderating influence appears in the later gospels to repair the reputation of the disciples and to temper that stark and original biblical reality that Jesus died alone, abandoned by all his followers. The need to explain this undoubted desertion was also well served by placing a text, once again from the prophet Zechariah, into Mark's passion story. "I will strike the shepherd and the sheep will be scattered" (Mark 14:27), Mark quoted the prophet Zechariah as saying. Even this less than admirable behavior of the apostles was understandable, Mark was explaining, because it was preordained. The Fourth Gospel picked up this same tradition of apostolic abandonment when this author had Jesus say, "The hour is coming, indeed it has come, when you will be scattered, every man to his own home, and will leave me alone" (John 16:32). This text suggested that the disciples, on Jesus' arrest, scattered separately, retreating to their own homes in Galilee. They were not around to view the crucifixion. This primitive understanding of the whereabouts of the disciples after the crucifixion informed the earliest version of the first Easter announcement. Recall that this announcement promised that the risen Christ would meet the disciples in Galilee, to which they had already fled! So the weight of these biblical texts indicates and reveals that primitive reality that in the final moments of Jesus' life he was alone, that he died alone, abandoned by his followers.

Now, for a moment, embrace the truth of that reality. Jesus died alone. Next, recall that the first written account of the last events in Jesus' life did not come into being for a minimum of thirty-five years after his death. By the time that this narrative was written down, the disciples were thought of as heroes, and heroes always have their embarrassing edges smoothed over by the passage of time. That would have been easy to accomplish, since by the time the Gospels came into written form all eyewitnesses had apparently passed away. A story that travels along a word-of-mouth route for thirty-five years usually abandons unpleasant or even irrelevant details. It also tends both to enhance and to exaggerate the more favorable accounts. So the fact that this negative portrait was still present, showing the unflattering behavior of the disciples who abandoned Jesus in the moment of their Lord's arrest and death, makes it ring with enormous authenticity. The disciples all forsook him and fled. Jesus died alone. When we can accept the reality of this fact on an emotional as well as an intellectual level, then we are forced to face the overwhelming probability that every detail in the biblical drama of the crucifixion is historically suspect. These are not the memories of eyewitnesses, for Jesus died alone. There were no eyewitnesses.

Now look at the gospel accounts of Jesus' passion. There we read of the arrested Jesus appearing before the Jewish council in an extraordinary late-night setting. We are even told what the high priest said to Jesus and the exact words with which Jesus responded. We are told what the high priest did, tearing his clothes and condemning Jesus for blasphemy. We are told that some of the members of the Jewish Council spat on Jesus and struck him while others mocked him with the shouts of "prophesy!" If the disciples had all forsaken him and fled, and if Jesus died alone, who or what was the source of all of these verbatim conversations and intimate details?

We are also told what the soldiers did to Jesus, what the bystanders said about him and to him. We are told of his conversation with Pilate. Once again, the actual dialogue is recorded. We are told the exact words with which Pilate spoke to the crowd and the exact words with which the crowd responded. We are told who bore Jesus' cross, what time he was crucified, how long he lingered, and what he said from the cross to the soldiers, to the crowd, to the penitent thief, and to the nonpenitent thief. We are told what others, including a centurion, said to him or of him. Since he died alone, abandoned by all his disciples and friends, I wonder why it has not occurred to us to ask who recorded these verbatims and who kept alive these intimate details. Did Pilate or Annas, Caiphas or the centurion, take notes and later put them into the hands of Mark, Matthew, or Luke? In a former age, it was even suggested that perhaps the risen Christ was the source of these details, that he had filled in these blanks in the narrative so that they were capable of being re-called later by the leaders of the Church. No one, however, today advances that theory with any seriousness. Indeed, no ex-planation is generally given today, for these questions are no longer raised by anyone. They have sunk beneath the horizon of our consciousness. They are the victims of those who take the words of the Bible literally and who do not want to hear any other possibility. So difficult is it for many Christians to face these issues and to recognize that these are not eyewitness ac-counts, that fearful Christians today have become part of what might be called "the conspiracy of silence."

But in an age of secularism, when the fires of faith and belief burn weakly, these questions must be raised and faced. For to view these narratives as literal history now stretches credibility to the breaking point. Please understand what this means. I am suggesting that all of the details of Jesus' last days, other than the fact that he was crucified, were unknown. So the Christian community created, after the fact, these narratives that now sur-round the story of the cross. They based these narratives on their newly developed understanding of Jesus as the paschal lamb of the Passover, who broke the power of death. I am fur-ther suggesting that the primary purpose of these stories of Jesus' passion was liturgical, not historical, and that they have been misread as the historical descriptions of literal events by the non-Jewish Christian world for far too long. The literal de-tails of the passion narratives are not descriptions of historically objective events. They were rather dramatic liturgical portrayals of the final moments of one who has already been acknowl-edged as Lord and Savior. When one reads the Gospels with Jewish eyes, it even becomes apparent that in the passion narra-tives, the evangelists were not writing history. They were rather writing faith stories to be read in the context of the worship life of the gathered community. These stories were created to pro-duce a memorable dramatic tale that would portray liturgically the essence of what they had come to believe about the man Jesus. They expressed the Christian conviction that God had been met in the life of this Jesus. That realization had dawned on them with startling power in the moment of Easter, and then it had, over the years, been read back into the memory of Jesus' earthly life. So the Gospels are not biographies. They are a series of faith proclamations. If read as biographies, they quickly become nonsensical.

The key to the understanding of this gospel portrayal of Jesus is twofold, and both insights require an understanding of things Jewish. First, the death of this Jesus had been interpreted, processed, and associated quite early in Christian history with the Jewish celebration of the Passover and shortly after that with the Day of Atonement, Yom Kippur. Both observances featured a lamb. The paschal lamb of Passover broke the power of death. The sacrificial lamb of Yom Kippur took away the sins of the people. The meaning of both lambs was quickly applied to Jesus. Paul's suggestion in 1 Corinthians, written ten to fifteen years before the First Gospel, "that Christ our paschal lamb has been sacrificed" (1 Cor. 5:7) made the Passover connection. His words that Christ died "for our sins" (1 Cor. 15:3) made the Yom Kippur connection. Both connections were clearly in place in the first generation of Christians. By the time of Paul, the death of Jesus, like the death of the paschal lamb and the death of the lamb of Yom Kippur, had already come to be seen as providing the benefit of destroying death and bringing salvation for the people who were believers. That was the faith commitment proclaimed in the liturgy of the Christian Church, but that faith commitment was not revealed in some fact of objective history.

Second, once this faith conviction was born, it was understood as an expression of the fact that Jewish people now identified the holy God of their sacred history as the presence they were meeting in Jesus. This was the realization that opened these first Christians to the enormous Jewish interpretive process. Now what they believed they were experiencing in Jesus could be understood and narrated through the lens of their sacred scriptures of antiquity, for there was a timelessness in the God who had been met in the history of this people. Paul's phrase from the aforementioned passage in Corinthians (1 Cor.

15:3) that Jesus not only died for our sins, but he died "in accordance with the scriptures," indicated that this typically Jewish method of using the scriptures had already been adopted by the first Christians in order to process their life-changing revelation. So we must begin to be aware that when we read the gospel story of Jesus' passion and death, we are not reading history. We are not even reading eyewitness accounts. We are not reading informed memories. What we are reading is a Jewish liturgical and *midrashic* interpretation of the reality of God that Jesus was believed to be as that reality broke into the human consciousness of believers. We are reading an interpretation of how this Christ affected the lives of those Jewish people who became the first Christians, and how it was that they came to understand that experience.

The shape and meaning of the biblical words that we possess are far more symbolic and liturgical than we have imagined. The content that is found in the gospel stories comes quite directly from the Hebrew scriptures in a manner far more overwhelming than most Christians have yet been able to conceive. The truth of this gospel story lay in the impact of his life, not in the liturgical or *midrashic* details that gathered about him. To get to this experience of God breaking into human history, we have to take these interpretive details quite seriously. We have to walk through these narratives that sought to explain the experience, but we cannot stop with these details nor can we assume that these narratives possess literal or objective truth. To literalize or even to debate the accuracy of these details of the biblical account of Jesus is to miss the point of the gospel story totally.

The drama of the end of Jesus' life began with the familiar account of Palm Sunday. We have celebrated this event on the Sunday before Easter for so long that we assume that this was where it actually happened originally. Each of the gospel writers has told us the story of that triumphant entry to the holy city of Jerusalem at the end of the winter season during the Jewish month of Nisan, which normally began in mid-March. But the details of that story do not fit that late-winter designation. We learn from Mark, written between 65 C.E. and 70 C.E., that the crowd waved leafy branches to hail Jesus' arrival in Jerusalem (Mark 11:8). In Matthew the text was altered slightly so that these leafy branches were called just "branches" cut from the trees (Matt. 21:8), but the presumption was that they were still thought to be leafy, for one does not normally speak of waving leafless sticks. Luke, probably suspecting a problem in this narrative, omitted from his Palm Sunday story all references to branches, leafy or otherwise (Luke 19:36). He rather had the crowd lay down their clothes along the pathway of Jesus. Strangely enough, it was not until John was written in the tenth decade that the suggestion that these were "branches of palm trees" (John 12:13) entered the tradition. Up until that moment, the palms that we tend to think are the heart of the Palm Sunday tradition had not ever been mentioned in this Christian story.

To put this data into a context of time and place, we need to note that there were no leafy branches in March (Nisan) in the land of the Jews, so this story begins immediately to totter if read in a literal time sequence as a prelude to Passover. Once we have embraced that anomaly, then we might move on to inquire if the waving of leafy branches while walking in a religious procession was a mark of any other identifiable Jewish liturgical observance. If we just take off our gentile blinders, we can discover that the great popular fall harvest festival of the Jews called Tabernacles, or Booths (Sukkot), had as one of its characteristic motifs the activity of pilgrims walking around the altar in the Temple in procession while waving a bundle of greenery made up of the leafy branches of willow, myrtle, and palm trees. This bundle of greenery was called a *lulab*. While those branches were being waved, the liturgy of Tabernacles called for the worshipers to chant the words of Psalm 118, which was the traditional psalm of that fall festival. This psalm proclaimed "Hosannah," which means "save us," "blessed is the one who comes in the name of the Lord" (Ps. 115:25–26). Suddenly, one has the procession, the waving of green branches, and the actual words attributed to the crowd that have been written into the Christian Palm Sunday narrative. But among the Jews these symbols were not the marks of the spring festival of Passover. They rather came out of the Jewish fall festival of Tabernacles, and, through some means, they seem to have been moved and adapted by the Christians to introduce the crucifixion, which was the climax of the Christian story. Since that crucifixion was indelibly connected to the early spring festival of Passover, the assumption was made that everything that preceded the liturgical memory of that event also had to have an early spring setting. Now our literal reading of the passion story begins to totter perceptibly.

The story of the entry of Jesus into Jerusalem riding on a donkey was also an adaptation to Jesus' life of yet another story from the book of Zechariah. This text was even quoted in the Gospels. Hence there is little reason to doubt today that all four gospel writers shaped their stories of the triumphal entry of Jesus into Jerusalem to fit the Zechariah account of the King coming to the Holy City. To this day this Zechariah text is read on the Sunday before Easter in Christian churches as a prophecy brought to fulfillment in Jesus' Palm Sunday procession. "Rejoice greatly, O daughter Zion!" Zechariah wrote. "Shout aloud O daughter Jerusalem! Lo, your King comes to you, triumphant and victorious is he, humble and riding on a donkey, on a colt, the foal of a donkey" (Zech. 9:9–11).

Was the Palm Sunday narrative a fulfillment of the prophecy of Zechariah, as later gentile Christians, who did not recognize how Jewish people created sacred stories, liked to assert? Did God really cause Zechariah, some 400 to 500 years before Jesus' birth, to write words that Jesus would fulfill in a literal way in his time? Or was the Jesus story of Palm Sunday written quite deliberately to conform to the narrative in Zechariah as a way of asserting that Jesus was the anticipated King about whom Zechariah had written? Do you see the difference this makes in how one approaches the scriptures?

Now go back and connect with the vignette with which I began this chapter. Zechariah actually described the fall festival of Tabernacles and said that when the Lord appeared in Jerusalem to claim his Temple, "There shall no longer be a trader in the house of the Lord of Hosts on that day" (14:21). Are we dealing with history? Or is this a Jewish way of asserting that Jesus must be understood "according to the scriptures" if he is to have the claim of messiah attributed to him? Clearly, the procession amid leafy branches, the shouts of hosannah, the cry "Blessed is the one who comes in the name of the Lord," and even the reenactment of the banishment of the traders from the house of the Lord were familiar observances to the Jews, but liturgically called to consciousness by them at the Feast of Tabernacles in the fall of the year. They had been borrowed from their natural habitat and used by the early Christians, operating on a one-year liturgical calendar, to make a statement about who Jesus was. The content of the Book of Zechariah had been transferred to Jesus. In that collapsing process, the customs from Tabernacles had been moved from the fall to the spring. History is shrouded and literal details are compromised, once we begin to identify the original setting of the narrative that we have, out of our ignorance, asserted was an objective part of the Jesus story or a remembered word or deed from the life of Jesus.

To lift this influential Book of Zechariah out of the ignorance to which Christians have assigned it, we need also to note that between the Zechariah story of the King coming to Jerusalem on a donkey and the promise that on that day no trader will remain in the House of the Lord, Zechariah has also told us about a shepherd king of Israel who was betrayed for thirty pieces of silver (Zech. 11:12 ff.). He has painted for us a picture of the inhabitants of Jerusalem looking "on the one they have pierced" and mourning for him as one mourns for "an only child" or as one weeps over "a first born" (Zech. 12:10 ff.). This prophetic work also alluded, as we noted earlier, to the shepherd who has been struck "that the sheep may be scattered" (Zech. 13:7). Zechariah's words even included a picture of the nations of the world gathered in Jerusalem in order to receive living water that would flow endlessly in that moment when the Lord became king over all the earth (Zech. 14:8–19). When one realizes that in the world of Jewish symbols water, especially "living water," was a sign of God's spirit, then almost all of the elements of

Luke's story of Pentecost (Acts 2) can be located here in the book of Zechariah. Jewish liturgical symbols and Jewish biblical content had been transferred to Jesus, and out of these artifacts the Christian story of the final moments in Jesus' life had been beautifully crafted. The accounts of Jesus' passion were not written to be literally accurate. They were rather written to interpret the life of Jesus and to proclaim the meaning of Jesus from within a Jewish perspective.

Does this mean that they are not true? No, but it does mean that the profound truth they embody must be understood from a theological point of view, rather than a literal, historical point of view. These narratives are just not literal descriptions of objective history. Does that mean that none of the things they describe actually occurred? No, Jesus was certainly crucified. That is the kernel of history behind the story of the passion. Jesus was certainly perceived to be alive after his death in some life-changing, experiential way. The effects of that experience can be objectively measured, even if the experience cannot. But it does mean that what we have in the Gospels is a theological interpretation of Jesus told in narrative form, based in large measure on the Jewish sacred story and seen as one more chapter in the unfolding drama of the revelation of Israel's God in the history of Israel's people. When we think about this, where else would these Christians, who were also Jews, get the content of their story of Jesus save from their sacred scriptures of antiquity? For remember that when Jesus was arrested, "the disciples all forsook him and fled." No one was present to chronicle the details of that death. They would later, because of that inbreaking, life-changing experience we call resurrection, be forced to interpret his death as having salvific meaning. That is, his death affected the world; or, in the words of Paul that got echoed in the epistle to the Hebrews, he died "for our sins" and, through his sacrifice, the salvation of the world was accomplished. We are thus just beginning to pull back from our eyes the scales that have blinded us for so long. Our search into the Hebrew Bible that shaped the story of his cross, however, has only just begun.

15

He Died According to the Scriptures II

We turn next to the story of the actual details of the crucifixion. I will leave the account of the betrayal out for a moment, for I want to look at the person and role of Judas, called Iscariot, in greater detail in a subsequent chapter. For now, our notice needs to be directed to the content of the Gospels' crucifixion tradition. The details are generally familiar, though most of us are not sure from which gospel each detail comes. Jesus was given over into the hands of wicked people. He was silent before Pilate and his accusers. He was mocked and abused. His clothes were divided among the soldiers. They cast lots to determine who would get what. He was crucified between two bandits or thieves. The crowd passing by derided him, shaking their heads and inviting him to save himself. He was taunted by his fellow victims, and he cried out,

"My God, my God, why have you forsaken me?" There was darkness over the land when he died. The veil in the Temple was split from top to bottom. A centurion proclaimed him God's son.

How many of these details are history? The story of Jesus' death is powerful. It is dramatic. It captures the imagination. It provides us with the means of entering into his suffering and his pain. It is true to the understanding we have of who Jesus was and who Jesus is, but we need to recognize that these details, in all probability, did not literally happen. If one had had a motion picture camera equipped with the ability to record sound, I do not believe that the "seven last words from the cross" would ever have been recorded, nor would the dialogue from the crowds, the crucified thieves, or the centurion that is in the gospel account ever have been heard. Remember, no one was there to record the words. Remember that thirty-five years, at a minimum, perhaps seventy years at a maximum, transpired before these words were written down.

The words, the actions, the dialogue from the cross may be an accurate interpretation of the meaning of Jesus' life, but these words are not literal history describing objective events. Is the gospel story, with these familiar details, then all made up? Are these accounts then nothing more than myths and fairy tales, legends and fantasies similar to those that have marked the exploits of other gods and heroic figures in the history of the human imagination? Is the Christian faith built on this kind of fragile sand?

Believers pose these questions with great anxiety and not infrequently with revelatory anger that betrays the fragility of their religious convictions. The answer to this anxious query, however, is no. These are not fairy tales created out of the subconscious imagination and related to nothing that is real. That does not mean, however, that these details are literal facts of objective history. These accounts are illustrative rather of the process by which the life of Jesus was incorporated into and interpreted by the traditions of the Jewish past. This was the Jewish account of the Jesus who "died for our sins *according to the scriptures.*" This was the faith affirmation of Jewish people driven by their experience of meeting what they believed to be the living God in Jesus of Nazareth and understanding that experience by references to their Jewish past in which they believed that the living God had regularly been active and present. The early Christians both applied these stories of their Jewish past to Jesus and expanded these stories into liturgical episodes, for that was the only way their vocabulary allowed them to speak of the holy God. And it was the holy God that they believed they had encountered in Jesus. So when they wrote the story of Jesus' crucifixion, they did so without knowing any firsthand details, since Jesus had died abandoned and alone. But they also wrote it with their Hebrew Bibles open to those passages they believed presaged this righteous and sacrificial death of the one they believed to be God's unique son and emissary. They worked out the details inside the faith conviction that what they now had come to believe Jesus was and the role they now believed he had acted out were in fact signaled in the Jewish scriptures. Above all, they searched the scriptures for validating words and phrases. Jesus did not fulfill the scriptures in some literal way, as we once thought. Rather, the first Christians, who were also Jews, had their sacred scriptures opened when his life was being interpreted, and the specific details of his life and death were actually written to conform to the ancient texts.

Psalm 22 was one of the primary sources of the crucifixion narratives. This psalm opened with the words attributed to Jesus on the cross: "My God, my God, why have you forsaken me?" (Ps. 22:1). This has led those who were captured by the reverse order of things to suggest that Jesus recited this psalm from his cross of pain! The fact is, these words were first written into the scene of the cross by Mark (15:34) and then copied by Matthew (27:46). Luke and John omitted these words for, when these later gospels came to be written, these words were thought to violate the enhanced divine status that increasingly was being attributed to Jesus in that period of time. A Jesus who knew himself to have come from God, to be a part of God, or to be destined to return to God, could hardly utter this cry of dereliction.

But Psalm 22 went on to say, "All who see me, mock at me; they make mouths at me, they wag their heads; he committed his cause to the Lord; let him deliver him, let him rescue him for he delights in him" (Ps. 22:7–8). Surely Mark had this psalm in front of him when he wrote, "Those who passed by derided him, shaking their heads and saying 'Aha. You who would destroy the Temple ... save yourself.' ... The chief priests along with the scribes also mocked him among themselves ... 'He saved others, he cannot save himself'" (Mark 15:29 ff.). Matthew made the connection with this psalm even more overt by adding, "He trusts in God. Let God deliver him now if he wants him" (Matt. 27:43).

The psalm went on to say, "I am poured out like water and all my bones are out of joint" (22:14). This was thought by the early Christian interpreters to be an actual description of the crucifixion, and the phrase "I can count all my bones" (Ps. 22:17), found near the end of this psalm, was the inspiration for the Johannine gospel tradition that suggested that in the crucifixion process, none of Jesus' bones had been broken (John 19:32–36). This text was augmented by another psalm, where it was said, "He keeps all his bones, not one of them is broken" (Ps. 34:20). It also revealed the growing identity between Jesus and the sacrificial lamb of the Day of the Atonement, which had to be physically perfect, that is, without blemish or broken bone for only a perfect offering could accomplish the task of atonement in the Jewish view of things.

The theme of thirst, or the desire for water, in this verse of the Psalm was referred to again a bit later when the psalmist wrote, "My mouth is dried up like a potsherd and my tongue sticks to my jaws" (Ps. 22:15). The Gospels suggested that Jesus was given wine mingled with myrrh to drink prior to the crucifixion and he declined (Mark 15:23, Matt. 27:34). Mark and Matthew said later that after Jesus cried out, "My God, why" someone filled a sponge with vinegar and put it to his lips so he could drink, but Jesus then breathed his last.

The Fourth Gospel, however, developed the story line behind this idea a bit further. Perhaps this part of Psalm 22 had already reminded John in *midrashic* style of Psalm 69:21, where the psalmist said, "For my thirst they gave me vinegar to drink." So John embellished the narrative by having Jesus cry out, "I thirst" or "I am thirsty" (John 19:28), and this accounted in the Fourth Gospel for that previously described action where someone gave him some wine (that is, vinegar) on a sponge for him to drink (v. 29); but John had moved it from the beginning of Jesus' execution to the end. The tradition was clearly growing.

Psalm 22 went on to say, "They divided my garments among them and for my clothing they cast lots" (v. 18). John took this text and made it the basis for another part of the developing tradition. He had the soldiers dividing his garments "into four parts, one for each soldier" (19:23). Then, to cover the second part of the psalmist's verse, "for my clothing they cast lots" (which in Hebrew was probably a repetitive doublet meaning the same thing but said in a different way), John developed the narrative that the tunic of Jesus should not be torn into four parts, but rather given to one soldier with the roll of the dice so he had the soldiers "cast lots for it" (19:24). Thus we see how the psalms in general and Psalm 22 in particular created again and again the details of the drama of crucifixion.

Most of the details of the crucifixion story that are not covered by Psalm 22 can be found in Isaiah 52 and 53. Here we encounter the mythological figure developed by 2 Isaiah as a symbol for the people of Israel.[1] Isaiah called this figure the servant of the Lord or the suffering servant. I suspect that this post-Exilic prophet developed this symbol so that he could help the defeated Jewish nation understand that their future did not lie in grandeur, power, or glory. The future of the Jewish nation as the people of God lay rather in being faithful even when that nation was the suffering victim of the hostility of the victorious peoples of the world. But this individualized portrait of a nation that was victimized, but nonetheless affirmed by God, was quickly incorporated by the early Christians into the story of Jesus. Luke seemed particularly fond of this association and intermingled the story of Jesus with the story of the servant figure of Isaiah on a fairly constant basis.

The servant was "lifted up and shall be very high" (Isa. 52:13). That became an allusion with a double meaning, for Jesus was first lifted up on the cross and then ultimately lifted up in exaltation to heaven. When the Christ, like the servant, was lifted up in either sense, he was made to say of himself, "I will draw all people [men] to myself" (John 12:32). Isaiah went on to describe the countenance of the servant figure: "Marred was his appearance, beyond human semblance and his form beyond that of mortals" (52:14). People would be astonished, nations would be startled, kings would shut their mouths (52:14–15). It was easy to imagine a crucified one writhing on his cross in terms of that particular description, and so it shaped the gospel tradition.

Isaiah went on with additional words that have been made immortal by George Frederick Handel in his oratorio entitled "The Messiah." Many people, influenced by this oratorio, think that these words were written to be descriptive of Jesus. They are, however, words describing Isaiah's mythical servant. "He was despised, rejected, a man of suffering [sorrows] and acquainted with infirmities [grief]. Surely he has borne our griefs. . . . he was wounded for our transgressions, he was bruised for our iniquities, upon him was the chastisement that made us whole and with his stripes we are healed. . . . the Lord has laid on him the iniquity of us all" (Isa. 53:3–6). Surely this was where Paul found confirmation for the content of his phrase, "He died for our sins in accordance with the scriptures." Behind these words also was the picture of Jesus as the human offering who achieved the atoning sacrifice so powerful in early Christian thinking. But we need to recognize that these images were derived, not from Jesus, but from out of the Jewish background of the early Christians, who tried to process their experience of Jesus in the only way they knew.

Theirs was a theological viewpoint destined to grow in sometimes strange and interesting ways throughout Christian history. It produced the words in hymns like "Saved by the Blood" or "Washed in the Blood," and it shaped the content of evangelical preaching that asserted that God had substituted Jesus for sinners like you and me—crucifying him in our stead so that "by his blood we are saved." This was a theological view that was born in the Jewish understanding of sacrifice and applied by Jewish Christians to Jesus, but when it became separated from that theological context, it transformed God into both a child-abusing heavenly parent and a malevolent sadistic deity. Modern people are hard-pressed to state just how it is that the crucifixion of Jesus has taken away their sins, for they have retained these ancient words but not the Jewish context in which alone the words made sense.

But Isaiah went on to portray his servant as silent before his accusers, "Yet he opened not his mouth . . . " (Isa. 53:7), which shaped the biblical portrait of Jesus before the Jewish Council, before Pontius Pilate, and even before Herod in that episode told only by Luke (Mark 14:61, 15:4–5; Matt. 27:14; Luke 23:9; John 19:9 ff.). Next, Isaiah said that the servant "made his grave with the wicked and with a rich man in his death" (53:9). This chapter in Isaiah concluded with these words: he "was numbered with the transgressors, yet he bore the sin of many and made intercession for the transgressors" (53:12).

These verses, under the skillful hands of the gospel writers, also helped to create narrative details in the crucifixion story. Mark started the narrative tradition based on these verses by asserting that "with him they crucified two robbers, one on the right and one on the left" (Mark 15:27). It is just a cameo appearance for the robbers. They do not speak, but Jesus was now "numbered among the transgressors" in his death. He was making "his grave with the wicked." But Isaiah had gone on to say that he was with a rich man in his death" (Isa. 53:9). This detail was turned by Mark into the Joseph of Arimathea burial story. In this narrative Joseph, "a respected member of the council" (Mark 15:43)—that is, a ruler of the Jews and thus a rich man—provided the tomb for Jesus. Thus the pain of the disciples leaving him alone and having his deceased body disposed of by his enemies was alleviated and it was all done "in accordance with the scriptures!" The tomb, we are told, "had been hewn out of rock" (Mark 15:46). The tomb was sealed with a stone. Thus the Isaiah-based narratives about Jesus both dying with transgressors and having his tomb located among the rich had entered the Christian story. Both stories were destined to grow through the years.

Matthew added a small bit to the story of the robbers. He had them join in the derision and taunting of Jesus (Matt. 27:44). Matthew also embellished the details in the Joseph of Arimathea story. He made overt the fact that Joseph was "rich," thus indicating even more clearly that the Isaiah text was shaping his story. Matthew also suggested that Joseph was actually a disciple and added not only that the tomb of Joseph was "new," but that Joseph had himself hewn it (Matt. 27:57–59). Even the stone that had been rolled up to its door seemed to grow, for Matthew described it as a "great stone" (Matt. 27:60).

Luke, having noted that Jesus made intercession for his transgressors as Isaiah had stated that the servant had done, developed the content of that intercession.

To those who crucified Jesus, Luke had Jesus say, "Father forgive them for they know not what they do" (Luke 23:34). Next he expanded the narrative of the two criminals (Luke 23:39–43). Only one was taunting and derisive in Luke. The other was remorseful and penitent. The penitent thief rebuked the non-penitent thief in the name of God, motivated we are told by fear. He requested that Jesus remember him when he came to his kingdom. Jesus then made intercession for him and promised him paradise "with me."

Joseph of Arimathea, under the influence of Luke's pen, became "good and righteous." Though a member of the council, he had not acceded to Jesus' conviction. He was waiting for the Kingdom of God to come. In this tomb, now we are told, no one else had ever been laid (Luke 23:53).

John also said that "two others" were crucified with him. He gave them no dialogue, however, since that was to be saved for the vignette of mother and beloved disciple at the foot of the cross. It was only to them that Jesus spoke, other than his word of thirst and his final triumphal affirmation that "It is finished." Few scholars today regard the story of Jesus' mother and the beloved disciple at the foot of the cross to be of history.

The Joseph story, however, was dramatically expanded by John. Joseph was a secret disciple "for fear of the Jews." He was joined in this burial by Nicodemus. They used one hundred pounds of aloes and myrrh and carried out the burial according to the burial customs of the Jews. The tomb was in a garden that was located at, or at least very near, the place of crucifixion.

All of this became the narrative form and development that rose out of the suggestion found in Isaiah that the servant figure made his tomb with the rich. The meaning of this part of the biblical story was that the Church had identified Jesus with the servant figure of Isaiah. So the details of the life of the servant were gathered into the "remembered" life of Jesus.

There were other parts of the Hebrew scriptures that shaped the story of the cross. There has even been a suggestion that the pharaoh's butler who was spared and the pharaoh's baker who was not spared from the Genesis story of Joseph and his brothers found reflection in the Lucan account of the penitent and nonpenitent thieves.

We do not have in the Gospels a literal story. Not even the most primary narrative of the cross was written to be approached as a description of what actually happened during the first Holy Week. What we have is a portrait, an interpretive painting if you will, that seeks to capture the essence of Jesus under the symbols familiar to Jewish people taken from their ancient Jewish scriptures. We look in vain if our search is for accuracy in literal details. By seeking literal details we will ultimately miss the point being made by the gospel writers. The gospel writers would have us seek rather, in the interpretive portrait that they have drawn, the impact of the life of Jesus. Our hope is to find a way into the Christ experience so that the living and eternal God might be revealed in Christ to us, that we too may know him to be part of who God is and might know ourselves to be raised to new life in him. If we enter deeply into this *midrashic* process, then and only then will we know what Paul meant when he wrote that "Christ died for our sins, according to the scriptures."

16

Judas Iscariot

A Christian Invention?

We have journeyed carefully through part of the story of the final week of Jesus' earthly life. We have come to an awareness of the way the narrative details of the biblical passion drama have been shaped by the Hebrew scriptures of antiquity. The story of our Lord's passion was thus not the miraculous fulfillment of the prophetic words from the past, as we have been led to think, as much as they were accounts written with the Hebrew Bibles open, so that the Jesus narrative could be made to conform to the expectations expressed hundreds of years before in the religious yearnings of the Jewish people.

Is there then no literal history that is reflected at the heart of the Christian story? Yes, of course there is; but it is not found in the narrative descriptions of Jesus' last days. The literal reality that stands behind the story of the final days of Jesus' life does not stretch to cover the descriptive details used to create the drama of the story of the cross that we now possess in the Bible. That is the powerful first insight that comes to us when we learn to read the passion story with Jewish eyes.

There are, however, other details in this narrative that need now to be considered. The major one invokes the anti-hero of the Christian tradition, a man named Judas and called Iscariot. In the drama of Holy Week, he is painted in dark and sinister tones. Throughout Christian history he has been vilified. No parents today use the name Judas when deciding what to call their son. His very name has come to be a synonym for treachery and disloyalty. This name does appear from time to time in the vocabulary of our political orations. Sometimes it is employed during painful moments of one person's disillusionment with another, when our principles have been violated or our personhood betrayed. At such a moment, the power of the curse we have laid upon the name Judas falls readily from our lips.

When the story of Jesus' passion is read in Christian churches during Holy Week, the figure of Judas takes center stage. Far more than most people realize, that figure has become the symbol of anti-Semitism. The emotions and rhetoric, the anger and hostility that surround the figure of Judas are symptomatic of the unspeakable evil that has historically flowed from Christians to the Jews. The most brutal, the darkest chapters in Christian history are revealed in our relations to the people of the faith tradition that gave Christianity its birth.

Through the ages Holy Week has been marked with increased anti-Semitic hostility. For in the churches of the world during that week, Christians hear a narrative read from a book thought to be the word of God that paints Judas as pure evil, that portrays him as a man of greed who would betray his Lord for money. That story also places the blame for the crucifixion squarely on the whole Jewish people. Those two facets of the passion story are deeply tied together.

It was not unknown in previous eras for Christians to emerge from their churches on Good Friday with their anger at a fever pitch, ready to invade the Jewish community to kill, to beat, and to deface the property of those evil descendants of Judas and the Jews. Jewish parents learned to hide their children and their treasures until the emotions of Holy Week subsided. Even today some of the echoes from the perceived character of Judas—treachery, disloyalty, and the willingness to do anything for money—shape the prejudiced stereotype of Jews in Western civilization that is carried so close to the surface in what we think is an enlightened age.

But who was Judas? Was he a person of history who did all of the things attributed to him? That is certainly one option. Or was there but a bare germ of truth in the Judas story, on which was heaped the dramatic portrait that we now find in the Gospels? Can we identify the *midrashic* tradition at work in the various details that now adorn his life? That is clearly another possibility. Or was he purely and simply a legendary figure invented by the Christians as a way to place on the backs of the Jewish people the blame for the death of Jesus? If so, why did the need arise to vilify the Jews? Did not Christianity begin as a Jewish movement? These are now the questions.

The first fact that needs to be filed was that Jesus was crucified and that crucifixion was a method of execution employed only by the Romans. If the Jews had executed Jesus, it would probably have been done by stoning. The very fact that Jesus was crucified means that he was executed by the Romans, not by the Jews. That bit of truth needs to be grasped very clearly.

Second, we must at least pose the question as to the meaning of the term "Iscariot." Does it point to Kerioth, the town of origin, or does it derive from the word *sicarious,* which means a political assassin? Today the weight of scholarship leans toward the latter of these options. With these issues and questions before us, we turn to the details of the Judas story and see what conclusions additional biblical data might lead us to consider.

The suggestion of betrayal received its first mention in Christian writings during the mid-fifties of the first century. It appeared in Paul's first epistle to the Corinthians in his recounting of the Last Supper. There was, however, no name attached to the note of betrayal; certainly not one of the twelve appeared to be associated with that act by Paul. Paul simply said, "I received from the Lord that which I also delivered to you, that the Lord Jesus on the same night when he was *betrayed* took bread" (1 Cor. 11:23). That is all the Christian Church had in writing about the betrayal until the seventh decade.

The name of Judas as the traitor makes its first appearance in Mark, somewhere between 65 C.E. and 70 C.E. The material in Mark, however, was scanty. First Judas was simply listed among the twelve (Mark 3:14–19) and identified with the words "who betrayed him."

The second mention of Judas in Mark came in the story of the betrayal (Mark 14:10–11). Mark recorded no motive for the act. We are only told that the chief priests offered him money, but this was after the fact, and it was hardly the reason that brought Judas to them. Nowhere are we told just what his betrayal would accomplish or why betrayal was necessary. A previous passage in Mark had suggested, however, that the chief priests were afraid that his arrest might bring "a riot among the people" (Mark 14:2). Judas, however, was not a party to that conversation.

Next in Mark came the account of the Last Supper, where Judas was not mentioned but the betrayal was discussed. Jesus here identified the traitor as one of the twelve, saying, "One of you will betray me, one who is eating with me" (Mark 14:18). In this passage Jesus went on to say, "The Son of Man goes as it is written of him"; that is, this script was preordained. None of the principals could escape their fate, but the curse on the traitor was nonetheless pronounced:"It would be better for that man if he had not been born" (Mark 14:21).

The supper having ended with a hymn, Jesus led the disciples out to the Mount of Olives, where the disciples were asked to watch while Jesus prayed. No mention was made in the text that

Judas ever left the disciple band. Finding them sleeping upon his return from prayer, Jesus admonished the disciples, announced that his "hour had come," and urged them forward, for "my betrayer is at hand" (Mark 14:42).

Immediately or suddenly, the text then said, Judas appeared with the chief priests, the scribes, and the elders (Mark 14:43–46). The whole Jewish establishment was to participate in the betrayal. The text identified Judas strangely as "one of the twelve," as if he had never been introduced before. Judas addressed Jesus as Rabbi "and kissed him." The kiss had been the prearranged sign. Jesus was arrested at that point, said the text, by the Jews. Judas then disappeared from Mark's gospel and was never heard of again.

The Judas story in Mark was embryonic. It left open questions, such as: How did Judas arrange to gather the delegation of the Jewish chief priests, scribes, and elders if he had never left the band of disciples? The story was also sparse on details. The Judas story sits on the text uncomfortably, as if it has been imposed on a text in which it was not original.

When Matthew wrote his gospel some ten to twenty years later, he added many details to the developing Judas story. Judas in Matthew went to the chief priests asking for money for the betrayal. Matthew supplied the motive that was lacking in Mark. It was greed, said Matthew. Yet the amount of money was rather trivial, since thirty pieces of silver was only the average price of a slave. This Matthean text, we need to note, was also the only time in the Bible that the exact price of the betrayal was mentioned.

At the Last Supper, Matthew also elaborated Judas' role. Judas actually spoke in this gospel, when Jesus announced that "one of you will betray me." "Is it I, Master?" said Judas. "You have said so," Jesus responded (Matt. 26:20–25).

This elaboration continued in the actual scene of the betrayal, where once again Matthew has expanded Judas's role. In the garden Judas greeted Jesus with the words "Hail, Master." Then he kissed him. Jesus responded, "Friend, why are you here?" Matthew then said that one of the twelve began to fight with his sword, wounding the ear of a servant of the high priest (Matt. 26:47 ff.).

Judas next appeared in Matthew on the following day. Having now seen Jesus condemned, Judas repented and returned the thirty pieces of silver. "I have sinned in betraying innocent blood," Judas was made to say to the chief priests (Matt. 27: 3–4). It was a fascinating confession, appearing nowhere else in any gospel. Judas was, however, rebuffed by the chief priests and elders with the words, "What is that to us?" So Judas threw the pieces of silver in the Temple, departed, and went and hanged himself. It was the first, but not the last, biblical account of Judas' demise. The chief priests, however, retrieved the silver, judged it unfit to be kept in the Temple since it was blood money, and then decided to use it to buy a potters' field in which to bury strangers. Matthew suggested that this action fulfilled a prophetic word spoken by Jeremiah, which he quoted: "And they took the thirty pieces of silver, the price of him on whom a price had been set by some of the sons of Israel and they gave them for a potters' field as the Lord directed me" (Matt. 27:9–10).

This was a very strained effort on the part of Matthew to ground this developing Judas story in the texts of the Jewish Bible. The quotation from Jeremiah was neither accurate nor appropriate (see Jer. 32:6–15), but it does provide us with insight into how the mind of the gospel writer worked as he sought to develop his narrative in the *midrashic* tradition of the Jewish people.

In Matthew's story of the betrayal, we need to observe that the following elements have been added to the developing Judas legend. Dialogue had been provided between Judas and Jesus in two settings, the Last Supper and in the Garden of Gethsemane; money had been made the motive; the price had been set at thirty pieces of silver; Judas had repented, returned the money to the chief priests, and been rebuffed by them; he had thrown the money back into the Temple; and finally, Judas had gone and hanged himself. We have also been told that the money, now called "blood money," had been used to buy a field in which strangers may be buried. The story of Judas, begun in Mark some ten to twenty years earlier, had clearly grown.

Some five to ten years after Matthew and fifteen to twenty-five years after Mark, the Gospel of Luke with its companion work, the Book of Acts, came into written form. Focusing only on Judas in this Lucan corpus, we find still more fascinating additions to the tradition. First, in Luke's list of the chosen twelve, there were two disciples who bore the name Judas. One was Judas, the son of James, and the other was Judas Iscariot, who, Luke says, "became the traitor" (Luke 6:13–16). This second Judas in Luke's list had taken the place of a man named Thaddeus in the lists of Mark and Matthew. There are scattered throughout the New Testament strong hints that there was a loyal disciple named Judas who was perhaps even the brother of Jesus. Mark said that Jesus had four brothers; James and Judas were two of the names (Mark 6:3). The Fourth Gospel referred to a disciple named "Judas, not Iscariot" (John 14:22). The epistle of Jude, included in the canon of the New Testament, claimed to be the work of an apostle who bore the Judas name and who identified himself as the brother of James. So the memory of a faithful follower named Judas becomes another piece of data to file in our attempt to gather the available biblical evidence that might help us understand the development of the character of Judas Iscariot.

Luke added other features to the story of the betrayal. His act of betrayal was the work of Satan, who entered Judas, Luke asserted (Luke 22:3). That was a new explanation for his evil. He went to the chief priests, not for money, but simply to put Jesus in their power or to betray him. They then offered him money. Judas next sought to betray Jesus in the absence of the crowd. The actual thing betrayed left vague in Mark and Matthew was now made explicit in Luke. Among the gospel writers, there was clearly some difficulty in understanding why a betrayer was necessary. Jesus was not difficult to identify. He was a public figure. But the fear of the Jewish authorities that there might be a riot mentioned in Mark (14:2) had now become the content of Judas' betrayal in Luke (22:6). Even this explanation was strained for it would have been no trouble to follow Jesus and to stake out a watch where he could have been arrested quietly. But the betrayal story needed content and this was the best that Luke could do.

Jesus announced at the Last Supper in Luke that "the hand of him who betrays me is with me on the table" (Luke 22:21), but no dialogue with Judas ensued. Other conversation ensued, but little of it related to Judas.

The meal over, Luke followed the familiar story outline and had Jesus go out, but he had him go not to Gethsemane, but to the Mount of Olives (Luke 22:39); the presumption is that Gethsemane was on the Mount of Olives. There Jesus prayed. The story has been heightened dramatically. We read of angels appearing and sweat like great drops of blood falling from Jesus' forehead (Luke 22:44).

Then the Lucan text had Judas appear leading a crowd. Judas approached Jesus to kiss him. Dialogue ensued. Jesus asked, "Judas, would you betray the Son of Man with a kiss?" (Luke 22:48). There was no reply. The arrest took place and then Judas disappeared from the Gospel of Luke.

He reappeared, however, in the first chapter of Acts, which was nothing but a second volume of Luke's gospel. That appearance was, however, not in person but by reference. In an address to 120 attributed to Peter, Judas was referred to as "a guide to those who arrested Jesus" (Acts 1:16). "This man," Peter went on to say, "bought a field with the reward of his wickedness; and falling down headlong, he burst open in the middle and all his bowels gushed out" (Acts 1:18). It was a story of the end of Judas that is not capable of being harmonized with Matthew's account of Judas' hanging. The tradition of the one called Iscariot was clearly growing.

In the Fourth Gospel, a few new details entered the tradition. There was no formal list of the twelve in John, but Judas was certainly a member of the disciple band. For John, the act of betrayal was the work of the devil, for he wrote, "The devil had already put it into the heart of Judas Iscariot, Simon's son, to betray him" (John 13:2). Other translations make that read,

"Judas, son of Simon Iscariot." Nowhere else in the New Testament had we yet been told that a man named Simon, who also bore the title Iscariot, was the father of Judas. So that too was a new element.

At this final gathering of Jesus with his disciples in John's gospel, Jesus foretold his betrayal. "One of you will betray me" he said (John 13:21). When Jesus told the disciples in John that one of them would betray him, the disciples inquired as to the identity of the traitor. Jesus said, "It is he to whom I shall give this morsel when I have dipped it" (John 13:26). The text went on to say that Jesus dipped the bread and "he gave it to Judas." Satan, John said, then entered Judas a second time, and Jesus said to Judas, "What you are going to do, do quickly" (John 13:27). The other disciples, we are also told, did not understand what this conversation meant. Judas, however, departed. John alone explained how Judas left in time to organize the treacherous act. Perhaps by the time John wrote, this inconsistency had been pointed out, so John corrected it. This part of the drama closed with John's editorial words "and it was night" (John 13:30). Darkness began, at that moment, to enshroud Judas in the Christian tradition.

Judas did not reenter the Johannine story until chapter 18, save for one reference in what has come to be called the high priestly prayer of Jesus in chapter 17. Here Jesus prayed for his disciples and said that he had lost none of them "except the one destined to be lost [sometimes translated the Son of Perdition or the Son of Destruction] so that the scripture might be fulfilled" (John 17:12).

When Judas did reappear in the Johannine text, Jesus was in the garden.[1] It was said that Judas knew this place "because Jesus often met there with his disciples" (John 18:2). Judas came with a detachment of Roman soldiers, but accompanied by Temple police. It was no longer a Jewish arrest party headed by the chief priests, scribes, and elders. This posse was made up of armed Roman soldiers. A dialogue ensued with the soldiers in the presence of Judas. That was the last Johannine appearance for Judas Iscariot. Of note, however, to complete the biblical analysis, was that in the Fourth Gospel there was no trial before the Sanhedrin. Jesus was taken first to Annas, then to Caiphas, and from there dispatched directly to Pilate's headquarters.

That is the entirety of the biblical data about Judas called Iscariot. It is not a consistent portrait. Where did the act of betrayal take place? In Gethsemane, said Mark and Matthew. At the Mount of Olives, said Luke. In a garden, said John. Who came to arrest Jesus? A crowd from the chief priests, scribes, and elders, said Mark. A "large crowd" from the chief priests and elders of the people, said Matthew. Simply a crowd, said Luke. A "detachment" of soldiers, who would have to be Roman, said John.[2] The soldiers were accompanied, however, said John, by police from the chief priests and Pharisees.[3] Did the Sanhedrin assemble that night to condemn Jesus? Yes, said Mark, Matthew, and Luke. No, said John. Did Judas repent of his treacherous act? Mark was silent. Matthew said yes. Luke said no. John was silent. How did Judas' life come to an end? Mark was silent. He hanged himself, said Matthew. He fell down headlong and his bowels gushed out, said Luke. John was silent.

The first fact that must be registered is that the Gospels do not paint a consistent portrait of the man called Judas. Even if he were a literal figure of history, there is little agreement about the details of his life.

The next question that must be raised is this: Can the details that have been attached to Judas in the gospel stories be found elsewhere in the Hebrew scriptures? How much of the Judas story can be seen as a *midrashic* reconstruction drawn from bits and pieces of the Jewish sacred tradition? The answer is, almost every bit of the story. So to document that possibility, we open up the Hebrew scriptures and the history of the Hebrew people and discover what is available there.

Christians need to recognize first that the name "Judas" was simply the Greek way of spelling "Judah," and that Judah was the name of the patriarch who was thought to be the father of the Jewish nation. From the tenth century before the birth of Jesus on, this nation was known first as Judah and later as

Judea. The designation "Jew," therefore meant originally a member of the nation of Judah. Jewish people in Hitler's Germany were forced to wear the identifying badge with the letters JUDE written on it. In the *midrashic* tradition, when the traitor was given the name of the nation that, by the time the Gospels were being composed, was perceived to be the enemy of the Christian movement, then our suspicions that something more than history is at work ought to be aroused.

Our second step in this quest is to recognize that the Jewish word for betrayal literally means "to hand over," especially to hand over to a recognized enemy. In the Jewish tradition, there was one other major story in which a gigantic Jewish hero was betrayed or handed over to an enemy. That was the story of Joseph in the Book of Genesis (37–50). In that story the "handing over" was done by a group of twelve who later became known as the leaders of the twelve tribes of Israel. In the Jesus story, the "handing over" also came out of a group of twelve who were designated the leaders of the Church that came to call itself the new Israel. In both stories the handing over or betrayal was into the hands of gentiles, and death was the presumed result of each act of treachery. In both stories God intervened to reverse that presumed outcome. In both stories the hero was imprisoned for a time—Joseph in the pharaoh's jail, Jesus in Joseph's tomb. In both stories money was given to the traitors—twenty pieces of silver for Joseph, thirty pieces of silver for Jesus. Not lost in this analysis was the fact that the one of the twelve brothers of Joseph who urged the others to seek money for their act of betrayal was named Judah or Judas (Gen. 37:26–27). In the light of these similarities, it is hard not to doubt that there was some intermingling of the stories.

Probing the gospel story of Judas for other *midrashic* connections, we discover once again that powerful connection between the Book of Zechariah, so little known by Christians, and the narrative account of the cross of Jesus. The Book of Zechariah certainly shaped the Christian story.

In Zechariah, for example, we find the reference to the specific price that Matthew employed in his betrayal story. This prophetic writer has told us about the betrayal of the shepherd king of the Jews for "thirty pieces of silver" (Zech. 11:13). This silver was later hurled back into the Temple treasury, which was a theme that Matthew said also occurred with the Judas money when Judas repented (Matt. 27:3–5).

Matthew said that Judas then went and hanged himself. This story also had echoes that point us to the Jewish past. Suicide was rare, indeed, in Jewish circles, but there was one story concerning a man named Ahithophel, who had betrayed King David and had given his loyalty to a rebel cause. When that cause failed, Ahithophel was said to have gone out and hanged himself. King David, like all kings of the Jews, was called "the Lord's anointed." As we have previously noted, the Hebrew word for anointed is the same word that came to be translated "messiah" or "Christ." So, later Jewish Christians reading this ancient tale would note that when Ahithophel betrayed the Lord's anointed, he went and hanged himself (2 Sam. 17:1–23). It begins to sound very much like the Judas story.

We also need to recognize that Matthew, who alone told us the story of Judas committing suicide, wrote his gospel within a decade after the Jewish war against Rome had ended. In that war, as we noted earlier, the forces of Rome destroyed the city of Jerusalem and everything in it. That war actually ended, however, not in Jerusalem, but in a massive suicide by the defeated and hopelessly surrounded Jewish soldiers on a battlefield named Masada to which they had retreated when Jerusalem fell. By the time Matthew wrote his gospel, the Jewish Christians had already begun to suggest that the destruction of Jerusalem was God's punishment on the strict Jerusalem Jews for their refusal to accept Jesus as the Christ. Jesus, they argued, had been betrayed by his own people. "He came to his own home and his own people received him not," was the way John would describe this a bit later (John 1:11). That betrayal, these Jewish Christians were asserting, had now resulted in the suicide deaths of the last remnants of the Jerusalem Jews in the Roman war. How easy it would be to interpret that Jewish behavior as betrayal, and together with its tragic suicidal results, relate this action directly to the life of Judas. This would be especially so if the traitor could be seen as a personification of the Jerusalem Jews.

But the search for ancient biblical clues that might have contributed to the creation of the Judas story does not stop there. In all four gospels, a description was given of an episode in which the traitor was designated at the Last Supper by the action of dipping a hand or bread with Jesus into the common table food supply. Mark (14:20), Matthew (26:23), and Luke (22:21) all had some version of this story identifying the traitor not by name, but simply as one of those who gathered at the table to eat that final meal together. John, however, had Jesus specifically identify Judas as the traitor by having Jesus say in response to the disciple's question, "Lord, is it I?" "It is he to whom I shall give this morsel of bread when I have dipped it." Then, the account continued, "When he had dipped the morsel, he gave it to Judas" (John 13:26). Earlier, John had stated that this action occurred simply to fulfill the scriptures, and John went on to identify the text that had inspired this story as coming from the Psalms, where it was written, "Even my bosom friend in whom I trusted, who ate of my bread, has lifted his heel against me" (Ps. 41:9). Thus even this detail from the Judas story also appears to have been the creation of a *midrash* tradition. It is of particular note to recognize that this psalm was originally thought of as a psalm of David bemoaning the betrayal of Ahithophel. These themes echo over and over again in the developing Judas tradition.

One final detail in the Judas story came when the traitor identified Jesus in Gethsemane with a kiss. That detail was in Mark (14:44, 45), Matthew (26:48–50), and Luke (22:47–48), but it was omitted from John. Can we find some parallel in the Hebrew scriptures to this kiss of the traitor? It is not as obvious, but it does appear to be present. For there is one other betrayal story in the Jewish scriptures in which echoes of this part of the Judas story may be found. This same Jewish episode might also be the source of the detail in Luke's story of Judas' death by disembowelment told in the Book of Acts. In 2 Samuel (20:1–10), Joab, David's captain, was replaced by Amasa during a period of civil war. Joab, enraged by his being replaced, approached Amasa under the guise of feigned friendship, very much as Judas had approached Jesus. Joab greeted Amasa with the words, "Is it well with you my brother?" and he drew Amasa, said the text, by the beard to kiss him. In that moment, however, Joab treacherously plunged his sword into Amasa's body and shed Amasa's "bowels to the ground without striking a second blow." It is not a vast stretch to suggest that the kiss of Judas part of the tradition grew out of this earlier Jewish narrative of betrayal, and that Luke's death by disembowelment had its origins also in this story. That would not have been unusual in the *midrashic* tradition.

When we put all the pieces together, a pattern certainly emerges. From Zechariah we get the account of the betrayal of the shepherd king of the Jews for thirty pieces of silver. From the story of Ahithophel we get the picture of the one who, when he betrayed the Lord's anointed, went out and hanged himself. Suicide was also freshly in the mind of Matthew, for Jewish resistance to the Roman army had ended in mass suicides of the final Jewish soldiers at Masada. From the story of Joab, we get the kiss of betrayal and the disembowelment of Amasa. From Psalm 41 we get the account of the friend who becomes the enemy after eating bread at the table together. From the Joseph story, we get the detail of the brother named Judah (Judas) who decided to seek money in exchange for "handing over" his brother to the gentiles and almost certain death. That accounts for almost every detail in the gospel tradition regarding one known as Judas and called Iscariot. This analysis, at the very least, makes the *midrashic* creation of the Judas story sound more and more probable. At the very least, it suggests that most of the details about the life of Judas may not be literal at all.

To cap off this lack of historic credibility in the story of Judas, we next observe in the Gospels a kind of inappropriate response from the disciples to a moment of pain and intense drama when the act of betrayal was broached. This note was struck in both John and Luke. The Fourth Gospel, which had Jesus publicly identify Judas as the traitor, portrayed the disciples as being unmoved in any way by that revelation. Jesus announced that the traitor was the one to whom he would give the bread, and he gave it to Judas. Judas then departed. No one made an effort to stop him and no one commented on Jesus' words about Judas. In Luke the description of the disciples' behavior when the traitor was identified was even more incomprehensible. After Jesus announced that "the one who betrays me is with me and his hand is on the table" (Luke 22:21), the disciples actually moved into a discussion as to which one of them would be greatest in the kingdom of heaven! Everywhere one looks, one discovers an inappropriate, confused context for the Judas narrative in the biblical tradition—which is exactly what one might expect to occur if a late-developing tradition like the story of Judas had been superimposed onto an ancient account where it did not originally exist. From many angles the story of Judas appears to be a late-developing Christian legend. When we confront the results of our study—which reveal that all of the biblical details of Judas' life appear to have been shaped by the Hebrew scriptures and therefore can hardly be regarded as literal and that the Judas story does not fit into the narrative of Jesus' passion as an original part of the story might be expected to do—then we ask with renewed urgency whether Judas himself could still be thought of as a literal figure of history.

While holding that question open to a growing conviction for a moment, we need to examine next another force so apparently at work in the story of the betrayal of Jesus that it too must be brought to consciousness. Why was there in the Gospels, especially in the later ones, such a rush to exonerate the Romans and to pardon the Roman procurator Pontius Pilate? Was this a part of the background, an unrecognized factor, that caused the Judas story to emerge? Examining these details we discover that while the death of Jesus was sealed when Judas planted the kiss of betrayal on his cheek, a man named Pontius Pilate, the Roman governor and the only one who could have legally ordered a Roman crucifixion, was being portrayed as seeking to free Jesus by offering to release a prisoner as part of the Passover celebration (Mark 15:6). What does this mean? First, we need to observe that the custom of releasing a prisoner as part of the Passover celebration is mentioned nowhere else in the literature of either Roman or Jewish history of which I am aware. This appears to be the sole reference to something called here "a custom." This custom seems to be a gospel invention, a literary device created to help exonerate the Roman governor. The irony of this story is so often missed by readers who do not understand that the name of the murderer who was offered for release, Barabbas, literally meant son of God (*bar*, son, and *Abba*, father or God). Three times in Luke's gospel Pilate was described as saying that this man Jesus was innocent (Luke 23:4, 14, 22). In all three synoptic Gospels, Pilate was portrayed as trying to release one whose very name meant the son of God, only to be thwarted by the Jews. What was going on in this biblical story? In Matthew's gospel Pilate was said to have gone so far as to wash his hands publicly and to declare himself "innocent of this man's blood." Matthew then went on to have the Jewish crowd say those terrifying words, "his blood be on us and on our children" (Matt. 26:25). Pilate was exonerated and the Jews were portrayed as calling down blame on themselves for all eternity. No text in any religious sacred literature has ever been the cause of as much pain and suffering in history as has this one. In these words a killing anti-Semitism found its biblical and therefore, in the eyes of many Christians, its justifying legitimization. The attempt to shift the blame from the Romans to the Jews is obvious, and it has been historically successful.

Some of the contradictory details in the gospel regarding Judas that we filed almost by title can from this perspective now be seen as a self-conscious attempt to document that shift of blame from the Romans to the Jews, to the people of Judah. Recall that in Matthew, Mark, and Luke, Jesus was not only arrested by the Jewish authorities, but also tried before a Jewish court that very night. Historically, both of these actions were quite unlikely, since each of these gospels had also insisted that the night of Jesus' arrest and trial was the most holy night of the Passover. It is almost inconceivable to suggest that on this particular night the leadership people of the Jewish nation, who formed the Sanhedrin, would be convened either to arrest or to condemn an agitator. Guards could have managed the arrest and the prisoner could always have been kept in jail until the celebration was over. The leaders of the Jews, the chief priests, scribes, and elders, would hardly leave their Passover celebrations for this purpose. Beyond this, the Torah commanded the Sanhedrin to render its judgments only in the light of day, so a meeting at night was actually a violation of the law. Clearly, something besides history was being described here.

John's gospel, however, contradicts the others by asserting that the arrest of Jesus was actually carried out by Roman soldiers who were only assisted by the Temple guard. Furthermore, in John, no gathering of the Sanhedrin was even mentioned. Hence, in this gospel, there was no trial. Though John was the last gospel to be written, it was the only gospel to claim to be based on an eyewitness memory, and it had an uncanny ability to correct the details of Matthew, Mark, and Luke that may well be working here. John, however, did express the growing negativity of the Christians toward the Jews by suggesting that, though it was a Roman arrest and a Roman crucifixion, it was nonetheless stage-managed by the Jews. While not exonerating the Jewish authorities, John still preserved what was clearly the memory of history that Jesus was arrested by the Romans and crucified by Pontius Pilate, the Roman governor. Even the Christian Church, in the service of its own anti-Semitism, dodged this issue by shaping its creeds so that Christians do not even today say that Jesus was crucified "by" Pontius Pilate, but rather "under" Pontius Pilate, as if Pilate were but an innocent bystander. In this evolving story, the blame for Jesus' death was clearly shifting from the Romans to the Jews, and as a part of that shift, the story of the traitor emerged. The traitor was then given the name Judas/Judah, which was historically the name of the whole Jewish people.

But what made that shift necessary or at least convenient in the minds of the early Christian writers who shaped the gospel tradition? Why was it thought to be essential that in order to exonerate the Romans, one must vilify the Jews? Why were Jewish people, and especially the rigidly orthodox and traditional

Jewish leaders who were associated with the Temple worship, a politically popular enemy? In order to address this issue, we need to remember that all four of the Gospels were written either during (Mark) or in the aftermath of the Roman war against the Jews (Matthew, Luke, John). This means that each gospel inevitably reflected either that war or the tensions of the anti-Jewish sentiment that followed that war's conclusion.

So bitter was this war that the Jews, especially the Galilean Jews and the orthodox Jewish leaders in Jerusalem, became anathema to the Romans for the next few generations. The Christian Church, already alienated from the rigid orthodoxy of Judaism and becoming less Jewish and more gentile during these years, thus attempted to gain for its members the favor of the ruling Roman authorities. Since Galilee was in particular thought by the Romans to be the hot-bed of revolution, the Galilean origins of Jesus were deemphasized. Perhaps that gave impetus to the Bethlehem birth stories that did not develop until the ninth decade. In every way possible, Christians busied themselves with the political task of shifting the blame for Jesus' death from the Romans to the Jerusalem Jews in any way that they could.

Earlier we noted that, in all the corpus of Paul, the name Judas was never mentioned. An argument from silence, however, can never be determinative. But when we search the Pauline material, we can also document the positive assertion that there was in Paul's writing no assumption that a defection from the ranks of the twelve on the part of one named Judas had been a part of his knowledge, and therefore it was not part of primitive Christianity as Paul represented it.

In the earliest account we have of the events of the Good Friday to Easter story, written sometime during the mid-fifties, Paul said, as if he were writing the primitive handed-down tradition, "I delivered to you as of first importance what I also received, that Christ died for our sins in accordance with the scriptures, that He [Christ] was buried, that He was raised on the third day in accordance with the scriptures, and that He appeared to Cephas, *then to the twelve*" (1 Cor. 15:3–5).

Please note that this Pauline text said that the risen Jesus appeared "to the twelve"! The traitor had neither been identified nor removed in these early years in the writings of Paul. The betrayal by Judas was clearly a late-developing tradition with which Paul was not familiar. By the time the gospels of Matthew and Luke had been composed and the Judas story had entered the tradition, this anomaly had been noticed and rectified so the appearance of the risen Christ was, in those narratives, said to have occurred only "to the eleven."

The authenticity of Paul's inclusion of Judas in the post-crucifixion band of twelve disciples is corroborated when we peruse the Gospels to see if at any place these authors assumed a tradition in which one of the twelve was not the traitor. Such assumptions might argue for the fact that the Judas tradition was not an original but a late-developing story.

We do find in Matthew a narrative in which Jesus was quoted as saying to the disciples with Judas present, "You who have followed me will also sit on *twelve* thrones judging the twelve tribes of Israel" (Matt. 19:28). In this text Jesus was portrayed as assuming that Judas would be one of those twelve judges. In the Lucan version of this saying, the gospel writer actually moved these words to the scene of the Last Supper, where we are told the disciples were present, presumably including Judas. To that special gathering of twelve, Jesus said, "You shall eat and drink at my table in my kingdom and sit on thrones as judges of the twelve tribes of Israel" (Luke 22:30). In this saying the author appears to reflect a tradition that knew no defection and no act of treachery. That is, this text reflects a time before the Judas legend arose. The story told in the Book of Acts (1:15–16) of one being chosen to take the place of Judas was a much later tradition, not written until the last years of the ninth decade at the earliest and probably as late as the tenth decade, and was clearly designed to address this apparent weakness. Everything about the Judas narrative screams that this was a late-developing legend created out of the *midrashic* method to serve the apologetic needs of the Christians in the last half of the first century in order to transfer the guilt and blame for Jesus' death from the Romans to the Jews.

Jesus was executed by the Romans, not by the Jews. That is a fact of history. Crucifixion as the method of execution was employed only by the Romans in the history of humankind. The exact reasons for Jesus' arrest and execution are forever lost in the dark recesses of ancient times, even if the facts of that arrest and execution are not. Thus we are left only with the ability to roam among the clues and on the basis of those clues to speculate.

I only want to register now that it is a tragedy of enormous dimensions that, by the time the story of Jesus' arrest and execution came to be written, the Christians made the Jews, rather than the Romans, the villains of their story. I suggest that this was achieved primarily by creating the narrative of a Jewish traitor according to the *midrashic* tradition out of the bits and pieces of the sacred scriptures and by giving that traitor the name Judas, the very name of the nation of the Jews. As a result, from that day to this, the blame for the death of Jesus has been laid on the backs, not just of Judas, the Jewish prototype, but of the entire people of the Jews themselves. "His blood be upon us and upon our children." That was a biblical sentence of death to thousands of Jews.

I raise this possibility to consciousness in the hope that as you and I are awakened to the realization of what this story of Judas has done to the Jews of history, we Christians might rise up and deal a death blow to the most virulent Christian prejudice that has for 2,000 years placed on the Jewish people the blame for the death of Jesus. If that result could be achieved, then the darkest cloud that has hung over the Christian Church in our history might finally begin to lift. At the very least, this is an idea that Christians need to entertain with great seriousness.

17

Raised According to the Scriptures I

We now bring our examination of the origins of the Christian faith to the very heart of that religious system. We confront the moment of Easter with its message of resurrection, in which Christianity was born. Without some defining reality attached to that moment, Christianity will certainly die. But, on the other hand, just because the stakes are so high, we cannot duck the critical questions that surround this moment, nor can we ignore the claims made throughout history for this moment. So into an exploration of the meaning of the resurrection we now go.

Whatever Easter was, it had incredible power. At first demoralized and scattered, the disciples were, in that experience, reconstituted and given a courage and a conviction that no pain or pressure of life could ever diminish. Before the Easter experience they all forsook him and fled. After the Easter experience, they were willing to die for their conviction.

Second, the very way in which a significant group of Jewish people actually envisioned God was transformed by the Easter moment. Whatever God was and whoever God is from that moment on had to include Jesus of Nazareth for these people. This shift in God consciousness revolutionized the theology of some Jewish people so dramatically that the world has never been the same since. Third, no matter how we describe the experience that we call "resurrection," we are also driven to admit that it had the capacity to create a new holy day, different from the Jewish Sabbath. That new holy day was designated "the first day of the week," and even today in this secular society Sunday still dictates the way that we experience and count the passage of time. Both the renewal of life and the energized force of the gospel that came to be associated with the story of Easter were so awesome and so attractive that Christianity grew from person to person and spread from generation to generation. It endured successfully countless trials and persecutions, until it finally became the established religion of the Western world. The continued experience of a God presence in this community of faith was so real that in time even this experience had to be defined. It was through this definition that the concept of the Holy Spirit and later its attendant doctrine of the Trinity came to be born as the very cornerstones of the Christian faith. No matter how one understands the meaning of Jesus' resurrection and the message of Easter, there must be about it something real enough to account for these measurable effects.

But can one affirm the reality of the Easter experience without the necessity of literalizing the narrative details of the gospel tradition that purport to describe the resurrection moment? That is a crucial and necessary distinction. Were these gospel stories of Easter written to capture a literal description of something that actually happened in a moment in time and space? Can Easter be real without this kind of objectivity? The objective reality of the events of Easter has obviously been the majority opinion among Christian believers for most of our 2,000-year history.

But today the literal truth of the Easter narratives raises more questions than it answers, as we shall see shortly. To put this question into perspective, we might dare to ask if this literal objective quality of the Easter stories would have been the assumption of Paul, Mark, Matthew, Luke, and John. Or is it possible that this assumption has risen, like so many other biblical assumptions, out of a loss of a Jewish perspective toward sacred stories? Going back to a key text we have looked at earlier, what, for example, do we think the Jewish Paul meant when he, as the first Christian author to write about Easter, stated, "He was raised on the third day *in accordance with the scriptures* and appeared to Cephas and then to the twelve" (1 Cor. 15:4–5) (italics mine)? What does "in accordance with the scriptures" mean?

To begin to answer this question, we must face first the fact that the biblical witness to the events it describes as taking place at the dawn of Easter day is significantly confused, contradictory, and, in some instances, mutually exclusive. If a literal reading of the resurrection stories of the Bible is required of Christian people as an article of faith, then one must confront the problems such a reading creates.

Look first at the fanciful details: Do angels speak? Do bodies deceased for at least thirty-six hours resuscitate and walk out of graves? Do these revived bodies have a functioning gastrointestinal system that enables them to eat? Do they have working vocal cords and a larynx that enables them to talk? Do they have a functioning skeletal system that enables them to walk? But even if all of these questions are answered positively, then we must ask how this kind of body can appear and disappear at will, as Luke seems to suggest the risen Christ did? Or how can such a body walk through the walls of a room with locked doors and barred windows, as the Fourth Gospel records? Can a body that walks through walls in one verse then, in the next instance, invite doubting observers to examine tactilely the wounds in its very physical hands and side?

Are we dealing, in these ancient biblical narratives, with a different level of reality and a different kind of language? How does one explore and seek to make rational sense out of experiences that occur at the edges of life? What words are adequate when one seeks to describe the reality of that experience in which the realm of spirit impinges upon the realm of human history? Is there any human language that can ultimately be used in a literal way when the subject of that language is God? These are the first questions that arise when we begin this journey into the awesome mystery of Easter.

Once we get beyond the simple inadequacy of human language or human concepts to enter or to describe the realm of the divine, we next must face the absolute contradictions present in the biblical texts of Easter. The Church has sought over the years to soft-pedal these contradictions, suggesting rather lamely that no five witnesses describe the same event in the same way. That is, of course, true; but when those descriptions are mutually exclusive, then our hold on any truth begins to be questioned. It is the magnitude of the differences—the mutually exclusive nature of key elements of the data in the Bible—that must be looked at closely.

Paul, whose description of the events of Easter was the first to be written, said that the order of resurrection appearances was to Cephas (Peter) first, then to the twelve, then to 500 brethren at once, then to James, then to all the apostles, and last "to me," that is to Paul (1 Cor. 15:1–6). In Mark, the first gospel to be written, there was no mention of an actual appearance of the risen Jesus to anyone. This gospel provided us only with an announcement and an anticipated reunion in an unspecified future (Mark 16:1–8). This reunion, however, was never recorded.

Matthew, writing more than twenty years after Paul, said that the first appearance was not to Cephas, but to the women in the garden. Much later he described an appearance to the eleven, not the twelve, but he never related any account of any moment in which an appearance to Peter was supposed to have occurred (Matt. 28).

Luke said that Peter was first, but just barely (Luke 24:34). Second in Luke's listing, however, was not the appearance to the twelve, as Paul had asserted. For Luke the second appearance was rather to an otherwise unknown man named Cleopas, who was traveling with a friend on the road to Emmaus. Only after this episode, said Luke, did Jesus appear to the disciples (Luke 24).

John, the last gospel to achieve written form, said the risen Christ appeared first not to Peter but to Magdalene, and only second to the disciples, but not all twelve of them since both Thomas and Judas clearly were absent (John 20). The last appearance described in the Fourth Gospel was not to Paul, but to Peter, though it was portrayed as being similar to Paul's experience in at least one detail. Both of these "final" appearances were said to have come at a point significantly past the first Easter (John 21).

No source in the biblical tradition corroborates Paul's mention of an appearance to 500 brethren, to James, or even to the apostles if we assume that this is a group different from the twelve, as Paul obviously believed.

The appearance of the risen Christ to Paul, mentioned in 1 Corinthians 15, was not narrated anywhere in his epistles by Paul himself. Paul talked of his conversion, but he never mentioned the road to Damascus, the bright light, or the heavenly voice. Those details were supplied to us by Luke some thirty years after Paul's death, giving Paul no opportunity to comment on their accuracy. When one reads this account in the Book of Acts (9:1 ff.), it is fair to say that, at least in the mind of Luke, the appearance to Paul was a vision from heaven and not a physical objective happening. Even those who were traveling with Paul did not see what Paul saw (Acts 9:7). If Paul's "seeing" of the risen Jesus was like all the others save that his was last, as Paul argues, then surely we must ask what kind of seeing Paul meant to imply. Claims that the resurrected body of Jesus had to be physical fall apart on this bit of biblical data.

The problems with literalism in the texts of Easter do not stop there. Was the messenger of the resurrection a young man dressed in a white robe, as Mark suggested (Mark 16:5), or an otherworldly angel dressed in dazzling apparel who traveled on the wings of an earthquake and who clearly had supernatural powers, as Matthew asserted (Matt. 28:1–4)? Was this messenger not one, but two, angels, as Luke and John both stated (Luke 24:43, John 20:12)? Did one of them turn into being Jesus, as John has hinted (John 20:14 ff.)?

Where were the disciples when the reality of Easter first dawned on the apostolic band? Mark said that the messenger directed them to Galilee with the promise that Jesus would meet them there (Mark 16:7). In Matthew the angel gave the same direction, but this author went on to describe that first appearance to the disciples, stating that it took place in Galilee on top of a mountain (Matt. 28:16 ff.). Luke directly contradicted Mark and Matthew and specifically denied that the messenger, angelic or otherwise, ever directed the disciples to Galilee. Luke rather insisted that every appearance of the risen Christ occurred in Jerusalem or in its environs (Luke 24). John agreed with Luke that the first appearances of the risen Christ occurred in Jerusalem (John 20), but he did admit that some time much later there was a Galilean rendezvous between the risen Lord and his disciples (John 21). Even so crucial a detail as where the disciples were physically located when the dawn of Easter broke upon their consciousness is confused in the gospel record.

Did the women see the risen Lord at the tomb at the dawn of Easter? No, said Mark. Yes, said Matthew. No, said Luke. Yes, said John, but it was not "the women." John has insisted that only one woman went to the tomb and her name was Magdalene. No one can harmonize this feature in the gospel witness.

What was the relationship between what we Christians now call resurrection, ascension, and Pentecost? Paul seemed to think resurrection and ascension were two parts of the same divine action and used various forms of the word "exaltation" to communicate that conviction. For Paul, God seemed to have raised Jesus from death to the presence of God—to God's right hand in glory (Phil. 2:5–11). Mark was not clear on any aspect of this debate. Matthew portrayed Jesus as the already ascended Lord of heaven and earth, invested with divine authority when he appeared to the disciples on the Galilean mountaintop (Matt. 25:16 ff.). Yet Matthew told no story of an ascension. So resurrection and ascension appear not have been separated for this author either. Luke, on the other hand, said that only the resurrected, but not yet ascended, Lord appeared to the disciples. When this Lord finally ascended, Luke said, that action took place some forty days later, and with that ascension all resurrection appearances ceased (Luke 24, Acts 1). The burden of Luke's argument was that only then, some fifty days after Easter, did the Holy Spirit come at Pentecost (Acts 2).

John said that the resurrected but not yet ascended Lord appeared only to Magdalene. When this Lord appeared to the disciples at the evening of that first Easter, he was the already ascended Lord who breathed on them, enabling them to receive the Holy Spirit. So resurrection, ascension, and the outpouring of the Spirit all occurred on Easter day for the author of the Fourth Gospel (John 20:19 ff.). Once again, no one can put these conflicting details into a consistent order.

Was the resurrected body of Jesus physical? Matthew seemed to think so when Jesus was portrayed as appearing to the women in the garden, for he said they grabbed his feet (Matt. 28:9). Surely, one cannot grab nonphysical feet. Yet the presumed physical nature of the Resurrected One was not clear at all in Matthew's narrative of the risen Christ when he appeared out of heaven to the disciples on the mountaintop. Luke had Jesus eat fish in the presence of the disciples and suggested that Jesus then invited the disciples to handle him, claiming that a spirit does not have flesh and bones (Luke 24:39–43). That sounds quite physical. But in the Emmaus road story this body could appear out of thin air and disappear into thin air (Luke 24:13–31). John had the same internal conflict in his text. John's risen Jesus could walk into a secured room, but once inside he could also offer his physical wounds for examination (John 20:19–25). Everywhere one turns in the literal examination of the biblical texts of Easter there is confusion, and various assertions made in one gospel are contradicted in another. So, if we have no alternative but to read these stories as objective descriptions of literal history, we have two choices: We must either close our minds to the world of reason and assert that we will believe in the literal physical account of the resurrection regardless of the biblical data, or we will reject the possibility that the resurrection could be real at all, based on the unbelievability and confusion found in this same biblical data. The first answer will produce a fundamentalism that is hysterical, irrational, and defensive and that will frequently erupt in life-threatening anger whenever it is challenged. It might even produce a heresy trial. The second answer will, however, move us beyond the edges of faith into citizenship in the secular city. Neither of these answers will help us walk into the mystery and wonder of God, nor will they long satisfy the deep spiritual yearnings that continue to burn inside the hearts of those hopelessly religious creatures we call *Homo sapiens*. So we must seek some other alternative, some other understanding of that transforming moment in which the Christian faith found its origin.

These problems, however, are not the only ones that modern interpreters face. Before beginning our journey into the language and style of the resurrection narratives, it is necessary to raise to our conscious awareness some more disturbing, perhaps, but nonetheless real, facts about the Easter stories of the Bible. Because our minds have for so long looked on these narratives only as presumably objective and literal accounts, we have been blinded to certain other obvious pieces of data.

First, if Paul's letter to the Corinthians is the first written record of the Easter happenings, it needs to be recognized that this was twenty-four to twenty-eight years after the fact. Next, we notice that when Paul talked about the resurrection/exaltation, in his mind it was an act of God, not an act of Jesus. God raised him, God exalted him, said Paul. Jesus did not himself rise. So the oldest biblical language of the resurrection suggested that whatever Easter was, it was an action of God and therefore it took place in the realm of God. Since human language has no facility to describe the realm of God, the Bible is asserting that the ultimate reality of Easter is beyond the capacity of human language to capture. Interestingly enough, nowhere in the Gospels is there any attempt to describe the moment of the resurrection. The only thing described is the human experience of the resurrection and its effects. The stone was removed, the tomb was empty, their eyes were opened, various witnesses emerged.

Second, in this first written witness of Paul, no narrative detail of any resurrection appearance was supplied. Paul simply listed those who were witnesses, but not once did he describe what any witness saw. This was true, as we have already noted, even for himself. Nowhere in the writings of Paul, for example, did he ever mention Ananias who, Luke suggested, had played such a large part in Paul's conversion (Acts 9:10–18). When we examine the text in the Book of Acts, we discover that even Luke described this Damascus road experience as being like "scales" falling "from his eyes." Since Paul was not blind before his conversion, we must ask what it meant for Luke to talk of scales falling from his eyes. If it was not physical sight that was being described, then what kind of sight was it? Does it have more to do with insight than with sight? With second sight more than first sight? Do not even the biblical texts themselves, when analyzed, carefully cry out against a crude kind of literalization?

Third, there is no appearance of the risen Christ at all in Mark, the first gospel to be written. The last portrait of Jesus to appear in Mark was that of a deceased body being given into the charge of Joseph for burial. He was never portrayed again in the first gospel to be written. Instead, all we have in this gospel is an account of the empty tomb and the announcement by a messenger that he had risen and that he would see the disciples in Galilee. But no story, no description of the risen Jesus, was recorded in this gospel. With that gospel we have reached a point in time some thirty-five to forty years after the events that concluded the earthly life of this Jesus. So we need to embrace the fact that no description of what anyone saw in regard to Easter has entered the written records of Christianity in the first forty years of its life.

I wonder why these simple facts have not entered the consciousness of Christian believers. Paul, who has given us no narrative details, even described this resurrected Jesus, not as a physical body, but as a "life-giving spirit" (1 Cor. 15:45). He went on to say that flesh and blood could not inherit the Kingdom either. Mark, following suit, has given us only an announcement being made and a promise being offered if the disciples would go to Galilee. If a physical resurrected body is an essential part of the Church's Easter claim, then one must wonder why no story about such a phenomenon had entered Christianity in its first forty years of life, for that is a fact.

The first narrative of Jesus' Easter rising that implied that the resurrection involved a physical body came in Matthew's gospel (80 C.E.–85 C.E.). Even then it was not a convincing story, but was rather crude and contrived. Mark had said that the women, upon receiving the resurrection announcement, fled the garden in fear, saying nothing to anyone (Mark 16:8). Matthew changed that line rather pointedly. In Matthew the women departed quickly with joy and went at once to tell the disciples (Matt. 28:8). It was almost as if to reward them for acting more faithfully than did the same women in Mark's story that Matthew related that "Jesus met them in the garden and said, 'Hail'" (Matt. 28:9). But the portrayal of this Jesus was both pale and disappointing.

One would expect the first account of the risen Jesus in Christian written history to be dramatic or that the first words spoken by this risen one would be memorable. Such was not the case, however, in Matthew's account. This Jesus simply stood in their path and the only words he spoke contained the verbatim message of the angel, nothing more. The angel had said, "Do not be afraid . . . behold he is going before you to Galilee. There you will see him" (Matt. 28:6–7). So what did Jesus say in his first post-death communication? "Do not be afraid," he said. "Go and tell my brethren to go to Galilee. There they will see me" (Matt. 28:10). How very dull and unoriginal!

Luke sided with Mark and denied that the women actually saw the risen Lord. In doing so, he raised great doubt about the authenticity of this late-developing Matthean narrative.

If the story of the risen Lord being seen by the women in the garden is to be dismissed as a strange Matthean aberration of history, as it is by most New Testament scholars, then we are driven to face the fact that the first nondebated narration of the risen Christ was Matthew's description of the mountaintop experience in Galilee (Matt. 28:16–20). That presents us with a fascinating speculative insight in that this was quite specifically not an account of a physical appearance. Jesus rather appeared in this narrative out of heaven. He claimed to possess all of the authority of both heaven and earth. He commissioned the disciples to a worldwide mission, and he promised to be "Emmanuel"—that is, a constant Divine Presence until the end of the world. He was clearly a heavenly Jesus, sitting at the right hand of God.

Stories of a physically resurrected Jesus do not really gain popularity until the writings of Luke (85–90) and John (95–100), some fifty-five to seventy years after the conclusion of the earthly life of this Jesus. These dates should be sufficient to cause us to suspect that these late-developing stories of a Jesus who appeared, disappeared, ate, walked, talked, and interpreted scripture were legendary and that they reflected a development of the tradition that was not original. It was clearly not these magical, supernatural, and miraculous narratives that created that burst of life-changing energy that so clearly revolved around whatever the first Easter experience was. That burst of energy clearly antedated any suggestion of a physical resurrection.

But despite that fact there are many Christians living today who feel that if these objective, physical elements of the resurrection story are dismissed as legendary, then the power of the Easter moment will also disappear. My view is exactly the opposite. I am convinced that, until these physical elements of the resurrection story are recognized as legends and dismissed as accounts of objective history, modern men and women will never understand, embrace, or even enter the power of Easter. When Paul wrote that "he was raised on the third day in accordance with the scriptures," he was not talking about physical resuscitations, bodies walking out of tombs, or the inspection of the wounds of crucifixion. None of that would be "in accordance with the scriptures."

There is certainly some evidence that some aspects of the resurrection stories were developed *midrashically* as so much of the content of the Gospels seems to have been. So we turn to look at that first.

We noted earlier[1] that there appeared to be a connection between the story of Joshua who led the children of Israel into the Promised Land and the Jesus who died, rose, and ascended into heaven. At least one of the details from Joshua 10 seems to have been in the mind of Mark when he wrote the story of the tomb. Matthew also seems to have embellished Mark while adding additional Joshua notes to his story. Joshua (the Old Testament way of spelling Jesus) had defeated five kings in battle, and after their surrender, he put them in a cave and rolled a great stone over the mouth of that cave to secure his prisoners. He placed a guard of soldiers around that tomb (Josh. 10:26–27, Matt. 27:65–66). After the battle this Joshua/Jesus opened the mouth of the cave by rolling back the stone and the kings came forth. Then Joshua executed the kings and hanged them on five trees until the sun went down. They were then removed from the trees and placed back into the cave and large stones rolled up once again to secure the tomb. A cave, a stone, hanging on a tree until the sun went down, a guard of soldiers around the tomb— these Joshua notes, reworked, of course, but still recognizable, seem to appear in Mark's and Matthew's burial/resurrection story.

Matthew had Mark in front of him as he wrote his account of Easter, but as a Jewish scribe he knew the scribal task of searching the scriptures to find details that could be used to heighten his story. When he found ancient texts that illumined his narrative, he used them to provide him with additional content. So from the account in Joshua of a cave secured by a stone, the author of Matthew turned to the Book of Daniel where he found a similar story. The den of lions in which Daniel was entombed was, for this Christian scribe, a kind of prefigured crucifixion. A stone was also placed at the mouth of the entrance to the lions' den. That detail certainly linked the two stories in Matthew's mind. The king had also sealed Daniel's "tomb" with his signet ring (Dan. 6:17–18). In Matthew the tomb of Jesus was likewise secured with a stone and was "sealed" by the authorities (Matt. 27:65).

At the break of day the king received Daniel alive from the place of death, just as Jesus was received at dawn from his sealed place of death.

Having made the Daniel connection, Matthew went on to develop his story. Matthew also found in the Book of Daniel a description of an angel that he used to transform Mark's messenger into one who was clearly a supernatural agent of God. In Daniel an angel appeared to the prophet "clothed in [white] linen whose face was like lightning" (Dan. 10:6–7). In the presence of this angel Daniel was said to have trembled and to have fallen into a trance (Dan. 10:9). So Matthew used this detail to describe the effect of the angel upon the soldiers guarding the tomb. "For fear of him the guards shook and became like dead men," said Matthew (25:4). The trembling was also read into the response of the women, but it was modified. They left the tomb with both "fear and great joy" (Matt. 28:8). Daniel was clearly important to the early Christians as they searched the scriptures to make sense out of their experience with Jesus of Nazareth, especially the experience of his living presence following the crucifixion.

Matthew stayed with the Book of Daniel to get much of the content of his account of Jesus appearing to the disciples in Galilee on top of the mountain. This connection is seen in Matthew's suggestion that at the time of Jesus' death "the tombs also were opened and many bodies of the saints who had fallen asleep were raised" (Matt. 27:52), which appears to be a direct play on Daniel (12:2), where the prophet wrote that "many of those who sleep in the dust of the earth shall awake." Matthew moved on to describe the risen Christ in terms of the Son of Man, another portrait drawn in the Book of Daniel. The Son of Man would come "with the clouds of heaven" (Dan. 7:13). He would be given "dominion and glory and kingship, that all peoples, nations and languages should serve him. His dominion is an everlasting dominion that shall not pass away" (Dan. 7:14).

Matthew's risen Christ came out of the clouds to the mountaintop. He claimed, "All authority in heaven and earth has been given to me" (Matt. 28:18). He directed the disciples to "make disciples of all nations" (Matt. 28:19), and he promised to be an eternal presence: "Lo I am with you always" (Matt. 28:20). It was a scene clearly drawn on the images of Daniel.

When we come to seek the *midrashic* origins of Luke's resurrection narratives, we acknowledge first that because his was the third gospel to be written, Luke had the benefit of many earlier writings, certainly Paul and Mark and I believe even Matthew. We have already examined the connections between the Emmaus Road story in Luke and stories of angelic visitors to Abraham and Lot in the Book of Genesis.[2] Now we notice that in the final resurrection episode in Luke, when Jesus appeared to the disciples, the language was quite reminiscent of a story in Mark (6:45–52) that Luke had omitted from his text, perhaps in order to use it here. That was the story of Jesus walking on the water. In Mark the disciples thought he was a ghost (Mark 6:49). In Luke's resurrection story they thought "they were seeing a ghost" (Luke 24:37). In Mark Jesus said, "Take heart, it is I; do not be afraid" (Mark 6:50). In Luke Jesus said, "Why are you frightened and why do doubts arise in your hearts? Look at my hands and my feet; see that it is I myself " (Luke 27:38–39). In Mark it was said that the disciples "did not understand about the loaves, but their hearts were hardened" (Mark 6:52). In Luke Jesus was portrayed as asking for something to eat and he ate it in their presence (Luke 24:41–43). This is evidence to me that the *midrashic* principle of creating a sacred story was not limited just to the Hebrew stories of antiquity, but Luke used Mark as a *midrashic* source.

When we turn to John, we find new possibilities. John started one resurrection episode with the words "on that day" (John 20:19). Back in the servant passages of Isaiah, the prophet had written "on that day they shall know that it is I who speak, here I am" (Isa. 52:5). John clearly regarded the day on which Jesus made the Spirit available as the eschatological day of the Lord.

It was the first day of the Kingdom of God. I suspect that this was the source of Easter's experience being identified with the first day of the week. The Holy Spirit that Jesus breathed on his disciples to inaugurate the newly created order was directly related to the creative breath of God that moved over the waters in the first creation story (Gen. 1:2) and the spirit or breath of God that brought the first man, Adam, into being in the second creation story (Gen. 2:7). The cry of Thomas in John's gospel, "My Lord and my God" (John 20:28), seems to be connected with the words, "My God and my Lord," uttered by the psalmist (Ps. 35:23).

The story of Mary Magdalene's search for Jesus might have found its origin in the Song of Solomon (3:1–4). In that narrative a woman searches for "him whom my soul loves. I sought him but found him not; I called him but he gave no answer." She sought him everywhere she went. She inquired of the sentinels. When she found him, she "held him and would not let him go." How very reminiscent of the Fourth Gospel's resurrection story featuring Magdalene. Recall that Jesus said to her, "Do not cling to me, Mary" (John 20:1–18).

The *midrashic* elements can be identified, explored, and even pondered. But that drives us to an even deeper question. Beyond the claims of literal truth for the narratives of the resurrection that are so obviously not adequate, beyond the contradictions and even the *midrashic* connections that help us to understand how the narratives were formed, there still remains the question of Easter's reality.

What caused people in that moment of history to seek to narrate what they clearly believed to be the action of God? What caused these Jewish folk to search the sacred record of their past for clues that might enable them to understand what they had come to believe that they had experienced? What was there that was real, that needed to be illumined? It was not the explanations of the experience that changed lives, redefined God, created a new holy day. It was the indescribable experience itself. Can we separate the explanation of the experience from the experience? Can we deliteralize the explanation without destroying the reality?

That is our first scary task. But once that radical surgery has been accomplished, then our search must continue to go more deeply yet. For we must somehow enter into that reality that clearly no words can finally describe.

18

Raised According to the Scriptures II

Having now begun the task of identifying where some of the details and perhaps even the shape of the biblical stories of Easter originated, we must press this analysis to its conclusion. In my book on the resurrection[1] I located many of the Easter details in the Jewish festival of Tabernacles. It was that location, the evidence for which I still find compelling, that led me for the first time to explore the connection between the Gospels as we know them and the liturgical traditions of the synagogues in which those Gospels were first used. It is this connection now that forces me to frame some additional questions that will guide us in this chapter to explore the biblical narratives of Easter from an exciting and fresh angle of vision.

I begin by asking: Could it be that while the moment of Easter was profoundly real, the biblical descriptions of that moment are both mythological and even legendary? Can we embrace the possibility that the resurrection narratives found in the Gospels are *midrashic* interpretations of a reality that human words could never really capture? Can we not now entertain the probability that the original gospel writers never intended their accounts of the first Easter to be viewed literally? Is it not becoming obvious that these evangelists were fully aware that it was the liturgical usage of their narratives for which their words were first composed that determined the actual shape of their composition, and that liturgical usage was far more important in the creation of the biblical narratives than was the memory of supposed eyewitnesses? Mark, Matthew, and Luke portrayed Jesus' ministry as lasting one year, not because it in fact lasted but one year, but because the gospels were composed for a Church that celebrated the life of this Jesus on a one-year liturgical calendar. Saying yes to each of these possibilities opens for us new doors into the Gospels in general, but for our purposes it also opens dramatic new insights into the meaning of Easter in particular. Into those insights I now intend to walk. For beyond this gateway, I believe we will begin to understand even more deeply what Paul meant when he wrote that Jesus was "raised on the third day, *in accordance with the scriptures*" (italics mine).

My starting place is to recognize the obvious. Christians have always assumed that the story of Easter in each of the Gospels was connected with the Jewish liturgical observance of the Passover. It is not so much the clear connection between the resurrection and the Passover in these texts that concerns me as it is the connection between the crucifixion and the Passover. There is a gospel consensus that Jesus was executed at the time of the spring festival of Passover and hence under the power of that Jewish holy day. This meant that the death of Jesus was very quickly interpreted in terms of the paschal lamb that was sacrificed at Passover. There was therefore an obvious liturgical necessity for the early Christians to add to the Passover celebration, as a final interpretive chapter, the victory of the living Jesus over his sacrificial death that had occurred on the cross. So it was that the story of Easter came to be celebrated as the final episode in the Christian observance of the great Jewish Passover festival, which had grown originally out of the Exodus. However, that does not mean that the moment in which the consciousness of Jesus' resurrection dawned in the human experience was also originally connected to the celebration of the Passover. When one recognizes the fact that the gospel narratives were organized and shaped by the liturgical observances of the Jewish calendar, one begins to understand that chronological time is not the primary component of the story, but liturgical remembrance is. In our liturgical life as Christians today we celebrate Jesus' temptation in the wilderness as a major theme of Lent, and it comes only weeks after we have celebrated his birth and only weeks before we will mark his crucifixion. The usage in worship has collapsed the literalness of time into a framework that makes sense only if it is understood liturgically. So once again we are driven to look at, read, and comprehend the Gospels in terms of their basic Jewishness and to seek the Jewish context in which they were in fact created. To separate the Gospels from their Jewish origins, and even to be blissfully ignorant of those origins as gentile Christians have done and been for at least 1,900 years, is to distort the gospel message dramatically. So we begin our journey into the truth of Easter by recognizing the liturgical necessity but not the chronological literalness of seeing Easter as the climax of the crucifixion and thus requiring both to be celebrated together at the time of the Passover observance.

Because the minds and understandings of Christian people have been trapped for so long inside the ignorance of a non-Jewish, gentile approach to the Gospels, we have been led to view the Easter stories as the literal descriptions of objective events told by eyewitnesses who believed that they were accurate observers of history. Even the variations, contradictions, and disagreements found in these Easter texts, which I have previously chronicled, have been used to support the supposed objectivity of the happening, for, it has been argued, subjective witnesses never agree in their memory with every detail of any occurrence, even where they have been eyewitnesses to the event. So Christian apologists have suggested that the confusion of the details was in fact a witness to the credibility of the narratives. But step back now for a moment from this generally discredited but all too familiar attitude and look at these Easter narratives from a fresh perspective and through a different set of presuppositions.

In my book *Resurrection: Myth or Reality?* I developed five clues that I believe can be documented from scripture itself that serve to obliterate the literal reading of the Easter narratives in the Gospels. I will not repeat those arguments here, but I do need to list the clues in order to build this present case.[2]

First, the reality of Easter, whatever it was, broke into the consciousness of the disciples after they had fled to Galilee. So Easter was not originally a Jerusalem phenomenon at all, but a Galilean one. This primary and simple assertion that would be agreed to by the majority of biblical scholars today means that some time must be placed between the events of Good Friday and the experience of Easter. At a minimum Galilee was a seven- to ten-day journey from Jerusalem. At a maximum, once the close proximity between cross and resurrection has been broken, a longer period of time separating the two occurrences can be entertained. Easter may well have been the experience that finally interpreted the crucifixion for Christians, but it does not have to be located historically in the same literal moment of time.

Second, the person who in scripture appeared to stand in a unique way inside the Easter experience was the one named Simon, who was later called Cephas or Peter. "He appeared first to Cephas" (1 Cor. 15:5) becomes a revealing hint that must be taken seriously. Since Peter was portrayed as both denying and forsaking Jesus, and since even the Bible records that his restoration took place in Galilee some time after even the description of the first Easter, it becomes important to allow a significant amount of time to enter our minds between the stories of the cross and the story of Easter (John 21).

Third, the experience of Jesus' resurrection was connected in some way to the reenactment of the Church's common meal. In that liturgical context, the eyes of people, who were not physically blind, were opened to see what they had never seen before. "He was made known to them in the breaking of the bread" (Luke 24:35) becomes yet another hint in the gospel record that must be given attention. Once again, before liturgy can be used to interpret history, time must pass. The Passover observance was not developed as soon as the people of Israel arrived on the other side of the literal Red Sea!

Fourth, the symbol of three days is, even in the Bible, a radically unstable symbol if literalized. The Gospels say "after three days," "on the third day," "three days and three nights," and on the "first day of the week." That is not a consistent record of counting chronological time. These designations cannot be harmonized to reach the same day. This is especially true when the Gospels state quite literally that only thirty-six hours or one and a half days came between the death of Jesus and his resurrection. So the measure of time represented by the symbol "three days" must be not a chronological measure, but rather a symbolic measure familiar to the Jews. This symbol was applied to Jesus by those Jewish interpreters who understood its mythological meaning. Yet, as time passed, it was misunderstood by those gentile Christians who read the text and who did not understand the Jewish symbolism embodied in the use of the phrase "three days." Gentile readers, for example, would not have been aware of the Jewish tradition concerning the end of the world. For the Jews, when the end of the world came, all life would die in the climactic battle of Armageddon. Then the still of darkness and death would reign over the earth for three days. Finally, at dawn, after three days, the Kingdom of God would descend from the sky to inaugurate the reign of God on earth. That dawning would usher in the first day of the new creation. So when Jesus came to be seen by his original disciples, all of whom were Jewish, as that special life through whom the Kingdom of God would be established on earth, the post-Armageddon darkness was applied to his death on the cross (Mark 15:33, Matt. 27:45, Luke 23:44), and the symbolic three days in Jewish mythology that would pass between the end of the world and the dawning of the Kingdom of God was applied to the time between his death and resurrection as a means of interpreting him as the inbreaking agent or first fruits of God's Kingdom. This mythological interpretive language was later thought by non-Jewish Western gentiles to be a literal description of reality, something the gospel writers, I suspect, could not have imagined.

Finally, the gospel stories of the burial by Joseph and the symbolic empty tomb of Jesus must be dismissed as nothing more than late-developing legends. These stories were first of all connected to the Jerusalem Easter tradition, which, since Galilee was determined to be the primary setting in which Easter dawned, relegates all of the Jerusalem tradition to a position of secondary importance. These burial stories were also so inconsistent and so fanciful as to be dismissable on those grounds also. Finally, it needs to be appreciated that a convicted felon in first-century Judea who was publicly executed was not likely to be given an elaborate burial. This was especially so if all his supporters had forsaken him and fled, as the earliest gospel texts have asserted. Dismissing the burial stories as legends also heightens the reality found in a sermon attributed to Paul and recorded in the Book of Acts that said that those who crucified him "took him down from the tree and laid him in a tomb" (Acts 13:29). If those who executed him also buried him, it would have been in a shallow, unmarked public grave shared by other victims. His body would have decayed quickly in the Middle Eastern heat unless it had first been devoured by the wild dogs that frequented public burial places in the ancient Jewish world.[3] The realization of this probable fate suffered by the body of Jesus was in all likelihood so painfully hurtful to the early Christians that their emotions drove them to create the comforting legends of a proper burial in a proper tomb located in a beautiful garden owned by a wealthy ruler of the Jews named Joseph. Since one Joseph with royal connections was created by the tradition to serve Jesus' safety and well-being at his birth, so another Joseph was created to serve Jesus' dignity and well-being at his death. But the discovery of the empty tomb on the first day of the week following the crucifixion was quite clearly not the catalyst to the original experience of Easter. The empty tomb does not create faith even in the gospel tradition for anyone save for the beloved disciple in the Johannine story (John 20:8), a story that few would regard as a description of history.

So we destabilize the literal claims that have been imposed on the biblical texts of Easter, and we are driven beyond these narratives to a place where we are freed to examine the reality or lack of reality in the experience itself. That is thought by many believers to be a scary place for a person of faith to walk. May I suggest, however, that it is not nearly so scary as the attempt to continue to locate our faith in Easter inside the literalized and deeply inconsistent gospel stories of the resurrection. For the ability to view those resurrection stories as literal history has already exploded into an impossibility. We have nothing to lose by looking at new possibilities unless we yearn to hide inside the hysterical prison of self-deception. For some religious folk, that is exactly what they seek to do. They no longer believe in God in any real or genuine way, but they still are convinced that they believe in believing in God. Hence they seek to protect, not their God, but their believing in God behind a fortress-like barrier of significant emotional defenses. Such an irrational belief system cannot be discussed openly, and incredible anger becomes obvious when such believing is disturbed. Yet even this hostility must be risked if we modern-day Christians are going to enter the experience of Easter to discover the reality and the power that this experience possesses.

Jesus was crucified. That is history. "There was darkness over the whole land" when he died (Mark 15:33). That is interpretive mythology. Human beings experienced Jesus on the other side of death as living and real. That is attested by the birth of Christianity and by the resurrected lives of those who had forsaken him and fled. The symbol of three days as the time span in which that experience occurred, however, is interpretive mythology. But quickly the hopes, dreams, aspirations, and legends of the Jews surrounded the reality of that experience. The Risen Christ would come to his Temple in glory. That was a hope vested in the Son of Man from the time of the Book of

Daniel (ca. 165 B.C.E.). The veil in the Temple would be split from top to bottom. That was a detail that Matthew added to the developing legend (Matt. 27:51). It symbolized that when the perfect sacrifice was offered, the barriers that kept human beings from approaching God through that sacrifice were obliterated. It was once again a powerful interpretive image, but not a literal one.

Matthew also added an earthquake to his resurrection story. It was not Matthew's first earthquake. In Matthew's story there was one earthquake at the moment when Jesus died (Matt. 27:51–52), and now he suggested that a second earthquake occurred when he rose (Matt. 28:2). For the Jews an earthquake frequently accompanied a divine revelation. That too is a mythological way of developing theology; it is not history. In both the death of Jesus and in his resurrection, the narratives were asserting that God had been seen in a dramatic new way. Eyes were opened, scales fell from believers' eyes, and a new dimension of reality was entered. It was real, but the words used to capture and to heighten that reality were symbolic and limited. If those words were literalized, as they were destined to be, the literalizations would inevitably become first a distorting presence, but then finally that literalization would destroy the truth to which the symbol was intended to point. Such is the fate of any process in which an act of the Holy Other is captured in the words of finite human beings. It is not the human description of the reality of God that is important and that must be protected. Human descriptions, no matter how deeply sanctified by the passing of time, are not reality. They are nothing more than human descriptions of reality. It is the reality itself that becomes the issue, and that reality can only be pointed to; it can never be captured by human words. Human words as pointers are always symbolic, always mythological, and always legendary in the sense that all words rise out of the human experience and can escape that limit only as they journey on the wings of human imagination.

The Messiah, the life through whom the Kingdom of God would be inaugurated, must be God's agent. His origins must be in God. His destiny must be to return to that divine source.

Through his access to God on one side and his availability to us on the other, the spirit of God would flow into our world. These were the symbols out of the Jewish past shaped now by the Jewish mind that gathered around the memory of Jesus, and in terms of these symbols the story of the life of Jesus was destined to be understood and ultimately communicated. All we can do is seek to trace this process.

A man named Jesus of Nazareth had lived among them. He had a unique capacity to be. His gift was to be whole, free, and giving, which in turn seemed to cause those around him to live more fully and more completely. He seemed to have an infinite capacity to love, to forgive, and to accept others. He appeared to enhance the personhood of every human being who touched his life. He broke every barrier that human beings erected to protect themselves inside their insecure world. Women, Samaritans, gentiles, lepers, those judged to be unclean felt his touch and were called into a new dignity. He had the capacity to live in the present moment, to drink from that moment all of its wonder, to scale its heights and to plumb its depths, to enable that moment to share in eternity. Stories of healing power gathered around his life. His teaching interpreted this power as a God presence, which his followers believed they had met in him. "He taught as one having authority," it was said of him. People felt that their lives were made whole when they touched him. The blind saw, the deaf heard, the prisoners were freed. All of these were signs among the Jews that the Kingdom of God was breaking into human history (Isa. 61:1 ff.). That was their experience with Jesus of Nazareth. Then he was crucified. Darkness descended. The light went out of their world.

His followers lived in that spiritual darkness for a period of time. They sought to make sense out of the God they believed they had met in Jesus as well as the stark reality of his violent execution in which God had not intervened, and in which God was even perceived as having forsaken him. "My God, why have you forsaken me?" they described him as pleading. They searched their ancient scriptures seeking to resolve this conflict, to lift the darkness, to ease their sense of defeat and loss.

At some point in this process the light dawned. I do not know what that point was, but I believe it was real. At some point the darkness of their minds lifted, the scales fell from their eyes, and they were able to stare into the reality of God; and Jesus was included in that reality. They saw him alive. They saw him in the very heart and life of God. Please do not minimize or trivialize that "seeing." It was not of a resuscitated body emerging from a tomb, but that was the only way they could narrate their conviction that death could not contain him. It was not in ghost-like appearances in an upper room or in the village of Emmaus, but that was the only way they could narrate their conviction that "we have seen the Lord."

Something about this Jesus, some powerful reality that they identified with him, caused his disciples at some point after his death to apply to him all of the symbols reserved in their mythology for the Messiah. He was atoning sacrifice, Son of Man, paschal lamb, Suffering Servant of the Lord, the life in which the world came to an end, and the life through whom the dawn of the Kingdom of God was to enter human history. So it was that the darkness of Armageddon, the three-day symbol, and the first day of the Kingdom of God, apocalyptic images all, came to be applied to the story through which they began to understand the events that brought his earthly life to an end. Some tremendous and powerful moment it must have been to force all of these symbols to gather around this life. Whatever it was, that became the moment in which the power of Easter exploded in the human consciousness.

Armed with those insights, the disciples searched the Jewish scriptures to flesh out the portrait of the Resurrected One whose first recorded words in the first gospel to be written were borrowed from that same apocalyptic literature: "The time is fulfilled, the Kingdom of God is at hand; repent and believe in the gospel" (Mark 1:15). This episode came immediately after we had been told that at his baptism the heavens opened, from which the Kingdom was to descend, and the sign of that Kingdom, the Spirit of God, was emptied on him and the heavenly voice was said to have pronounced him the beloved Son in whom God was well pleased. These words were but a para-phrase of Isaiah 42:1, "Behold my servant whom I uphold, my chosen, in whom my soul delights; I have put my spirit upon him; he will bring forth justice to the nations." Justice was, of course, one of the marks of the Kingdom of God. Of whom was Isaiah speaking in this verse? None other than the figure known as the Servant, or the Suffering Servant of the Lord, from whose portrait we have already noted the details of the narrative of the crucifixion have been so generously copied. The details of the crucifixion, we have observed, came primarily out of Isaiah 53. But note how this servant figure was described in that portion of Isaiah leading up to that crucial fifty-third chapter. Of this same servant figure, it was said in Isaiah: "And where is the fury of the oppressor? He who is bowed down shall speedily be re-leased. He shall not die and go down into the pit, neither shall his bread fail" (Isa. 51:13–15). Is it not clear that these details were used to shape the Jesus story?

Isaiah then exhorted the oppressed nation of the Jews, person-ified in his suffering servant, who was viewed as the individual representative of the whole nation, "Rouse yourself, rouse your-self. Stand up, O Jerusalem" (Isa. 51:17). It was lost on no one that the Greek word used to translate "stand up" in the Septu-agint was akin to the word used to refer to Jesus' rising from the dead by the gospel writers. Later this prophet continued, "Shake yourself from the dust, arise, O captive Jerusalem, loose the bonds from your neck" (Isa. 52:2). Then he stated of the one who was to proclaim the reign of God, "How beautiful upon the mountains are the feet of him who brings good tidings." Could Matthew have gotten from this source the genesis of both his mountaintop resurrection story and his account of the women who grasped these beautiful feet of the ultimate Messen-ger of God while still in the garden? For Isaiah said that in this moment eyes would see "the return of the Lord to Zion. . . . and all the ends of the earth shall see the salvation of our God" (Isa. 52:9–10). Echoes of the language of resurrection are found again and again in these servant passages from Isaiah. This prophet went on to suggest, "Behold my servant shall prosper.

He shall be exalted and lifted up and shall be very high" (Isa. 52:13). If the first and most primitive human understanding of Easter was that God had raised Jesus from death to God's right hand and that out of this heavenly place he had appeared to chosen witnesses, as I believe Paul documents, then we have taken a giant step beyond the late-developing legends of Easter into that Easter reality that changed the world. Please note that when Paul was describing the work of Jesus near the end of the great apostle's career, he said, "and being found in human form, he humbled himself and became obedient unto death, even death on a cross. Therefore God has highly exalted him and bestowed on him the name which is above every name" (Phil. 2:8–9). In this passage Paul moved from death to exaltation into heaven. There was no Pauline mention of a resurrection back to this earth.

This theme was replicated in the epistle to the Hebrews, where once again there was not a single mention of a resurrection and of Jesus' return back into the life of this world after his death. There was in Hebrews only the sense that the sacrifice of Christ on the cross was the eternal act of atonement that resulted, not in a resuscitation of Jesus' body, but in his being "seated at the right hand of the throne of the majesty in heaven" (Heb. 8:1). The author of Hebrews related this act of Jesus to the promise recorded in Jeremiah (31:31–34) that God would some day establish a new covenant (Heb. 8:8–12). Then he argued that the blood of Christ, that is, the cross by itself, secured this eternal redemption and made this Christ the mediator of the new covenant (Heb. 9:12, 15). Christ had entered, this author concluded, "not into a sanctuary made with hands . . . but into heaven itself, now to appear in the presence of God on our behalf" (Heb. 9:24). From heaven, the epistle to the Hebrews concluded, this Christ "would appear a second time . . . to save those who are eagerly waiting for him" (Heb. 9:28). This remarkable book, difficult to date, but primitive and deeply Jewish in its structure, talked about Jesus as the divine agent of salvation, likened his cross to the sacrifices offered on the day of the atonement, and then, like Paul in Philippians, asserted that he had been lifted to the right hand of God. All of this without ever mentioning a bodily resurrection from a grave of death.

Once again, the miraculous content that we have come to think of as the source of Easter's power appears quite secondary when we probe the earliest records of our faith. The power of Easter was originally related to things far more primitive than speaking angels, empty tombs, and appearing and disappearing apparitions. He was raised on the third day "according to the scriptures."

The prophet Isaiah in his work continued to attribute to God the source of Spirit and to identify spirit as the breath of life. This theme also echoed in the resurrection narratives and fueled the God claims being made for Jesus because Jesus was perceived to be the source of the spirit, an incredible claim for Jewish people to make. Yet in Matthew the promise of the risen Christ was that of his eternal presence. "Lo, I am with you always," Matthew's Christ asserted, equating himself with the Spirit of God. In Luke the Spirit who descended at Pentecost was the gift of the ascended Lord Jesus to the gathered community. It was he who would send the promise of the father upon them if they waited in trust in Jerusalem (Acts 1:4). In John Jesus promised not to leave them comfortless, but to send the Holy Spirit who would teach them all things and lead them into all truth (John 14:26 ff.). The first act of the risen Lord in John's narrative was that after greeting his disciples with the words, "peace be with you," he breathed on them and said, "Receive the Holy Spirit" (John 20:22). The heavenly exalted Jesus present at God's right hand became the source of God's outpoured and embracing spirit. This spirit was the ultimate symbol of Jesus' living presence among the disciples. Empowered by this spirit they could act in Jesus' name as "the Body of Christ" in the world. It was when they acted thus as the Body of Christ that they were empowered. Again and again throughout the texts of the Gospels we find the echoes of the primitive Christian experience. The essence of resurrection was not located in a man raised from the dead back into the life of this world. It was rather discovered when their eyes were opened to see who Jesus was and is, exalted to the right hand of God, the source of life-giving spirit, incarnate in each person as comforter and guide into all truth, enabling that person to live for others, to feed the sheep of Christ, to be an agent of the ongoing life of Christ. Resurrection was thus both beyond and within these original Christians, forcing them to describe Easter as both objective and subjective.[4]

Is that, as some of my critics have suggested, insufficient to account for the incredible eruption of power that marked the dawn of Easter? May I suggest that such a criticism has validity only if those who employ it do not understand the power of the Spirit, or the presence of the living Christ in the least of these our brothers and sisters. Nor do they understand the power of the love of God that destroys human barriers that seek to block its path as it rushes toward universalism. The barrier between Jew and Samaritan was the first to fall. Next came the barrier between Jew and gentile. As this life in the spirit rolled on through history, other barriers of race, ethnicity, gender, and sexual orientation have all fallen before its inclusive dimensions. Every barrier erected by proponents of a rigid orthodoxy has fallen. The barriers that suggested that God's love was limited to Catholic Christians only or to Protestant Christians only have fallen. The barriers that defined Jews, Moslems, Hindus, Buddhists, and the other great religious systems of the world as beyond the reach of the love of God are today tottering before our eyes. This enormous power comes not from ancient tales that suggest that three days or so after the crucifixion of Jesus people saw him alive; it comes rather from the realization born at Easter that Jesus was and is a new revelation of God—an incarnation, if you will, that he has entered into the meaning of God, that he is the source of the life-changing, life-enhancing Spirit of God that will finally bind us into one human family. It was not a ghost-like apparition that convinced human beings of this truth. It was an eye-opening new consciousness that enabled some of our spiritual forebears to peer beyond the boundaries of time and space into the reality of God where Jesus was now perceived to be alive and from whom a divine and holy spirit flowed to those who had the eyes to see. This spirit called its recipients into new dimensions of life. It was life that was transformed, whole, open, risky, and vulnerable. It was resurrected life, new consciousness, new awareness. It was a life of "peace," but not as the world gives. It was not the peace of no conflict but rather the peace of a transformed new consciousness that delivers us from the sources of the conflicts of the past.

This was reflected in John's gospel (chapter 7) where, in the midst of the celebration of the Feast of Tabernacles during which it was said that the Messiah would someday return to his Temple, John said that Jesus stood up and declared himself to be the source of living water. Isaiah had said of his servant figure, "I will pour water on the thirsty land and streams on the dry ground" (44:3). He had also issued the invitation, "Ho, everyone who thirsts, come to the waters" (55:1). In the Feast of Tabernacles the Temple was to be the source of this living water. In the Book of Zechariah, when the Messiah came to his Temple, "living water shall flow out from Jerusalem. . . . it shall continue in summer and winter. And the Lord will become King over all the earth. On that day the Lord shall become one and his name one" (Zech. 14:8–9). These were among the scriptures of the Jewish past that enabled the first Christians to understand their experience of Easter, whatever it was, and to be able to say because of that experience, "He was raised on the third day *in accordance with the scriptures*."

The Easter story of Jesus' resurrection was thus not an action that occurred inside history, though when it was embraced, its effects were inside history. Resurrection was rather a revelation that emanated from the heart of God. It was not an event that occurred three days after the crucifixion. It was rather a window through which could be seen the timeless reality of the love of God as that love had been incarnate in Jesus of Nazareth. To see Jesus as part of God was to see him beyond the boundary of human finitude. In time, stories of Jesus' divine conception and of his resuscitation from death at the dawn of Easter would be the literalized way through which people would believe that they had captured in the objectivity of their words an understanding of the literal truth of this Jesus. They had not. They could not. The truth of Jesus could not have been captured by any human tale. For his life was and is of God, and his death was seen as his re-entry into God, and the life of God can never be entered with the words and stories of human beings. His was a life in whom the Holy God was pleased to dwell. His was a life through which the spirit of the living God found access to the human family. He broke the barrier that separated the human from the divine, the mortal from the immortal, and he called us to journey through him into the mystery and wonder of God that he had revealed. He was and he is the way, the truth, and the life. He is the door through which we walk to touch the meaning of God. He is the source of living water, that wonderful Jewish metaphor for the Spirit. He is the bread of life, for he satisfies the deepest hunger, the God hunger that dwells in the heart of every human being.

The essence of Easter is thus far beyond angels, tombs, messengers, and apparitions. All of those traditions and legends developed well after the primal experience of Easter had broken into the human consciousness. The human mind groped for the means to process this experience adequately. It did not lend itself to that, so it drove the first Christians back to their Jewish religious roots in a search for some frame of reference. They found it in their sacred scriptures, in the portrait of the servant, in the image of Messiah as Son of Man, in the sacrificial offering of the paschal lamb, who banished the angel of death from the household, and in the sacrificial lamb of the Day of Atonement, whose blood reconciled a sinful people to the alienated Deity. They also found it in their dreams of a new heaven and a new earth that would be ushered into history by the Son of Man, who would ride the clouds of heaven to inaugurate the rule of God. They saw a new birth of the same spirit that had once hovered over the waters in the first act of divine creation. That spirit they now asserted hovered over the womb of Mary and now hovers over the world in the second act of divine creation in which a new heaven and a new earth would be born and the human family would be invited to live as one people in the Kingdom of God.

These were the staggering revelations that broke on the disciples of Jesus at some point after the crucifixion. It was a revelation processed first by seeking insights from the scriptures, which opened hearts and lives to incredible new possibilities, and then by wrapping those narratives around the new revelation in the tradition of *midrash*. That is the reality that lies behind Easter that we will discover when we have the courage to break the literalisms in which we have tried to capture this Jesus.

Perhaps now we can see that unless we deliver the gospel of Jesus from these literal distortions, that gospel might well die.

He was crucified. That is the one objective historical truth in the creeds. All else in the creeds is but commentary on who it was who was crucified and what his life meant and means. Death could not contain him. Jesus, you are the Christ. We have seen the Lord. Those are the ecstatic faith affirmations that seek to capture that meaning.

So it was "in accordance with the scriptures" that he was raised. That text was the original invitation to seek the truth of Jesus in symbol and story. We seek it there still today. For it is not the description of the experience of Easter, but the experience itself that beckons us. That is the confusion that still haunts the Church. The experience of Easter is timeless. The description of the experience is always time-bound and therefore transitory. The Jewish way into that experience was to search out the timeless word of God that the Jews believed was provided for them in the symbols and the stories of their sacred past. But that could be so only if these stories and symbols are open-ended, only if they are vehicles through which one journeys into the mystery, the wonder and the wordlessness of God. It is and it will be eternally so only if one is able to resist the perpetual human tendency to think that literal words capture truth, when all they can ever do is point toward it.

19

Ascension and Pentecost

How the Life of Jesus Was
Shaped by the Figure of Elijah

Beyond the resurrection, Christians speak of the ascension and Pentecost, or the outpouring of the Holy Spirit, as defining experiences. In reality these three moments in the Christian story are deeply intertwined, but over the years they have been isolated and thought of as three separate events. We have already noted that while they are spread out over fifty days in Luke, they are each said to be part of Easter day itself in John.

We turn now to look specifically at the later two aspects of this trilogy. To do so opens us to the differing ways in which the gospel writers used the figure of Elijah. We also become aware yet again that if we are to understand the Christian story, then we must read it with Jewish eyes.

It must be noted once again that Luke and John, the last two gospels to be written, seem to have had some difficulty identifying Elijah with John the Baptist. That identification was, however, powerful in both Matthew and Mark. Mark indeed had Jesus announce that Elijah had already come (Mark 9:13). The dress, the setting, and the diet of John the Baptist were shaped by Elijah in these earlier gospels. In Luke, however, the suggestion was offered that John was not really the new Elijah, but that he came only with "the spirit and power of Elijah" (Luke 1:17). In John (1:21 ff.), the crowd put the direct question to the Baptist, "Are you Elijah?" and received the specific denial, "I am not!"

The reason for this shift in the later gospels is clear. Both intended to portray Jesus himself as the new and greater Elijah. Neither wished to expend the rich capital of this heroic figure of the Jewish past on one like John the Baptist, whom they viewed as of less worth "than the least in the Kingdom of God" (Luke 7:28).

So, walking through the Gospels, we discover Elijah increasingly hidden underneath the stories of Jesus. Elijah was present in the account of the raising to life of the widow's son at Nain (see Luke 7:11–17, 1 Kings 2:1–12). He was also present in the story of the feeding of the multitudes (Mark 6:31–44, Matt. 13:13–21, Luke 9:10–17), which seems to reflect not only the manna in the wilderness story that featured Moses (Exod. 16:13–25) but the account of the inexhaustible food supply from the story of Elijah (1 Kings 17:8–16). Elijah was once again present, along with Moses, in the story of the transfiguration, which I have suggested shaped the Christian observance of the Feast of the Dedication.

It was the Gospel of Luke, however, that seemed to have the greatest investment in Elijah as a prototype figure for his Christ story. Luke wanted to save Elijah to enable him to tell about the climactic moments in the life of Jesus. In the service of this agenda, Luke specifically contradicted Matthew in his identification of the Baptist with Elijah. To see that contradiction clearly becomes a revealing clue to our understanding of Luke's gospel.

Both Matthew and Luke, we have observed, used a flashback technique to reintroduce John the Baptist as the figure and content of their Christianization of the Jewish celebration of New Year, or Rosh Hashanah.[1] Matthew, however, made his textual reference to wrap the Elijah identity around John the Baptist even more tightly, while Luke specifically blurred that identification of John the Baptist with Elijah.[2] That distinction becomes the clue that illumines for us the way in which Luke saved the Elijah image in order to provide himself with the content for both the ascension and Pentecost stories with which he would open the second volume of his narrative, called the Book of Acts.

To develop this story line, we must return briefly to the original appearance of John the Baptist in Mark. In that narrative Mark referred to the fact that John the Baptist had been imprisoned by Herod. In their flashbacks both Matthew and Luke have John send messengers from prison to Jesus (Matt. 11:2; Luke 7:18). In John's questions and in Jesus' response, the themes of the Rosh Hashanah message revealing the signs of the inbreaking kingdom of God are repeated. Mark had also, a bit later, told the story of John's execution. That story suited Matthew's agenda well, for it linked John the Baptist quite specifically with Elijah (see Mark 6:14–29, Matt. 14:1–12). So Matthew used that Marcan story in substantial detail. However, Luke abbreviated that narrative so thoroughly that it all but lost its Elijah content (see Luke 9:7–9). Yet most people still read the story of the death of John the Baptist in Mark and Matthew without ever seeing Elijah in it at all, and so they miss the depth of the drama. Elijah is there, however, shaping the narrative.

John, according to the Mark/Matthew account, had preached against the wickedness of Herod, the king of the land. He had accused Herod of improperly taking to wife the widow of his brother Philip. That wife, whose name was Herodias, exercised enormous influence on her husband, the king. John the Baptist thus infuriated Herodias and was destined to become the victim of the king's wife. In this account, there was a birthday party given for the king. At this party a pleasing, perhaps erotic, dance was offered by the daughter of Herodias. This dance, immortalized in later fantasies as the "dance of the seven veils," elicited a lavish royal promise and even a royal oath from the king to reward his step-daughter with anything she desired.

Upon instructions from the queen, her daughter asked for the head of John the Baptist on a platter. The king ordered the request to be carried out. John was beheaded with a sword and his head was presented to Herodias, the queen, in the company of party revelers.

But where in this story was Elijah? Well, he is there if one is familiar with the Jewish scriptures and if one reads the gospel story with Jewish eyes. In order to find Elijah in the account of John the Baptist's death, one must turn back to the Book of Kings and read there the narrative of Elijah and Queen Jezebel.

Elijah had confronted on Mt. Carmel the prophets of Baal who were allied with Queen Jezebel (1 Kings 18). He had won this contest and had celebrated his victory by slaying all of the prophets of Baal with the sword. When this was reported to Queen Jezebel, Elijah became her implacable foe. She sent a message to Elijah that read, "So let the gods do to me and more also if I do not make your life as the life of one of them by tomorrow at this time" (1 Kings 19:2). That is, Elijah was to be beheaded with a sword at the order of the wife of the king. It was a solemn oath. It could not be rescinded. It was, however, according to the Book of Kings, a sentence that was never carried out, for Elijah fled. So this oath remained in the sacred story awaiting its fulfillment, perhaps by a new Elijah. In the *midrashic* tradition, the oath was certain, but there was always a timeless quality about any text. It could be fulfilled generations later.

Jezebel's wrath toward Elijah was further exacerbated when she coaxed King Ahab, her husband, into murdering Naboth and taking possession of his vineyard (1 Kings 21:1 ff.). On this occasion Elijah confronted the royal family personally with their sin. So just as John the Baptist would later confront Herod about the sin of marrying Herodias, Elijah had pronounced the death penalty at the hand of God on both King Ahab and his Queen Jezebel. Both of them did meet violent deaths. Hence the word of Elijah was fulfilled, but the word of Jezebel against Elijah remained open and waiting.

Mark and Matthew, casting John the Baptist in the Elijah role, used this Elijah story to expand on the tradition of how John the Baptist met his death. The vow of Jezebel to remove the head of Elijah with the sword became the theme of this story. So John the Baptist became Elijah and Herodias became Jezebel. Then the vow of Jezebel was carried out on John the Baptist in exact and specific detail. With the death of the Baptist, Jesus, as the life in whom the Kingdom of God was to dawn, emerged in Matthew's gospel a second time. Elijah had become quite solidified as John the Baptist for Matthew.

Luke omitted the salient details from his account of the Baptist's death as he found them in Mark, for he wanted to reserve the Elijah role for Jesus, the ultimate hero.[3] He accomplished this in a brilliant and dramatic way at the climax of his gospel by telling the stories of Jesus' ascension and the outpouring of the Holy Spirit. No other gospel writer gave content to these moments in the Jesus story.

The narratives of both Jesus' ascension and the gift of the Holy Spirit were graphic. Both were told by Luke against the framework of a three-tiered universe, with the flat earth at the center of that world. As the story developed, we were told that Jesus led his disciples on a journey out of Jerusalem toward Bethany (Luke 24:50). He gave them instructions about where to stay after his departure. He told them to wait for an empowering gift from the Father, and he promised them that they would be baptized with the Holy Spirit (Acts 1:4, 5). After answering their questions (Acts 1:6,7), he charged them to be his witnesses in Judea and Samaria, and to the ends of the earth (Acts 1:8). Then, we are told, the disciples watched as he was taken up into heaven. A cloud hid him finally from their sight; clearly it was the cloud of God, out of which God had spoken at the transfiguration. Two angels appeared, like the two who had appeared in Luke's story of the empty tomb,[4] to interpret the phenomenon being observed as a divine action, and to promise that his second coming would occur "in the same way that you saw him go into heaven" (Acts 1:11). The disciples then returned to Jerusalem. They prayed and waited. One organizational story was added by Luke. He was preparing in this second volume of his story to tell of the Church's expansion from "Judea to the ends of the earth," so he had to perfect his institutional instrument. A gaping void existed where Judas had once been. So Luke told us that while the disciples waited in obedience to Jesus' command, they chose Matthias, and the holy number of twelve was restored. The new Israel, like the old Israel, would have twelve tribes.

Then the Spirit fell upon them. It was, said Luke, like the noise of a rushing wind. The Hebrew word for spirit was *ruach*, which meant wind. The wind was the great breath of the great God that animated life and shook the trees of the forest. Next came tongues of fire, which lighted upon the faithful to cleanse and purge but not to destroy. It was like a refiner's fire. Then they were filled with the Holy Spirit, and the language barrier that separated one human being from another was overcome. They spoke a language of universal understanding. Once again in this narrative we have an Elijah story. "But Elijah is never mentioned!" you respond. Where is Elijah in this gospel tradition?

We note first that the content of both the ascension and Pentecost stories appears to be drawn from the narrative in the Book of Kings that described the ascension of Elijah and the outpouring of the spirit of Elijah on his single disciple, Elisha (2 Kings 2:1–18).

In that narrative Elijah, like Jesus, went forth from the city with his disciple, toward a preordained destination. It was Bethel for Elijah and Bethany for Jesus. As each journeyed he talked with his disciple or disciples. Elijah ordered his disciple, Elisha, to return and not to accompany him, but Elisha insisted on going with him (2 Kings 2:4). On Elijah's journey his disciple Elisha was faithful to the end, whereas on Jesus' journey all of his disciples defected at some point along the way. Elijah and Elisha came to the barrier of the Jordan River. Elijah removed his cloak and struck the water with it. The waters split and Elijah and his disciple walked through on dry land. It was the Moses at the Red Sea story being told all over again, a powerful sign that God who was with Moses was now with Elijah. Presumably, Elijah and his disciple were now free to enter the Promised Land.

Next came an unusual request of Elijah from his disciple Elisha. I want a share of your power, he said, in order to be your successor. Will you give me a double portion of your gigantic, but nonetheless human, spirit? It was a difficult request, Elijah contended, one he was not certain could be granted, but he answered, "If you see me when I am taken up, you will receive it" (2 Kings 2:10).

Then there was a whirlwind, a mighty rushing wind no less, and fire, a chariot of fire pulled by horses of fire, and Elijah was transported up to heaven. Elijah disappeared into heaven, never to be seen again (2 Kings 2:12) in the Hebrew scriptures.

But Elisha, his disciple, had seen his master ascend just as the disciples of Jesus were to watch their master as he disappeared into the sky. That was the prerequisite for the promise to be fulfilled that the disciple or disciples would receive the spirit of their master. In the Hebrew scriptures, we are told that Elisha picked up Elijah's cloak and approached the Jordan River. With that cloak he struck the waters, and once more the miracle of the Red Sea occurred. The waters parted and Elisha walked back on dry land. He had Elijah's power, perhaps a double portion. He next met the larger group of fifty prophets, who confirmed that the power of Elijah "now rests upon Elisha" (2 Kings 2:15). This group of prophets then looked for Elijah but did not find him. In the later gospel tradition, Jesus would be quoted as saying, "You will seek me, but you will not find me, for where I am you cannot come" (John 7:34). The stories have so many points of connection.[5]

Luke took this Elijah story and expanded it dramatically in order to portray his understanding of Jesus. Jesus had also risen into God. He did it without whirlwind or fiery chariot. As one greater than Elijah, he used his own divine power. His disciples watched and then waited for the fulfillment of the promise. When that promise came, the divine Christ expanded the gifts of the human Elijah a thousandfold. Elijah was able to pour a double portion of his large, but still human, spirit on his single disciple. The ascended Jesus could pour the infinite power of God's Holy Spirit on the entire gathered community of believers. It was a Spirit that would transcend both time and place. It was the Emmanuel presence, God with you. God had been incarnate in Jesus, the gospel writer was saying, and now the same God was to be incarnate in the body of Christ, the body of believers for all time. That body of believers would know who they are when they give this love away to "the least of these." The incarnate Spirit of God was to be the ultimate gift of the one now seen to be the incarnation of the Holy God. The only way that Luke, the gospel writer, could find language big enough to make sense of his experience was to take and expand a well-known story from the sacred past of the Hebrew people. It was a story of a hero of gigantic proportions, who walked with God so deeply that God lifted him into heaven. Then he applied that story to Jesus but raised it to a whole new dimension of reality and hoped that this would capture a bit of the essence of the reality he believed that he had met in Jesus of Nazareth.

The whirlwind and the chariots of fire that marked the Elijah story became the mighty rushing wind and the tongues of fire in the Pentecost story. The ability to call down fire from heaven had been a primary distinguishing mark of the biblical portrait of Elijah. Yet Elijah's fire destroyed, first the prophets of Baal and then the emissaries of Queen Jezebel. The fire of the new and greater Elijah, named Jesus and called Christ, would purge, purify, cleanse, ignite the life of the believer, and call him or her into the fullness of the stature of Christ Jesus, which was within the believer. It would not destroy. This was a stunning, dramatic story. It had nothing to do with a literal description of an objective occurrence. It had everything to do with an attempt to define a powerful experience of God within a peculiarly Jewish frame of reference.

The climax of Luke's Pentecost story came in the ability of the Spirit-filled believers to communicate across the boundaries of human language. The peoples of the world—Parthians, Medes, Elamites, and residents of Mesopotamia, Judea, and Cappadocia, Pontus and Asia, Phrygia and Pamphylia, Egypt and parts of Libya belonging to Cyrene, and visitors from Rome, both Jews and Proselytes, Cretans and Arabs (Acts 2:9–11)—they each heard, we are told, in their own language, the marvelous works of God. Was this a miracle? Did Peter suddenly become competent in German, English, and Chinese? Hardly!

However, if one has Jewish eyes, if one understands the *midrashic* principles employed by Jewish people to tell their sacred story in scripture, then one finds a new angle of vision on this narrative. It drives the Jewish interpreter first to the book of Daniel, where the prophet wrote "all people, nations, and languages shall serve him" (Dan. 7:24). Next it drives the interpreter back to the book of Genesis, where a correlation can be made with the descendants of Noah's grandsons in Genesis 10, from whence Jewish mythology suggested that all the people of the earth had been derived. The people who Luke said were present at Pentecost can be correlated very specifically with that Genesis list.[6]

Finally, it drives the interpreter back to a narrative known as the story of the Tower of Babel (Gen. 11:1–9). There the divisions in the human family created by human brokenness destroyed the human attempt to build a tower into heaven where humanity and divinity could be united. The symbol of that division was the confusion of languages. Now Luke was saying that in the outpouring of the Holy Spirit, the human family was invited anew into God. And in that divine presence human divisions ceased, the barrier of different languages was overcome, oneness with God and with one another was established. The Tower of Babel's confusion was finally overcome because the language of love is universal. It was a great story, a great truth being communicated in a Jewish style.

Elijah found his way time after time into the process that Jewish Christians used to tell the story of the Christ. By lifting him out of the shadows of the Gospels, we see again and again the profundity of the Jewish meanings long lost to our gentile eyes. Instead of debating the meaningless question, "Did this really happen?" which dominated the Church's approach to scripture for most of Christian history, we now ask with Jewish insight, "What does it mean that the stories of Elijah magnified a thousand times have been wrapped around Jesus of Nazareth as the only way the first Christians knew how to say that 'God was in this Christ reconciling the world unto himself'"? The call of the Gospels is a call finally to enter the Christ experience. That is the call that we need to hear if the word of God is to speak to this generation.

That is why I suggest that reading the Gospels with Jewish eyes will lead us to see that truth for which so many of us hunger and thirst every day.

Epilogue

Entering the God
Presence of the Bible and Jesus

This particular journey through the New Testament is now complete. It has been an unusual journey, I suspect, for many. It may have driven you toward conclusions that are not typical of most books on the Bible. You may have found this journey radical and shocking, even fearful and depressing. But I hope, indeed I pray, that you have also found it exhilarating and life-giving: for my purpose has been to deliver you from that which you know you can no longer believe no matter how hard you pretend, and to invite you into a whole new religious perspective. My assurance to you is that though this perspective may be different from that with which you are familiar, it still points us to something powerfully real.

To journey into the content of this book is to entertain some unusual ideas and possibilities. A literal view of the Gospels becomes untenable. There might well have been no such person in history called Joseph, the spouse of Mary, the earthly father of Jesus, who was said to have guarded the manger when Jesus was born. Indeed, there was in all probability no manger. There were also no literal shepherds, no angels, no guiding star, no magi, and no flight into Egypt. There was not even a journey to Bethlehem by one who was "great with child." But to dismiss these parts of the biblical tradition as nonhistorical legends is not particularly radical. That has been done hundreds of times before, including once by this author.[1] That has become almost tolerable, even among religious conservatives. The birth narratives are not the heart of the Gospel.

But my studies, shared in this book, point to far more startling conclusions than these. I have also suggested that there was no Temptation during forty days in the wilderness; nor did Jesus ever preach the Sermon on the Mount. Both of these narratives were designed, I have suggested, to portray Jesus reliving the life experiences of Moses. There was no literal raising of Lazarus from the dead. This was a Johannine attempt to turn a Lucan parable into history. There was no miraculous feeding of the multitudes. This was part of the early Christian effort to bring Elijah and Elisha material into the story of Jesus, blending it with the manna in the wilderness story of Moses. I have also suggested that in all probability Jesus did not himself either create or deliver such parables as the prodigal son, the good Samaritan, the Pharisee and the publican, or even the judgment day account of the sheep and the goats. These were the creations of the early Church as it tried to relate Jesus first to the Book of Deuteronomy and later to parables found in the Latter Prophets. Even that story of Jesus' visit to the home of Mary and Martha is not a remembrance of history but is rather a story designed to illustrate the Torah text that human beings "do not live by bread alone, but by every word that proceeds out of the mouth of God."

I have also argued that there was no literal triumphal entry of Jesus into Jerusalem just a week before his death. That part of the tradition was shaped by the work of the prophet Zechariah. There was also no betrayal by Judas, because the character called Judas Iscariot was, in all probability, as I have suggested, created by the early Christians in order to shift the blame for Jesus' death from the Romans to the Jews. Thus Judas may not have been a person of history at all.

I have even posed the possibility that, though the crucifixion of Jesus was real, most of the narrative events of Holy Week, including the Last Supper and the words from the cross, were creations of an interpretive liturgical process and not literal acts that Jesus ever did or literal words that Jesus ever spoke. Furthermore, just to complete the cycle, the Joseph who was said to hail from Arimathea, and to have provided the tomb in the garden to receive the body of Jesus when he died, was also a legendary character, designed to show that Jesus not only made his grave with the rich but was also guarded by a Joseph on both sides of his life.

If this were not enough, I have also argued that though Easter was a powerful and life-changing experience, there were no literal Jerusalem resurrection appearances, in an upper room or elsewhere, no Emmaus road episode, no invitation to touch the wounds in the hands or side of the risen Christ. Each of these accounts was a late-developing legend that arose long after the fact of Easter in an attempt to give content to the experience of Easter that was beyond the early Christian's capacity to doubt.

My studies have also concluded that there was no cosmic ascension of Jesus that began its flight from a spot just outside Jerusalem and carried him into the heaven of a Ptolemaic universe. There was also no literal Pentecost experience of wind and fire in which people spoke in a variety of foreign languages. These were rather expansions of the Elijah cycle of stories, combined with a throwback to the Tower of Babel story in Genesis.

When these assertions are taken altogether, indeed along with so much more, then it becomes clear that I have placed that which literal people assert is the traditional understanding of Christianity very much into question. Those who identify Christianity solely with this understanding of that faith will become uncomfortable and probably angry. They will quote this list of nontraditional conclusions as justification for not considering the deeper aspects of this book. That will be, however, to misunderstand this book totally.

Do these things mean that I believe that Christianity is somehow a hoax or a delusion, or am I suggesting that there is no history, no firm objective truth on which the Jesus story stands? That will be the way the questions are posed by some. To those questions my answer is, "Of course not!" Others will wonder if one can still be a Christian and at the same time entertain the insights presented in this book. Those who have identified the essence of their faith with a literal reading of the Gospels will inevitably make this charge. Still others, wondering if these insights are true, will ask whether Christianity has any future. Once more to both questions I would answer with a ringing, "Yes!" Yes, my commitment to Jesus as my Lord and my understanding of the future of Christianity are both significant and positive realities in my life. However, as this book, I trust, has revealed, such approaches to Christianity are not for me the proper questions to raise and are designed primarily to avoid the deeper issue. That issue addressed in these pages is whether Christianity, as it has been traditionally presented, is the only way one can view Christianity. That is the real question for me, because I have serious doubts as to whether that literalized traditional understanding was the original meaning of Christianity or whether it has any realistic future. To put flesh on that assertion, as well as to develop a new way to approach Christian truth, was my purpose in writing.

When I began this book, I promised a new perspective on the Bible, a new point of entry into biblical truth. I stated my hope that I would cut beneath the sterile divisions that separate the liberal and conservative perspectives on holy scripture. Those alternatives both arise, I have suggested, out of asking the wrong question of these Jewish books that have come to be called the New Testament. The question historically posed of the Bible was, "Did it really happen?" This question, I have argued, resulted from a misunderstanding on the part of non-Jewish readers and interpreters of the origins of the Gospels. For Jewish authors of Jewish sacred stories would never have approached their gospel-writing task from this perspective. This was rather the question of a Western gentile mentality, and it served to impose the illusion of objective history on the gospel tradition.

But what does it do to our religious convictions if many of the people mentioned in the tradition prove to be literary creations, or if many of the events we celebrate in the life of Jesus never occurred or never occurred the way they have been portrayed, or if many of the words and parables attributed to Jesus were never spoken by him? Would that not effectively put an end to Christianity as we have known it? I do not think so. Yet I do understand that these questions and conclusions are devastating if one is still trying to hold on to some vestige of a traditional literal objectivity, or if one still insists on a yes answer to the question of the historicity of events described.

There is, however, another side to this issue. These conclusions might also help the searching and questioning Christian avoid the faithless despair that engulfs the person who feels that "no" is the only honest answer one can make to the question, "Did it really happen?" when that question is asked of the Bible in our postmodern world. For in such a world as ours, virgin births, cosmic ascensions, physical resuscitations, and people who are capable of walking on water do not occur, and assertions that they do or that they have are less and less believable by anyone.

I have tried to present the possibility that the Gospels were written not to be objective vignettes, describing things that occurred in literal history. Rather they represent the attempt by Jewish people to enter into and to interpret the God experience encountered in Jesus of Nazareth. This God experience was so real and so powerful as to be undeniable, but it was also not capable of being spoken about easily in the ordinary language of human beings. So when Jewish people sought to process that God experience, the content for the life of this Jesus came inevitably not only out of what they remembered but also and perhaps primarily out of the God experiences that had been recorded earlier in the Jewish scriptures. These scriptures were read as lections in synagogue services where Jesus was being preached as Lord. That is how it happened that sacred God experiences of the Jewish past were wrapped liturgically and homiletically around the God experience found in Jesus of Nazareth. This was the highest compliment Jews could pay to Jesus. That was the deepest commentary they could write on the integrity of what they believed they had met in Jesus.

What the Gospels were designed to do was to measure the impact of this Jesus on a community of believers by using the content of the sacred past of that community to describe the reality they were experiencing in the present. So the Gospels were not written to be history. The Jews who created the Gospels knew they were not history, but they also knew that their experience was true—not literally true, but profoundly true. The Gospels were *midrashic* interpretations of the meaning of Jesus told in the traditional way of the Jews. The great pity is that later non-Jewish, Western readers had no idea what that meant, and so they literalized these texts.

Was there, some might wonder, a real person named Jesus of Nazareth? Of course there was. I cannot conceive of a way that would lead me to dismiss his historicity. His impact on life, especially the lives of certain first-century Jews, was so deep, so real, and so profound as to be undeniable. This impact spread from life to life, and its profundity was not diminished. The people who encountered Jesus could not make sense of that experience without making the assumption that human beings alone could never have produced this life. What they had encountered in him was of God. So when they tried to explain this reality, they did so inside the traditional legends of a supernatural birth complete with signs in the sky and with visitors who came via supernatural communications to acknowledge the inbreaking presence of God, or else they conceived of him as the preexistent word of God that was enfleshed in Jesus. But behind these legends and explanations there was a person who was real and an experience of God that was profound.

Not only was Jesus real, but he was also an insightful and inspiring teacher. Those moved by his words applied the teaching of the holy Jews of the ages to his life. They came to believe that he had fulfilled all that was anticipated and called sacred in the Jewish past, and more than that, he had opened to them the reality of God so that all people could journey into that sense of holiness.

Because his first disciples were Jews, inevitably they reinterpreted their familiar Jewish liturgical festivals so that this Jesus became the content of those celebrations. They saw Jesus as Moses, Joshua, Samuel, David, Solomon, Elijah, and Elisha, and yet he was in their minds greater than any or all of these heroes put together. There is enormous reality in these experiences, if not literalness in the content.

This Jesus also broke barriers for them. He overcame sickness and separation. He called people into wholeness and oneness. He opened the ultimate sign of human finitude, the reality of death, and transformed it with a resurrection power that human beings found themselves incapable of doubting, but neither did they know what words to use to speak about it. So resurrection tales were designed to fill that vacuum. Am I now saying that what came to be called the resurrection of Jesus was not actually real? Of course I am not saying that! Can the resurrection be real if the descriptions of it are not? I would bet my life on it! The words employed, the legends used, and the attempts to make that moment rational do not capture the truth of the resurrection. They point rather to Jesus' risen presence. For that moment was a God moment, not an earthly moment, and we do not have a God language available to us. So the words they used were neither objective nor literal. These words did not even attempt to be historic descriptions of objective reality. They were much more like curtains drawn apart to reveal the mystery of a living God, a God who was for them real beyond the power that any words could finally describe.

Some who cannot escape the traps of their literal minds will surely think that this is an attack on traditional Christian piety and beliefs, but I do not! Could it be that the Church, in its traditional literalism, has been so wrong for so long? Yes, I think we Christians have tried to claim too much for our revelation. I think the Bible has endured a gentile captivity. I think the Church has sought to accumulate power beyond its deserving. Today the underpinnings that support those claims are no longer firm, and so the power is being rapidly withdrawn. I have suggested that Christianity as presently understood is being destroyed, not by new possibilities, but by the fearful clinging to these dying traditional approaches. The institutional forms of Christianity are clearly in decline, perhaps even dying. Its conservative voices, both Catholic and Protestant, are increasingly nonsensical, and its liberal voices are increasingly empty. A premodern message simply cannot be heard by postmodern ears.

I believe that Christianity is more, far more, than its popular public voices would have us believe today. I want to provide our world with a new way to look at and to enter the essence of this faith. I want to find a new way to embrace the reality of this Jesus. I do not believe that there is only one version of Christianity that is the correct version. I do not believe that the Christian life can be so narrowly defined that those who probe and question traditional conclusions are to be judged, by the narrow-minded believers of yesterday's popular Christian assumptions, to be non-Christians or even heretics. I do not believe in the infallibility of popes, or the inerrancy of literal scriptures, or even the indefectibility of sacred traditions. History teaches me that popes and churches alike can be corrupt and evil and that traditions based on and derived from the sacred scriptures can be used as weapons of oppression to enforce and justify human prejudices.

I recognize the tremendous need for religious security that is present in every human heart. I know that yearning for a sense and a conviction that one is the recipient by revelation of the ultimate truth of God. I too am driven by that yearning. I see illustrations of the fact that this yearning rises again and again in human history in times of great stress and social upheaval. A frightened world seeks answers, and the religious movement builds its authority and power by suggesting that it is capable of giving those answers. The more authoritative those answers seem to be, the more power that religious system seems to possess. But the security of certain answers is always fleeting, and it always comes at the great cost of the sacrifice of human freedom and even human maturity. In this book I have sought to raise our consciousness to this cost, even as I confront the idolatry present in this religious mentality. To do these things constitutes the negative part of my agenda. From this comes my willingness to embrace the scholarship that destabilizes the religious convictions that undergird so much of the popular religious agenda of yesterday.

I confront this mentality overtly and publicly. I do not want Christianity to be identified in the public mind only or even primarily with the narrow and sometimes mean-spirited religious agenda that is produced by those who seek security at the price of truth. I am embarrassed when the word "Christian" has been applied publicly to that hostile negativity that creates the environment in which murder at family planning centers is actually encouraged by some religious voices. I am offended when homosexual people are still abused and scapegoated by "Christian" groups who seek to raise money by exacerbating the ignorance that justifies this prejudice. I am angry when all-male gatherings of decoratively dressed ecclesiastics solemnly pronounce moral judgments, in the name of an exclusively male deity called "father," concerning what a woman can and cannot do with her own body. I resent anyone who defines a woman in the name of the Christian God primarily in terms of her reproductive functions. I am distressed when Christian words are used to justify and to encourage violence against the poor and the weak under the euphemistic title of "necessary welfare reform." I am saddened when entities that are called "Christian bookstores" have their shelves filled with material that not only is lacking in intellectual competence but also allows and even justifies hostility toward other religious groups, especially toward the Jews. I am despairing when I observe that major themes in the books on the shelves of these bookstores define homosexual persons and women inside the prejudiced stereotypes of the past and even unwittingly encourage child abuse under the general rubric of justifying corporal punishment and upholding "traditional family values."

I regret that those politicians who have aligned themselves with what has been called "the Christian agenda" have also been a voice against society's willingness to care for young mothers, a voice against immigrants, a voice against health care for the poor and especially against health care for poor children. I flinch when I see my Christ used this way, and I want to cry to the public that this must not be and it certainly must not be as an expression of the Christ I know, the Christ I serve, and the Christ I worship. These are the negative concerns, which prompt me to be as confrontational as some parts of this book reveal me to be. But as urgent as these negative concerns are, they are still a minor and not the major reason that I am driven to probe the origins of the Christian story, as I have done in this volume.

Most deeply of all, I am led by my study to move away from the dying theological structures of the Christian past because I am convinced that they do not capture the ultimate truth of either God or Christ. So I now am convinced that I can abandon dying traditions without abandoning the living God. Indeed, once I have scraped the barnacles of the past from the God I worship, this God is seen with a far more compelling insight. I do not create the religious fears and religious insecurities that my critics suggest that I do. I simply articulate those that are all about us and thus raise them to consciousness. Denying reality is never a way to God. I cannot destroy a religious system that is not already crumbling. That power is not my possession, no matter what the voices of the frightened religious right might suggest. The God I worship cannot be threatened by scholarship or truth. My theology professor once said to me, "Any God who can be killed, ought to be killed, as a public service."[2] A God who is capable of being killed or even threatened by the explosion of knowledge is already too weak to command our allegiance or our worship. I engage in this task that some call "deconstruction" because I am convinced that the view of the Bible being deconstructed is neither the correct nor the original meaning of that sacred text. That is why I have sought to propose this new alternative for looking at the traditional belief systems in which I was raised and that are collapsing all around me. The Western gentile captivity of the Gospels has, in our time, finally run its course, and it is increasingly revealed to be absolutely empty.

So I have tried in these pages to open the eyes and the minds, perhaps even the hearts, of the spiritually hungry but Church-alienated generations of this postmodern world. I have sought to introduce them to the essence of the Christian gospel that has been so smothered in the literalistic past of Christianity. I write to shout to those who have abandoned their household of faith or to those who hang on by their fingernails to a religious system that long ago ceased to make sense to them that there is more to Christianity than they have yet imagined. I write to invite them anew into the Bible, and once there to view that Bible with a different set of eyes. For when I am asked, "Who is Jesus for you?" or "What is the essential meaning of the one you call Lord?" my answer is something like this.

Jesus is for me the life of God being lived out in the human arena. His was a life so full and whole that it was not diminished when he was abused. It is the kind of life that removes the barriers that impede others and calls them to abundant living. That is why the Gospel writers, when trying to describe the moment Jesus entered the world, found themselves speaking of an angel who announced his coming and of a multitude of angels who sang to greet his birth. They wrote that when he was born the heavens were aglow with an unearthly light and that even the stars guided a seeking world to his point of entry. That is also why they wrote that angels announced his triumph over death and why angels were also present at his return to the heavenly realm. How better can one say that Jesus was God living among us? This divine life had but one purpose, namely, to invite you and me into the fullness of our own lives. A disciple of Jesus will thus live with zest.

Jesus is also for me the conduit through which the love of God was loosed into human history. Jesus lived the love of God. This love was and is wasteful love, embracing love, inclusive love. It is a love that overflows every human boundary. That is why Jesus was portrayed by the Gospel writers as stepping across the racial divide to heal the Samaritan; or as stepping across the cultural divide to engage the woman at the well in conversation; or as stepping over the cultic purification laws to embrace the lepers; or as moving past that intensely human divide that enabled him to forgive his executioners. These are the kinds of things that the love of God does. That is also why the biblical portrait drawn of Jesus pictures him as loving the one who betrayed him, the one who denied him, the ones who forsook him and fled, and even the ones who killed him. The love of God is boundless. God loves in the face of every affront, every abuse, and every denial of love. That love of God which Christians believe they meet in Jesus has one purpose: It is to invite us to be and to love us into being loving people. A disciple of Jesus will be known by his or her love.

Jesus is also for me a human expression of the "Being" of God. This is the Being expressed under the human limits—inside both time and space. It is the kind of Being that people stare at in awestruck wonder. It is a Being who never apologizes, nor does it ever brag. Watch Jesus as he is portrayed by the gospel writers in the passion story. It was said of him that he came to Jerusalem amid the shouts of those who hailed him as a king. However, he was not turned from his Being by the praises of the crowd. Later he was pictured as hanging on the cross amid the jeers of his tormentors. However, his Being was not diminished by their condemnation. Jesus was portrayed simply as having the courage to be himself under any set of circumstances. The Being of Jesus thus issues in enormous freedom. It delivers us from the need to impress, to win, or to protect ourselves. It calls us only to be the self we are, the deepest self, the most real self.

Being one's most real self is a God quality, and that is why the Gospel writers portrayed Jesus as doing the things that only God could do. Like God, he walked on water, fed multitudes, forgave sins, defeated death, and ascended into heaven. How else could this truth be described in human language? A disciple of Jesus will have the courage to *be*.

The life that is touched by Jesus does not become pious, righteous, or defensive for God. Rather, true discipleship is seen when we imitate this God presence by living fully, loving totally, and having the courage to be all that God has created each of us to be. This is the power of Jesus and the presence of Jesus that for me lies behind the literal words of holy scripture. This is the treasure that awaits us after we have cracked the literal images found in the Gospels. This is the mystical presence that beckons to us when we follow the pointers in the biblical symbols, in the myths, in the the legends, and in the *midrashic* traditions toward their destination. These were the creative but inevitably human ways that people used to capture in timebound words the God presence they met in Jesus. This is the ineffable wonder that Jesus offered that can only be seen when our eyes are opened and our consciousness is raised to the realm of the holy. That realm surrounds us constantly but is rarely seen. Yet when our lives are touched by a God presence, scales do fall, as it were, from our eyes, and we see far beyond our own limits into the realm of the holy. It is in that realm that we begin to understand the essence of this Christ.

It should surprise no one who has entered this realm of truth when I say that the God I worship today does not resemble the God with whom I grew up. This is not a statement designed either to threaten the religiously insecure or to create institutional fear. It is rather a statement for rejoicing. For if I had not escaped that literal and limited God with whom I grew up, if I had not become convinced that the reality of God went far beyond the definition of God to which the majority of church people still pledge their allegiances, then I, long ago, like so many of this generation are now doing, would have abandoned the faith of my fathers and mothers.

But that is not where I am today. I am, rather, one who is frequently overwhelmed by my God consciousness. I am one who believes that it is by living fully, loving wastefully, and daring to be all that I can be that I act out the meaning of Christian discipleship.

Yet beyond this, Jesus calls me and all others who constitute "the body of Christ" to take one additional critical step. "Feed my sheep" was Jesus' command, according to the Fourth Gospel. Ultimately, the role of the Christian is to build a world in which all people might be given the strength that would enable them to live, to love, and to be all that God created them to be. So disciples of Jesus must finally live for others.

That is the God experience that lies beyond the literal words of the Gospels. It is into this God experience that I have sought to invite my readers. I believe that the future of that intensely human enterprise called religion lies here. Religious experience, the presence of God, is mystical at its core, and because it is mystical, then creeds, doctrines, scripture, and sacred stories will never be ultimate. For ultimacy belongs to God, not to the words that only point to God.

I have done and will continue to do my searching for God inside that system we know as the Judeo-Christian faith tradition. Jesus will always be for me the way to God. I am not able to approach God except by him. That does not mean, however, that I regard this tradition as the only legitimate place in which all the people of the world must search. The God consciousness in all human life beckons us *Homo sapiens* to a religious pilgrimage in every land, culture, and social order all over this world. But my journey must be inside the traditions of the world where I was raised. For this reason the Christian scriptures are part of that God consciousness for me, and a lifetime of roaming within them has not exhausted their profundity for me. Because I have been faithful to the study of this rich resource, I have discovered in this holy book realities that I never dreamed existed. And it keeps expanding. Finally, I discovered the wonder of what was surely their original Jewish perspective. So by entering that Jewish world, truth seemed to open and widen and deepen for me until I could swim endlessly in the sea of God where all barriers and all literalisms disappear. That is the perspective I have offered in this book. It is, in my mind, the first step that Christians must take if we are going to reclaim our religious heritage for the postmodern world. The second step, which is how we Christians can continue with integrity to say the premodern words of the creeds in a postmodern world, will have to await my next volume.

Shalom.

Notes

1 The Crisis in Faith Today: Finding a New Question

1. Robert Funk, Roy Hoover, and the Jesus Seminar, *The Five Gospels* (New York: Macmillan, 1993), 36–37.

2 The Gospels Are Jewish Books

1. Jerry Falwell, *Finding Inner Peace and Strength* (Garden City, NY: Doubleday, 1982).

3 How These Jewish Books Became Gentile Captives

1. There was a brief and short-lived revival of the Jewish nation that ended in 135 C.E. But it never succeeded in reestablishing the nation in a significant way.
2. John Dominic Crossan, in his book *Jesus: A Revolutionary Biography* (San Francisco: HarperSanFrancisco, 1994), argues this point quite powerfully.

3. Some scholars suggest that "Canaanean" was an attempt to translate an Aramaic word that might also mean zealot, so that the issue was not certain.

4. From the word *kairos,* which means a turning-point moment in the fullness of time.

5. See Norman Golb, *Who Wrote the Dead Sea Scrolls?* (New York: Scribner, 1995).

6. See Michael D. Goulder, *A Tale of Two Missions* (London: SCM Press, 1994).

7. These were commentaries by the rabbis on the Torah and on certain writings that were compiled and studied by the Jews in the early centuries of the Christian movement that explained the meaning of ancient texts in the light of present experience.

4 The Jewish Calendar and the Jewish Liturgical Year

1. There were two deportations: one in 598–96 and one in 587–86, so it is not possible to be exact.

5 Mark: The Story of Jesus from Rosh Hashanah to Passover

1. Recent scholarship (e.g. Robert Funk and John Davidson) suggests that Jesus was able to communicate in Greek. The jury is still out, however.

2. Michael D. Goulder, *The Evangelist's Calendar* (London: SPCK, 1978), 297.

3. In Greek, *deutero* means second, and *nomas* means law.

4. An early fifth-century Greek manuscript of the Bible now in the British Museum.

5. Mark 1:1 and 2:22, to be specific.

6. Mark 3:13 and 4:41, to be specific.

6 Matthew: Setting Matthew into a Jewish Framework

1. B. W. Bacon, *Studies in Matthew* (London: University of London Press , 1931), 80 ff.

2. D. E. Nineham, *Studies in the* Gospels (Oxford: Basil Blackwell, 1955), chapter entitled "On Dispensing with Q," 55–88.

3. Michael Goulder, *Midrash and Lection in Matthew* (London: SPCK, 1974), 171.

4. The major penitential observance was Yom Kippur, the Day of Atonement. A minor penitential observance was the Ninth of Ab.

5. Goulder, *Midrash and Lection in Matthew,* 172, 173.

6. Michael Goulder, *The Evangelist's Calendar* (London: SPCK, 1978).

7. See chapter 10 for more substance to this suggestion.

8. I recognize that I am repeating here material previously covered. I do so quite deliberately to get this framework into our conscious minds. Because this dating process is so crucial, I will repeat it yet again when we get to Luke.

9. Christians began their worship of Jesus as members of the Jewish worshiping community. This would have occurred in ancient times on Sabbath evening (Friday) or on Sabbath morning (Saturday). When Christians began to move into a separate identity, they gathered on Saturday evening, which by Jewish reckoning was the first day of the week. We see references to this custom in 1 Cor. 11 and Acts 2:7. Saturday night obviously was not the Sabbath. Justin Martyr mentions the fact that Christian worship in the early second century included readings both from the Torah and from the Prophets, as well as Gospel Teachings (1 Apol. 67).

10. We do see women in the hellenized Christian worship of Acts 16:14 and 18:26.

7 Matthew: Reading Matthew Through a Jewish Lens

1. Steeter counted 660 verses. Following the RSV, I count 664 verses. Following the Greek text, I count 666. In neither case does this include 16:9–20, which are universally dismissed as part of the original Marcan text.

2. The King James Version uses the colorful phrase "not a jot or a tittle."

3. Joshua, Judges, 1 and 2 Samuel, 1 and 2 Kings. (In time, Chronicles, Ezra, and Nehemiah were added.)

4. Isaiah, Jeremiah, Ezekiel, and the Book of the Twelve Minor Prophets. (In time, Daniel was added.)

5. As I noted in the preface, it is beyond the scope of this volume to argue the Q hypothesis. In the preface I directed readers to Michael Goulder's detailed study in his preface to *Luke: A New*

Paradigm (Sheffield: Sheffield Academic Press, 1989). I can also recommend Austin Farrer's work, "On Dispensing with 'Q,'" in a volume edited by D. E. Nineham entitled *Studies in the Gospels* (London: B. Blackwell, 1955).

6. Matthew used animal images forty-four times in his gospel. He employed farming images twenty-two times.

7. Recall that as Christianity developed in the second century, the octave of Easter then involved us with two Easter Sabbaths. Matthew was easily adapted to this usage since his Easter narratives have both a Jerusalem and a Galilee account.

8. Recall that there are actually three biblical versions of the Ten Commandments: Exodus 20, Exodus 34, and Deuteronomy 5.

9. Depending on whether one or two Sabbaths were dedicated to Easter.

8 Luke: Seeking the Jewish Clue That Will Unlock the Third Gospel

1. Christians began as Jews who observed the Sabbath. As the Christian identity became more distinct, they both worshiped on the Sabbath (either Friday night or Saturday morning) and then gathered again on Saturday evening to observe the first day of the week with the uniquely Christian celebration of the supper of the Lord. As the Jewish connection faded, so did Sabbath worship. Finally, the gathering on Saturday evening (the first day of the week since the new day began at sundown) shifted to Sunday morning. It has been so since.

2. The Greek word is καθεξῆς *(kathexes)*. It always means "in order," said Michael Goulder. Goulder, in defense of this translation, cites four other occasions on which Luke used this word (Luke 8:1; Acts 3:24, 11:14, 18:11). It never meant an orderly account in any of its usages. It always meant in order or in sequence. See Goulder, *Luke: A New Paradigm* (Sheffield: Sheffield Academic Press, 1989), 198–99.

3. Preserved in the writings of Eusebius H. E., *The History of the Christian Church from Christ to Constantine* (New York: Dorset Press, 1965), e.39.1, 14–16.

4. The Greek word is ἀσφάλειαν *(asphaleian)*.

5. The Greek word is κατήχηϑης *(katechethes)*.
6. The Greek word is Θεόφιλε *(Theophile): theo(s),* God, and *phile,* love.
7. Luke 8:3–26 is actually an overlap between Mark and Matthew.

9 Luke: The Story of Jesus Told Against the Order of the Torah

1. Many of these connections I will develop more completely in chapter 11.
2. The word translated here by the RSV as "men" is ἀνϑρώπους *(anthropous),* which means men, not human beings or persons. It is a plural of the singular "man." In the plural it is meant to include both genders, but it nonetheless reflects the patriarchy of the ages. For this reason I have chosen to use the NRSV "people."
3. See chapter 20 for a further exposition of this theme.
4. The dead being raised as a sign of the kingdom was not a major note in Isaiah, but it is found there. It becomes important in later Jewish history, is a major note by the time of the Maccabees, and is found in Jewish apocalypticism.
5. This connection will be traced more extensively in chapter 5 on Mark.
6. Of the servant figure Isaiah it was said, "Therefore, I have set my face like a flint" (Isa. 50:7), which might be a better connector even for Luke.
7. "The Central Section of Luke's Gospel," by C. F. Evans, published in *Studies in the Gospels*, edited by D. E. Nineham (London: Blackwell Press, 1955).
8. See Evans, "The Central Section of Luke's Gospel," 37–50.
9. St. Cyril of Jerusalem's lectures on the Christian sacraments by F. L. Cross (London: Univ. of London Publishing Co., 1951).
10. Michael Goulder, *The Evangelist's Calendar* (London: SPCK, 1978), 92.

10 Acts and John: A Very Brief Glimpse

1. Strictly speaking, Hebrews is not an epistle since it is not a letter addressed to anyone in particular. Its form appears far more to be that of a homily.

2. The measure of the year as the amount of time it takes the planet earth to make its full journey around the sun was not yet known to the human mind.

3. Unpublished paper by Michael Goulder entitled "The Paschal Liturgy in the Johannine Church," delivered in Gottingen, August 27, 1989.

4. See the bibliography for books on John by such distinguished scholars as Hoskyns, Temple, Dodd, Bultmann, Brown, Fitzmeyer, and Lightfoot.

11 Jewish Stars in the Stories of Jesus' Birth

1. Please see chapter 9, where additional references to sheep, angels, journeying to Bethlehem, and childbirth are developed, connecting the experience of Jacob and Rachel to the experience of Joseph and Mary in Luke's birth story.

2. See chapter 9.

3. See chapters 5–9.

12 Joseph: The Shadowy Figure

1. W. H. Auden, *The Collected Longer Poems of W. H. Auden* (New York: Random House, 1969).

2. See chapter 9.

3. See Michael Goulder, *Midrash and Lection in Matthew* (London: SPCK, 1974).

4. I shall trace Jesus/Joshua connections more extensively in chapter 17.

5. See chapters 14, 15, and 16, where the Zechariah themes are spelled out.

6. I did that in my book *Born of a Woman* (San Francisco: Harper-SanFrancisco, 1992).

13 How the Virgin Birth Tradition Began

1. The best history of the development of doctrine that I have ever read is the multivolume *The Emergence of Catholic Doctrine 100–600*, vols. 1–6, by Jaroslav Pelikan (Chicago and London: Univ. of Chicago Press, 1971).

2. See chapters 14 and 15.
3. This was detailed more fully in chapter 12.
4. See George Wesley Buchanan, *To the Hebrews* (New York: Anchor Bible Series, Doubleday, 1972).

15 He Died According to the Scriptures II

1. For a fuller exposition, see my book *Resurrection: Myth or Reality?* (San Francisco: HarperSanFrancisco, 1994), chapter 12, and *This Hebrew Lord* (San Francisco: HarperSanFrancisco, 1993), chapters 7 and 8.

16 Judas Iscariot: A Christian Invention?

1. Only John turns Gethsemane into a garden.
2. The word, translated as "detachment," literally means a cohort of 600 soldiers.
3. A reference from chapter 7 of John's gospel identified these police as "Temple police" and also in that earlier text had them sent by "the chief priests and the Pharisees . . . to arrest him" (John 7:32). I have suggested in *Resurrection: Myth or Reality?* (San Francisco: HarperSanFrancisco, 1994) that John chapter 7 is a narrative that makes no sense outside the context of the crucifixion/resurrection/Pentecost climax of the Christian story.

17 Raised According to the Scriptures I

1. See chapter 12.
2. See chapter 9.

18 Raised According to the Scriptures II

1. See *Resurrection: Myth or Reality?* (San Francisco: HarperSanFrancisco, 1994), especially chapters 19 and 20.
2. For the full explanation, see *Resurrection: Myth or Reality?* chapters 14–18.
3. See John Dominic Crossan, *Who Killed Jesus?* (San Francisco: HarperSanFrancisco, 1995).
4. I think of the primate of Scotland, the Most Reverend Richard Halloway, in particular.

19 **Ascension and Pentecost: How the Life of Jesus Was Shaped by the Figure of Elijah**

1. See chapters 5 through 9.
2. Compare Matthew 11:2–15 (note especially verse 14) with Luke 7:18–30 (note the absence of the content of verse 14).
3. Yet Luke revealed his knowledge of this death by referring to it as a beheading in Luke 9:9.
4. Or even as Moses and Elijah appeared in the story of the transfiguration.
5. We do need to note that Elijah and Elisha split the Jordan River, while Jesus split the heavens to allow himself to be received into the presence of God.
6. Michael D. Goulder, *Type and History in Acts* (London: SPCK, 1964).

Epilogue: Entering the God Presence of the Bible and Jesus

1. See my book *Born of a Woman: A Bishop Rethinks the Virgin Birth and the Treatment of Women by a Male-Dominated Church* (San Francisco: HarperSanFrancisco, 1992).
2. The Rev. Dr. Clifford L. Stanley, the late Professor of Theology at the Virginia Theological Seminary in Alexandria, Virginia.

Bibliography

Ashcroft, Mary Ellen. *The Magdalene Gospel.* Garden City, NY: Doubleday, 1995.

Auden, W. H. "For the Time Being," in *Collected Longer Poems of W. H. Auden.* New York: Random House, 1969.

Barton, John. *Reading the Old Testament: Method in Biblical Study.* Philadelphia: Westminster Press, 1984.

Blackman, Edwin Cyril. *Marcion and His Influence.* London: SPCK, 1948.

Brown, Raymond E. *The Birth of the Messiah.* Garden City, NY: Doubleday, 1977.

———. *The Death of the Messiah.* Garden City, NY: Doubleday, 1995.

———. *The Gospel According to John,* vols. 1–2. Garden City, NY: Doubleday, 1966.

Bruce, F. F. "To the Hebrews or to the Essenes." *New Testament Studies* 9 (1962–63): 217–32.

Buber, Martin. *On the Bible—Eighteen Studies.* New York: Schocken Books, 1968

Buchanan, George Wesley. *To the Hebrews.* Garden City, NY: Anchor Bible Series, Doubleday, 1972.

Bultmann, Rudolf, translated by G. R. Beasley-Murray. *The Gospel of John: A Commentary.* Oxford: Oxford University Press and Basil Blackwell, 1971.

Burkett, F. C. "Codex Alexandrinus," *The Journal of Theological Studies XI* 44 (July 1910): 603–6.

Caird, George B. *St. Luke.* Baltimore: Penguin Books, 1963.

The Cambridge History of Judaism. Cambridge: Cambridge University Press, 1984.

The Cambridge History of the Bible, vol. 1, 1970, and vol. 3, 1973. Cambridge: Cambridge University Press, 1963–1970.

Childs, Brevard. *The Book of Exodus.* Philadelphia: Westminster Press, 1974.

Conzelman, Hans. *The Theology of Luke.* London: Faber and Faber, 1960.

Crossan, John Dominic. *Jesus: A Revolutionary Biography.* San Francisco: HarperSanFrancisco, 1994.

———. *Who Killed Jesus?* San Francisco: HarperSanFrancisco, 1995.

Daube, D. *The New Testament and Rabbinic Judaism.* London: Athlone Press, University of London, 1958.

Derrett, J. D. M. *Midrash in Action and as a Literary Device.* Leiden: E. J. Brill, 1978

———. *Studies in the New Testament,* vol. 2. Leiden: E. J. Brill, 1986.

Dodd, Charles H. *The Epistle of Paul to the Romans.* London: Hodder & Stoughton, 1949.

———. *The Interpretation of the Fourth Gospel.* Cambridge: Cambridge University Press, 1953.

Drury, J. "Midrash and the Gospel." *Theology* 77: 291–96.

Eusebius. *The History of the Christian Church from Christ to Constantine.* New York: Dorset Press, 1965.

Evans, C. F. "The Central Section of Luke's Gospel," an essay in D. E. Nineham, *Studies in the Gospels,* 37–54.

Farrer, A. M. "On Dispensing with 'Q,'" an essay in D. E. Nineham, *Studies in the Gospels,* 55–88.

Finkel, Asher. *Midrash and the Synoptic Gospels—An Introductory Abstract.* Atlanta: Society of Biblical Literature, Seminar Papers, 1997, 251–56.

Fitzmyer, Joseph A. *The Gospel According to Luke.* Garden City, NY: Anchor Bible Series, Doubleday, 1985, 1987.

Foakes-Jackson, Frederick John. *Christian Difficulties in the Second and Twentieth Centuries: A Study of Marcion and His Relation to Modern Thought.* Cambridge: W. Heffer and Sons; London: Edward Arnold, 1903.

Fuller, Reginald. *The Formation of the Resurrection Narratives.* New York: Macmillan, 1971.

Funk, Robert W., Roy W. Hoover, and the Jesus Seminar. *The Five Gospels: What Did Jesus Really Say?* New York: Macmillan, 1993.

Gertner, M. "Midrash in the New Testament." *Studies in Honor of G. R. Driver* (1962).

Goldin, Judah. *Studies in Midrash and Related Literature.* Philadelphia: Jewish Publication Society, 1988.

Goldstein, Morris. *Jesus in the Jewish Tradition.* New York: Macmillan, 1950.

Goulder, Michael D. *The Evangelist's Calendar—A Lectionary Explanation of the Development of Scripture.* London: SPCK, 1978.

———. *Luke: A New Paradigm,* vols. 1 and 2. Sheffield: Sheffield Academic Press, 1989.

———. *Midrash and Lection in Matthew.* London: SPCK, 1974.

———. "The Paschal Liturgy in the Johannine Church," a private paper delivered in Gottingen, August 27, 1989.

———. *A Tale of Two Missions.* London: SCM, 1994.

———. *Type and History in Acts.* London: SPCK, 1964.

Guillaume, A. "The Midrash in the Gospels." *Expository Times* 37 (1925–26): 3928.

Guy, H. A. *The Fourth Gospel: An Introduction.* London: Macmillan, 1972.

Hartman, Geoffrey H., and Starford Burdick. "In Midrash and Literature," article by James L. Kugel, in *Two Interpretations of Midrash.* New Haven: Yale University Press, 1986.

Haenchen, Ernst. *The Acts of the Apostles: A Commentary.* Philadelphia: Westminster, 1971.

Herford, R. Travers. *Christianity in Talmud and Midrash.* Clifton, NJ: Reference Book Publishers, 1966.

Hoskyns, Edwin. *The Fourth Gospel.* London: Faber & Faber, 1947.

Knox, John. *Marcion and the New Testament—An Essay in the Early History of the Canon.* Chicago: University of Chicago Press, 1942.

Kung, Hans. *On Being a Christian.* Garden City, NY: Doubleday, 1976.

Lake, Kirsopp, and Silva, eds. *Studies and Documents,* vol. 5. London: Christophers, 1936.

Lightfoot, R. H. *St. John's Gospel.* Oxford: Clarendon Press, 1956.

Mann, Jacob. *The Bible as Read and Preached in the Old Synagogue.* New York: KTAV Publishing House, 1971.

Meier, John P. *A Marginal Jew: Rethinking the Historical Jesus.* New York: Doubleday, 1991.

Milgram, Abraham E. *Jewish Worship.* Philadelphia: The Jewish Publication Society of America, 1971.

Miller, M. D. "Targum, Midrash and the Use of the Old Testament in the New Testament." *Journal for the Study of Judaism* 2 (1971): 29–82.

Montefiore, Claude Goldsmid. *Rabbinic Literature and Gospel Teachings.* New York: Macmillan, 1930.

Moore, George Foot. *Judaism in the First Centuries of the Christian Era, The Age of the Tannaim.* Cambridge: Harvard University Press, 1927–30.

Moule, Charles F. D. *The Origins of Christology.* Cambridge: Cambridge Press, 1977.

Neusner, Jacob. *The Canonical History of Ideas, The Place of the So Called Tannaite Midrashim.* Atlanta: Scholar's Press, 1990.

———. *Christian Faith and the Bible of Judaism.* Grand Rapids: Wm. B. Eerdmans Publishing Co., 1987.

———. *The Foundation of Judaism.* Philadelphia: Fortress Press, 1983.

———. *Invitation to Midrash—The Workings of Rabbinic Bible Interpretation.* San Francisco: Harper & Row, 1989.

———. *What Is Midrash?* Philadelphia: Fortress Press, 1987.

Nineham, D. E. *St. Mark.* Baltimore: Penguin Books, 1963.

————. *Studies in the Gospels: Essays in Memory of R. H. Lightfoot.* London: B. Blackwell, 1955.

Noth, Martin. *The History of Israel.* London: A. C. Black, 1960.

Pelikan, Jaroslav. *The Emergence of the Catholic Doctrine 100–600,* vols. 1–6. Chicago and London: University of Chicago Press, 1971.

Reinke-Heinemann, Uta. *Putting Away Childish Things.* San Francisco: HarperSanFrancisco, 1994.

Ricoeur, Paul. "The Conflict in Interpretations," essay in *Essays in Biblical Hermaneutics.* Philadelphia: Fortress Press, 1980.

Sanders, E. P. *Jesus and Judaism.* Philadelphia: Fortress Press, 1985.

————. *Judaism: Practise and Belief 63 B.C.E.–66 B.C.E.* London: SCM Press, 1992.

————. *Paul and Palestinian Judaism: A Comparison of the Patterns of Religion.* Philadelphia: Fortress Press, 1977.

————. *The Tendencies of the Synoptic Tradition.* Cambridge: Cambridge University Press, 1969.

Sanders, E. P., and Margaret Daniels. *Studying the Synoptic Gospels.* London: SCM Press, 1989.

Sanders, E. P., ed. *Jesus: The Gospels and the Church.* Essays in Honor of William R. Farmer. Macon, GA: Mercer University Press, 1987.

Sandmel, Samuel. *Judaism and Christian Beginnings.* Oxford: Oxford University Press, 1978.

Schillebeeckx, Edward. *Christ—The Experience of Jesus as Lord.* New York: Seabury Press, 1980.

————. *Jesus—An Experiment in Christology.* New York: Seabury Press, 1979.

Spong, John S. *Born of a Woman.* San Francisco: HarperSanFrancisco, 1992.

————. *Living in Sin?* San Francisco: HarperSanFrancisco, 1992.

————. *Rescuing the Bible from Fundamentalism.* San Francisco: HarperSanFrancisco, 1992.

————. *Resurrection: Myth or Reality?* San Francisco: HarperSanFrancisco, 1994.

————. *This Hebrew Lord.* San Francisco: HarperSanFrancisco, 1993.

Stenning, J. F. *The Targum of Isaiah.* Oxford: Clarendon Press, 1949.

Strack, Harmann Leherecht. *Introduction to the Talmud and Midrash*.
Philadelphia: Jewish Publication Society of America, 1931.

Temple, William. *Readings in St. John*. New York: Macmillan, 1945.

Vermes, Geza. *Bible and Midrash: Early Old Testament Exegesis*.
Cambridge: Cambridge University Press, 1970.

———. *Jesus the Jew: A Historian's Reading of the Gospels*. London:
Collins, 1973.

———. *The Religion of Jesus, the Jew*. London: SCM Press, 1993.

Von Harnack, Adolf. *Marcion: The Gospels of an Alien God*. Translated by John E. Steely and Lyle D. Biermen. Durham: The
Labyrinth Press, 1990.

Wiesel, Elie. *Messengers of God: Biblical Portraits and Legends*. New
York: Random House, 1976.

Index

Stephen's speech (Book of Acts), 138–41
Studies in the Gospels (Nineham), 90
Studies in Matthew (Bacon), 87
Sukkot. *See* Festival of Tabernacles (Sukkot)
Swaddling clothes, 189
Symbols: Jesus as sacrificial lamb, 50; Jewish liturgical, 245; Lazarus used as, 179–80; living water, 244, 307; reserved for the Messiah, 302; of three days, 297–300; used in Gospel of John, 179–80; used for Holy Spirit/Tower of Babel, 319
Synagogue liturgy, 60–63, 171, 178
Synoptics Gospels: described, 54; as lectionary books, 91–95; portrayal of Pilate in, 272. *See also* Gospels

Targum, 104, 105
Temple (Jerusalem): destruction of, 44, 49; rededication of (164 B.C.E.), 78; replaced by Jesus, 80–81
Ten Commandments, 113, 340n8. *See also* Law
"Tent of Meeting," 80
Theophilus, 126
Thirty pieces of silver story, 262, 268, 270. *See also* Judas Iscariot
Three days symbolism, 297–300
Three wise men, 187–88
Torah: festival to give thanks for, 113–14; Gospel of Matthew compared to, 89–91; influence on Gospel of Luke, 131–67;

Luke use of, 127, 131–67; rigid understanding of, 49; on violation of betrothed virgin, 214; yearly reading of, 60–63, 120
Tower of Babel, 319
Transfiguration: Gospel of Luke on, 155; Gospel of Mark on, 78–81; Gospel of Matthew on, 88; *midrashic* style on, 78–80
"Two ways, the," 164

Uncleanliness: Gospel of Luke on, 153–54; Judaism customs on, 84–85

Virgin: Mary as, 188–89; violation of a betrothed, 214. *See also* Mary, mother of Jesus
Virgin birth tradition: Christian development of, 221–32; religious legends of, 220. *See also* Birth narrative (Jesus)

"Way of the cross, the," 75
Widow's son (raised from the dead), 147
Wilberforce, Samuel, 9–10
Wisdom of Solomon, 189
Women: during Easter events, 282–83, 286–87; purification of, 152
Word of God, 4–5. *See also* Bible
Wycliffe, John, 198

Yeshuah, 24. *See also* Jesus
Yom Kippur, 62, 65, 82, 85, 148, 150, 240

Zealot movement, 42–43
Zechariah, 192–93, 195–97, 234